KRISHNA and the Later Avatars of Vishnu

KRISHNA and the Later Avatars of Vishnu

The Galaxy of Hindu Gods
Book 4

PLUS MAHABHARATA DEMYSTIFIED

SWAMI ACHUTHANANDA

Copyright © 2021 Swami Achuthananda

All rights reserved. No part of this book may be reproduced or transmitted in any form or by any means, electronic or mechanical, including photocopying, recording, or by an information storage or retrieval system, without the written permission of the author, except for the inclusion of brief quotations in a review.

The author can be contacted at *swamia@mmmgh.com*

Editor: *Pothi.com*
Page Layout and Design: *Wordzworth.com*
Cover Design: *Pothi.com*
Photo Credit: *www.shutterstock.com, www.depositphotos.com* and public domain (Wikimedia Commons)

ISBN: 978-0-9757883-5-6 (paperback)
ISBN: 978-0-6483482-2-1 (ebook)

Relianz Communications Pty Ltd,
Queensland 4035, Australia.
Email: *contact@relianz.com.au*

Other books by Swami Achuthananda:
Many Many Many Gods of Hinduism
(A Concise Introduction to Hinduism)

Volumes in **The Galaxy of Hindu Gods** series:
Book One: The Reign of the Vedic Gods
Book Two: The Ascent of Vishnu and the Fall of Brahma
Book Three: Rama and the Early Avatars of Vishnu
Book Four: Krishna and the Later Avatars of Vishnu
Book Five: The Awesome and Fearsome Shiva
Book Six: Devi—Goddesses from Devious Kali to Divine Lakshmi
Book Seven: Bhagavad Gita—An Odyssey of Self-Discovery

Dedicated to my daughter Jisha,
Abundantly talented, yet unsparingly humble

Contents

KRISHNA — 1

Chapter 1	The Divine Birth of Krishna	3
Chapter 2	Avatar #8 – Krishna or the Dark One	9
Chapter 3	The Slaying of the Big-bosomed Infant Killer	15
Chapter 4	The Butter Thief of Gokula	19
Chapter 5	Taming the Monstrous Serpent Kaliya	25
Chapter 6	Krishna Lifts Mount Govardhana	29
Chapter 7	Krishna Steals the Clothes of Gopis	33
Chapter 8	Rasa Lila – The Dance of Divine Love	39
Chapter 9	Krishna and Radha – A Pastoral Love Story	43
Chapter 10	Did Krishna Have Many Wives?	51
Chapter 11	The Downfall of Kamsa	57
Chapter 12	The Golden Touch That Healed a Hunchback	65
Chapter 13	Krishna – The Lord of Dvaraka	69
Chapter 14	The Eternal Bond of True Friendship	73
Chapter 15	Dvaraka – The Atlantis of the East	79
Chapter 16	Chaitanya Mahaprabhu – The Dancing Saint	85
Chapter 17	A Thousand-Year-Old Stotra of Krishna	93

MAHABHARATA — 99

Chapter 18	The Greatest Epic of All	101
Chapter 19	Ganga Kills Her Own Children	105
Chapter 20	The Ultimate Sacrifice of Bhishma	109
Chapter 21	The Birth of Pandavas and Kauravas	115
Chapter 22	Feuding Cousins	121
Chapter 23	The Deadly Game of Dice	127

Chapter 24	The Declaration of War	133
Chapter 25	The Rules of War	137
Chapter 26	The Dynamics of the War	141
Chapter 27	Fierce Fighting Breaks Out at War	149
Chapter 28	Raging Krishna Charges at Bhishma	155
Chapter 29	The Downfall of Bhishma	159
Chapter 30	Abhimanyu Is Trapped in the Chakra Vyuha	163
Chapter 31	Krishna Conjures an Eclipse	167
Chapter 32	Rumor Leads to Drona's Undoing	171
Chapter 33	A Fatal Memory Lapse	175
Chapter 34	Duryodhana Hides in a Lake	181
Chapter 35	Midnight Massacre by Ashwatthama	185
Chapter 36	Aftermath of the War	189
Chapter 37	The Cruel Destiny of Karna	193
Chapter 38	Why Drona Is a Controversial Guru	199
Chapter 39	Amba Is Reborn as Shikhandi	207
Chapter 40	Samba – The Black Sheep of the Family	211
Chapter 41	The Tragic Death of Krishna	215
Chapter 42	Yudhishthira and the Dog	219
Chapter 43	Bhagavad Gita – The Song of the Lord	223
Chapter 44	Why India Is Known as Bharat	231

BUDDHA & THE LATER AVATARS — **237**

Chapter 45	The Curious Avatar of Buddha	239
Chapter 46	Ajanta Caves – Louvre of Ancient India	243
Chapter 47	Padmapani – The Mona Lisa of India	249
Chapter 48	Avatar #9 – The Balarama Avatar	253
Chapter 49	Avatar #10 – The Kalki Avatar	261

Index	265
What's Coming Up?	275

Dear Reader,

If you are a lover of trivia, then the feats of the Englishman Charles Burgess Fry will be of utmost interest. A cricketing legend of the 19th century, Fry became well-known as the captain of the English Cricket team that never lost a match. Besides cricket, he represented his country in soccer and was also a solid rugby player. At 20 years of age, he broke the British long jump record. A year later he went on to equal the world record in long jump that stood for over 21 years. And that's not all. In the second innings of his life, he led an ordinary life as a journalist and wrote a novel. Later, he represented India at the League of Nations and also authored the technical book, "A key book of the League of Nations." A man of diverse talent, Fry was undoubtedly one of the greatest all-rounders both on and off the field.

I mentioned Fry to introduce you to Krishna, for no deity in the Hindu pantheon is as multi-talented as Krishna. For many, Krishna is an adorable child, a divine lover, a romantic dancer, an outstanding flute player, and so on. Volumes have been written about Krishna and his deeds in the Hindu scriptures. Although his childhood pranks and amazing feats of strength made Krishna endearing to his devotees, it was the spiritual advice of the highest order given in the Bhagavad Gita that defined his legacy.

This book is a continuation of the Dashavataras, the top ten incarnations of Vishnu. For those who have followed the *Galaxy of Hindu Gods* series, you may recall that the avatar saga began in book 3 where we discussed seven of the ten avatars. The remaining avatars are covered in this book starting with Krishna, the eighth avatar of Vishnu. Because of his importance in Hindu mythology, Krishna is discussed in extensive detail—about three-fourths of this volume is about him. Also described in depth is the Mahabharata, the greatest epic of all times, where Krishna plays a major non-combat role. If Bhagavad Gita constitutes the theory, then its application is the Mahabharata. But the epic is also the place where the water gets really deep. While the storyline of Ramayana is simple and straightforward, the Mahabharata is complex with a myriad of intriguing characters. My treatment of Mahabharata, however, is different from other books. While most works start with descriptions of the feuding families—the Pandavas and the Kauravas—I step further back and provide the backdrop for the conflict. This vantage point, I believe, should help you and I understand how actions at one time can have karmic comeuppance on what comes next.

And that brings us to one of the key doctrines of Hinduism—karma. So, karma is what goes around comes around, right? True, but for most people karma may mean different things, such as right action, fate, or consequence of past action. The Mahabharata shows that humans themselves are the masters of their own destiny until the gods make them responsible for their actions. In this context, karma is like a rubber band. It can only stretch so much before it breaks and slaps you in the face. The Mahabharata is replete with characters trying to manipulate karma only to find the karma rubber band strike back in unexpected ways. Krishna himself was not exempted from the consequences of karma.

This book is much thicker than the other volumes in this series. For that reason, it took me more time to do the final touches. I was humbled by many lovers of mythology who emailed me asking, "Hey, what happened to the fourth book?" Because of its breadth, this volume is divided into three sections: Krishna, Mahabharata, and the later avatars. While this book is mostly about Krishna and the Mahabharata, the remaining avatars, particularly Buddha, are also described in detail.

Now let's dive into the story of Krishna's extraordinary birth.

Take ~~care~~ action.

Swami Achuthananda

Actions are the seeds of fate. Deeds grow into destiny.
—HARRY S. TRUMAN, 1884–1972

Krishna prodding Arjuna in the Kurukshetra War

KRISHNA

1

The Divine Birth of Krishna

Rain clouds rumbled softly. Fierce winds grew calm. Devaki was about to deliver her eighth child. Hand in chains, Vasudeva paced nervously across the prison cell, trying to conceal his anxiety so as to not attract the attention of the guards stationed outside. The baby could arrive any moment. He trembled uncontrollably at the thought of Kamsa, the ruler of Mathura, who had vowed to kill this child.

Vasudeva was married to Devaki, the sister[1] of Kamsa. Mathura was the capital of the Yadavas, a clan of pastoral people of northern India. It was a peaceful town during the reign of King Ugrasena until a mishap befell upon the queen. One day while returning from the forest, she was waylaid by a wicked demon who assumed the form of her husband. He ravished her and foretold that her soon-to-be-born son Kamsa would become a tyrannical ruler and could only be stopped by one called Krishna. Nine months later Kamsa was born. Since the queen chose to remain silent about the incident, Ugrasena believed Kamsa was his own child.

Kamsa grew up among the peace-loving Yadavas. His demonic tendencies were evident from an early age. He defeated the neighboring king of

---

[1] In some versions of story Devaki is the cousin of Kamsa and they share the same paternal grandfather instead of the father.

Magadha and forced two of the king's daughters to be his wives.[2] He fought with his father, imprisoned him, and usurped the throne. Once in power, Kamsa banned the worship of Vishnu and began committing atrocities at such an alarming rate that even the patient Mother Earth could not remain silent. Assuming the form of a cow, she approached Vishnu and reminded him of his promise to incarnate when righteousness on Earth declined. At her request, Vishnu decided it was time to put the demon in his rightful place. He created a master plan for the destruction of Kamsa. According to the plan, Kamsa's sister, Devaki, would marry Vasudeva. Plucking a black hair from his body and a white hair from his serpent Ananda Shesha, Vishnu placed them on Devaki's womb, declaring that the white hair would become her seventh child Balarama, and the black hair, her eighth son, Krishna.

Devaki and Vasudeva were soon married. Kamsa was driving the bridal car on the wedding day when a voice thundered from the sky. "Fool! The eighth son of the lady you are driving shall end your life." Kamsa was shocked. His first impulse was to slay Devaki immediately. But Vasudeva begged Kamsa to let his sister live on the condition that he would himself deliver every child born to her to Kamsa. Devaki was spared, but both she and Vasudeva were placed under guard.

Six children were born to Devaki and Vasudeva in due course. At birth, each one of them was smashed to death on a rock before their horrified eyes. As ordained, Devaki conceived for the seventh time. This time before the baby was born, the divine powers of Vishnu transferred the embryo from the womb of Devaki to that of Rohini, the first wife of Vasudeva. Only a few days ago, Vasudeva had sent Rohini to the house of Nanda, a fellow cowherd who lived in the town of Gokula. Kamsa was led to believe that fear caused Devaki to miscarry her seventh child. Shortly thereafter, Devaki conceived for the eighth time. The news that Devaki was pregnant reached the king. Immediately he issued orders to imprison both Devaki and Vasudeva. Taking no chances, Kamsa had them manacled, and the prison security was reinforced.

---

[2] The neighboring king was Jarasandha, who will feature in this book later.

Suddenly, the cry of a baby interrupted Vasudeva's thoughts. In the pitch darkness inside the jail cell, the divine child Krishna had taken birth at the auspicious astrological midnight hour with the star Rohini in ascent. A mysterious soft light emanating from the baby filled the prison. As Devaki held the bundle of bliss in her hands, she momentarily forgot about the cruel death that awaited her son. Realizing that Kamsa's men would arrive any second, Vasudeva panicked. But miraculously, the chains that held his hands broke, and the heavy doors of the prison swung open. Vasudeva glanced at the baby. Astounded, he saw the image of Vishnu speaking to him. The voice commanded Vasudeva to take the baby to the house of Nanda. Wrapping the baby in his garments and tenderly placing him close to his heart, Vasudeva walked past the prison doors only to find the guards snoring softly. Finding a threshing basket, he hid the child in it and set off to Gokula, as ordained by Vishnu.

Outside, thunder cracked in the midst of a heavy storm and raging winds. The roar of the turbulent waters of the Yamuna river could be heard in a distance. Vasudeva stepped out in the rain, but not a single drop fell on him. The celestial serpent Ananda Shesha followed him with its raised hood resembling an umbrella, protecting Vasudeva and the baby from the torrents of rain. The water level of the Yamuna was rising with the rain, but as Vasudeva came nearer, the waters magically parted allowing him to cross to the other side with only a trickle washing his feet. It didn't take too long to reach Gokula. Meanwhile at Nanda's house, his wife Yashoda had just given birth to a baby girl. When Vasudeva entered the house, both Nanda and Yashoda, suddenly overcome with exhaustion, were fast asleep. Without disturbing the sleeping couple, Vasudeva bent down and swapped the babies, as he was ordained, and then safely returned to the prison with the baby girl. Inside the prison, he found himself in chains again. The prison doors closed and bolted, as if nothing had happened.

Hearing the cry of a newborn baby, the guards woke up and at once announced the birth of a girl to Kamsa, who rushed into the prison. "It's a girl," protested Devaki. "She deserves to be spared, for the prophecy mentioned a boy. What harm can she do to you?" In spite of the mother's earnest appeal, Kamsa seized the baby by its feet and tried to smash the body on a rock. But the child slipped out of his hands and escaped into the sky. The baby transformed into the goddess Devi and she spoke from above, "O fool! What use is it to kill me when your killer has already taken birth and is alive and well!" With that, she vanished into thin air.

Kamsa felt powerless and gloomy. He decided to free his sister and husband from captivity. But at daybreak, he was back to his evil self. He sent out an order for all male children in the kingdom to be killed. Vasudeva was terrified. Both his sons were safe in Gokula under Nanda's care for now, but he wanted to warn Nanda to be vigilant. Meanwhile both Nanda and Yashoda were overjoyed to learn that their child was a boy, after all, for they thought they had heard the cries of a baby girl before succumbing to fatigue.

Vasudeva crossing the river with the baby amidst heavy rainfall

The apsaras danced, and the gods in heaven showered flowers upon the Earth. Krishna, the eighth incarnation of Vishnu, had taken birth. The infants Krishna and Balarama would soon grow up together in Gokula in the same house without knowing they were brothers. If you are a student of comparative mythology, you will at once realize the parallels between the birth of Krishna and Christ. While Christ was born in a cave, Krishna was born in a cave-like dungeon. Like Kamsa, Herod sent out troops to kill newborn infants on learning about the birth of a future king. Both had royal genealogies and both miraculously survived at birth. In fact, the circumstances around Krishna's birth were so similar to that of Christ that Christian theologians at first thought Hindus had stolen parts of the story of Jesus' birth. But they soon discovered that Krishna's story was at least a century older and the matter was left aside altogether.

2

Avatar #8 - Krishna or the Dark One

A tremendously god friendly country, India is home to a vast assortment of gods. Among them, Krishna is one of the most beloved deities and rivals Ganesha and Shiva in popularity. Such is Krishna's popularity that he is often considered the God in Hinduism. Even the average outsider who knows nothing about Hinduism has heard about Krishna. He is more popular than Vishnu himself and receives far greater worship even though he is only an avatar of Vishnu. Among the avatars, the largest body of mythology is dedicated to Krishna, beating Rama, the seventh avatar.

Vishnu has many avatars, but the Dashavataras, or Vishnu's top-ten incarnations, hold a special place in Hinduism today. The purpose of the eighth incarnation, Krishna, was relatively straightforward—to end the life of the demon king Kamsa, the tyrannical ruler of Mathura. To accomplish this mission, Krishna manifested on Earth through a miraculous birth that has many similarities with the birth of Jesus. Along with his older brother Balarama, Krishna grew up in the city of Gokula as a mischievous but adorable child. In his youth, he became a divine lover and flute player par excellence. The annihilation of Kamsa followed soon thereafter. With Kamsa's death, Krishna served the purpose of his incarnation, but he stayed back on earth, and went on to play a major noncombat role in the Mahabharata War, acting as an adviser and dispensing timeless wisdom that was recorded in the Bhagavad Gita. By sheer weight of his popularity and the volume of mythology, Krishna is sometimes considered a deity in his own right, while Balarama is recognized as an avatar of Vishnu.

In mythological terms, the entire life of Krishna can be categorized into four main parts: childhood, youth, adulthood, and middle-age. As a child, Krishna was fond of pranks and was given the moniker "butter thief." He also proved to be an extraordinary child who performed great feats of strength during this period. As Krishna reached his youth, he dallied with the cowherd girls and became famous for the circular romantic dance known as Rasa Lila, which is a constant theme in Indian classical dances. Among the Hindu deities, Krishna, like Shiva, was artistically inclined. The flute was Krishna's favorite instrument. During his adulthood, he became the guardian of his clan and eventually overcame his tormentor, his own uncle, Kamsa. In the fourth and last part of his life, Krishna became the ruler of Dvaraka,[3] now a submerged island in the Indian Ocean, and took part in the Mahabharata War, playing the role of Arjuna's charioteer but also handing down his prodigious teachings. Maybe he overstayed his visit on earth. Like Rama, Krishna also ended his duties and left the earth in less than perfect circumstances, for the miraculous birth and extraordinary life culminated in a tragic death.

The mythological elements in the tales of Krishna may give the impression that these stories were written by a fiction writer for entertainment. On the contrary, scholars have found that these legends are grounded in some reality. Like Rama, Krishna is considered a historical figure and is believed to have lived somewhere between 3200 BCE and 3100 BCE. No archeological or documentary evidence in support of that date exist other

---

[3] The mythological city, Krishna's Dvaraka, is believed to have been submerged into the Indian Ocean. This city is different from the city of Dwarka in the state of Gujarat, India.

AVATAR #8 - KRISHNA OR THE DARK ONE

than the fact that the epics list 3102 BCE as the year of the Mahabharata War. Since the Mahabharata is teeming with deceit, greed and chicanery, the Puranas marked that year as the beginning of Kali Yuga (the dark ages) in which society experiences a breakdown in ethical values.

Over the years many scholars have dissected the life of Krishna in meticulous detail. According to them the various elements associated with Krishna—mischievous child, amorous youth, and spiritual master—probably did not originate from one deity, but were the byproduct of an amalgamation of many deities existing at that time. However, they were unable to separate these various elements. One prominent theory suggests that the present Krishna combined elements of Krishna-Gopala, a deity worshipped by the Abhira clan of that time, and Vasudeva-Krishna, the deity of the ancient clan Vrishnis from the city of Mathura, Krishna's fabled birthplace.

Just like Rama, Krishna is not mentioned in the Vedas. While the details of Rama's life lacks adequate sources, Krishna's is teeming with them, for accounts of Krishna can be found in many texts. The main source of information, however, comes from the Mahabharata, particularly its appendix Harivamsa, which was perhaps inserted into the epic in the fifth century CE. Notably the Mahabharata does not say that Krishna is an avatar of Vishnu. Krishna's identity as an avatar,

The eighth avatar Krishna

however, is established in the appendix. The sixth chapter of Mahabharata is the Bhagavad Gita, which celebrates the teachings of Krishna in 18 chapters. Besides the Bhagavad Gita, the Puranas, particularly the Vishnu Purana and the Bhagavata Purana, have also contributed greatly toward the mythology around Krishna.

You will be surprised to learn that unlike Rama, Krishna is never considered morally perfect by worldly standards. Hindu scriptures repeatedly assert that the gods should not be judged by human moral standards, which are variables of time and place. The greatest gift of Krishna to humanity, however, has been the Bhagavad Gita. In it, he addresses deep philosophical questions about human existence. The Gita is a refreshingly honest book and tells you how to make hard choices when the obligations of life push you in different directions. The Gita does not recommend you to adopt a herd mentality and imitate the actions of a morally perfect individual like Rama, Christ, Buddha, or Mohammad. Rather Krishna emphasizes that you must adhere to certain core principles, such as remaining detached from expected outcomes. According to the Gita, moral motivation for action should not be based on expected outcomes.

If Shiva is associated with meditation and Rama with dharma, then Krishna is often linked with bhakti (devotional love). The rich assortment of legends associated with Krishna has led to a profusion of representation in painting, sculpture, and arts. As a child, Krishna is depicted crawling on his hands and knees or dancing with joy over a ball of butter in his hands. The most common representation of Krishna is as a divine lover in which he is seen playing the flute surrounded by admiring *gopi*s (milkmaids). Krishna is also the focus of numerous bhakti cults, such as the Hare Krishna movement, which has produced a wealth of religious poetry over the centuries. Although the word *krishna* means the "the dark one," he is generally depicted as having a blue complexion—which is common across all Vishnu avatars. He is seen clad in a yellow loin cloth, a fact brought to the national attention by the Indian pop singer Usha Uthup in her famous song "Pitambara, O Krishna." Furthermore, most depictions of Krishna have a peacock feather tucked into his crown.

Among his many names, Govinda (protector of cow), Keshava (one with long hair), Mukunda (one who liberates), Vasudeva (lord of Vasus), and Achutha (infallible) are widely popular. Krishna is enthusiastically worshipped on many Hindu festivals, the most popular being Krishna

Janmashtami and Gita Jayanti. In descriptions of Krishna, you will often encounter the term Vraj (or Braj), which is a mythical region comprising heaven and earth. The earthbound region of Vraj is believed to be situated within the golden triangle of Delhi, Jaipur, and Agra and includes cities of Mathura (Krishna' birthplace), Vrindavan (Krishna's youth), and Gokula (Krishna's childhood). Most texts, however, refer to the historical city of Vrindavan when they talk about Vraj. You won't find Vraj in maps since it is entirely mythical.

In teachings of Krishna, you will often encounter the words "love" and "attachment." These twin words may appear inseparable in meaning, but the leading Tibetan Buddhist scholar Ponlop Rinpoche came up with this to illustrate their difference: *Love is when you are thinking, "How can I make you happy?" Attachment is when you are thinking, "Why aren't you making me happy?"*

3

The Slaying of the Big-bosomed Infant Killer

If Putana was in the fashion world today, she would have been a plus-sized model gracing the covers of Vogue or Harper's Bazaar. Brazenly overweight, Putana was sensually attractive with broad hips and heavy breasts connected by a slim waist. Often casting sidelong glances while walking, she had such an infectious smile that people who saw her often mistook her for the goddess of prosperity.[4] In mythology, however, Putana is famous for using her pendulous breasts to kill a number of infants.

Originally, Putana was a hideous ogress who was an expert at infanticide. With his future slayer still at large, Kamsa ordered Putana to slaughter all infants regardless of their sex or age. To carry out this task, she transformed herself into a gorgeous woman and moved through cities and villages in search of infants. Her attack weapon was her over-sized breasts that extended to her waist. She did not kill by crushing or choking her victims with her bosom. Rather, she smeared poison on her breasts and turned them into twin deathtraps. Posing as a wet nurse, she tended the babies of unsuspecting parents, managing to kill the infants instantly.

---

[4] The goddess of prosperity is Lakshmi, the wife of Vishnu.

After wandering through towns and villages and accounting for a number of unexplained infant deaths, Putana arrived at Gokula. When she heard about the birth of a baby boy, she was eager and headed to Nanda's house at once. As luck would have it, Nanda had gone to Mathura to pay taxes and was away from home. With Putana's goddess like stature and air of authority, both Rohini and Yashoda welcomed her wholeheartedly and were embarrassed to ask who she was. After exchanging pleasantries with her hostesses, Putana chose a quiet moment to slip into the child's room. She picked up the sleeping infant and placed it gently on her lap. She undid her blouse swiftly, and releasing a large breast, she pushed the poison-smeared nipple into the baby's mouth. As she suckled the infant, Putana smiled to herself for executing the plan to perfection. She knew it would take only a matter of minutes for the baby to succumb to the effects of the poison. Her patience, however, grew thin with the passing of an hour. Unlike other babies, this baby was sucking milk with gusto, becoming stronger and stronger. Her complacency turned into anguish, when the child strengthened its hold on her breast and slowly sucked all the milk and then her vital energy. Frantic, she rushed out of the house in distress, turning into her true demonic form. Outside, she labored to the middle of the courtyard and then dropped dead with a thunderous roar of pain, destroying the cowshed and haystacks with her fall.

Alarmed by the screams, the neighbors and cowherds rushed to the house only to find the monstrous cadaver of the demon. They looked around for the baby. Yashoda started to tremble expecting the worst. They spotted the infant kicking his limbs in delight and lying on top of the demon with her deflated breasts dangling like popped balloons. The evil devourer of children had finally met her match in a tiny infant. The foster parents and cowherds were amazed that the baby was still alive, for they never thought he could be the one responsible for the monster's death. None was more relieved than Yashoda herself. After this incident, she was frightened to leave the child alone even for a minute.

Putana was only the first of the many demons sent by Kamsa to kill the baby. Not one of them returned alive. At first the parents and cowherds thought the baby was remarkably fortunate. After many such incidents, however, they began to get a sense of the tremendous reservoir of power packed in that tiny body. Slowly it dawned to them that Krishna was no ordinary child and there was something extraordinary about him.

4

The Butter Thief of Gokula

In the book *Yoga for Beginners*, Swami Gnaneswarananda recollects an incident where a Christian missionary, who, after listening to stories about Krishna, says to his fellow Indians, "Your Krishna is a thief, yet you still worship him as God." The deceased Northern Californian yoga swami did not elaborate the circumstances that led to this remark. Maybe the missionary suffered from diarrhea after indulging in Indian food. Or maybe he found it odd that Krishna was not perfect and yet devotees in throngs were attracted to him. Let's be clear. There's no denying Krishna was a mischievous child, prankster, and philanderer at various stages of his life. But to reduce Krishna's entire life to a thief is akin to saying Gandhi was an incorrigible liar or Nelson Mandela was a hard-core terrorist.

The basis of many such misinformed views is the Western notion that God is a perfect being, who does not play pranks or throw tantrums or indulge in philandering. In this concept, God maintains a clean image and is the epitome of frozen perfection that is remote, static, and unsociable. In contrast, in Hinduism, God is not considered perfect even when endowed with supernatural powers. For instance, the higher gods like Vishnu, Brahma, and Shiva are known for their strengths and shortcomings. Krishna is no different. He is endearing to his followers because of his unstinting love. Although Krishna demonstrates flashes

KRISHNA AND THE LATER AVATARS OF VISHNU

of supernatural behavior throughout his young life, he does not project the image of a perfect being at any time. In this chapter, we look at a series of childhood incidents in Krishna's life that earned him the popular moniker, the butter thief.

Let's visit Krishna's birth story again. Nanda and Yashoda did not have a child for a very long time. The couple had almost given up hope of ever having a child, when Yashoda, at 45 years of age, was blessed with a baby. During childbirth, Yashoda was certain the baby was a girl. After she recovered from labor fatigue, she was astounded to find that the baby was actually a boy. Her family and friends were ecstatic at the arrival of the new baby. The chief priest of the Yadavas named the baby "Krishna" at a secret ceremony since the parents were worried that news about his birth might reach the ears of Kamsa. As a baby, Krishna was a hearty milk drinker, a trait he shared with other milk-loving divinities of the Hindu pantheon. For instance, it is widely known that Ganesha had a thing for milk.[5] His brother Kartikeya was another feisty drinker, who feasted on milk from six pairs of breasts to quench his thirst.

Although Krishna was born in Mathura, he grew up in the town of Gokula along with his brother Balarama. Both Nanda and Yashoda believed Krishna was their own child. Having had a baby in the later part of her life, Yashoda was, understandably, an overanxious mother. When Krishna started crawling, Yashoda was on her toes and could rarely find time for household chores. Krishna and Balarama would hold on to the tails of calves, and the calves would drag the boys back and forth in the pasture much to the delight of the women who gathered around them. One day Krishna noticed a calf drinking the milk of its mother. So he crawled up to the mother cow, pushed the calf away, and started drinking milk straight from its udder. The mother cow raised its horns at Krishna. From far away Yashoda saw the aggrieved mother and was petrified. Her anxiety, however, turned to relief when the mother cow spread its big tongue and licked the boy affectionately as if he was its own calf. As

---

[5] See the chapter "Milk Miracle" in the book *Many Many Many Gods of Hinduism*.

Krishna began to toddle, Yashoda became even busier. Once she found him leaning precariously over the well. Pointing to his image in the water, Krishna pleaded with Yashoda, "Mother, there is a boy inside the well. Get him out." Yashoda rushed and grabbed the child with both hands. She admonished him never to go near the well again.

The *gopi*s, or cowherd girls, developed a fondness for Krishna and invited him to their houses. But they had no inkling how naughty he could be. Once he had been to a house, he would go uninvited and help himself to their prized possessions like ghee, curd, and milk. It was akin to your refrigerator being raided by your neighbor's kid repeatedly. Soon the *gopi*s had enough of these pranks and confronted Yashoda with a laundry list of complaints. "Krishna unties the calves before milking time and scampers away. He steals butter and curd and gives them to pups and kitten. He upsets the pails of milk and blames others for his mischief. If something is beyond his reach, he stacks pillows or mortars and gets it. When milk or curd is placed in suspended pots, he makes holes in the bottom and drinks whatever is pouring down. If we scold him, he laughs at us. What should we do?" Yashoda looked at the child questioningly. Seeing his frightened face, she could not bring herself to admonish him. Turning toward the *gopi*s, Yashoda pleaded, "Why don't you give him what he wants? After all, he's only a child." The *gopi*s protested in unison, "That we do. He still comes to our house unseen and steals more."

With a doting mother protecting her child, the *gopi*s chose not to air their grievances any more. Instead, they decided to prove their point by catching him in the act. They didn't have to wait too long, for one of the *gopi*s caught Krishna red handed with his hands fully immersed in … guess what? A pot of butter. Fearing the little one might give her the slip, the *gopi* locked him up inside a heavy chest. She then dragged the chest to Yashoda's house. "The butter thief is inside," she announced triumphantly. "Here's your innocent son caught in the act of stealing." But Yashoda protested, "That can't be him. He's playing in the backyard." Without a moment's hesitation, the *gopi* took out the key and opened the lock. Both of them peered into the chest only to find the *gopi's* own daughter, Radha,[6] sobbing inside. The poor *gopi* was at a complete loss of words at what had happened. She was certain she had caught the butter thief this time.

Krishna, the butter thief

By now, Krishna was officially known as the butter thief of Gokula. Not a day went by without some complaints from the *gopi*s. To put an end to his mischief, Yashoda thought of confining him to the house. So, she tied him around his waist with a rope and fastened the rope to a

---

[6] Radha later became Krishna's intimate lover.

heavy kitchen mortar.[7] *Now he would not be able to make his house visits*, thought Yashoda, as she went about her daily chores. Meanwhile Krishna sat quietly, the mortar severely restricting his movement. After some time, he got bored and began crawling. Lo and behold, the mortar gave way and wobbled obediently after him. Out the back gate they went, the child on all fours, and the mortar behind him. They went up the path for some distance until they approached a pair of tall trees standing close together. Krishna tried to crawl between the twin trees, but the mortar got stuck. Then something amazing happened. As Krishna lunged forward, the mortar followed the child, uprooting the trees in the process. The trees fell on either side with a heavy thud. Hearing the commotion, Yashoda came rushing out of the house. She almost fainted at the sight, but was thankful to find Krishna had emerged unscathed. *The child could have been killed*, thought Yashoda. It's a miracle he survived.

Back home, Yashoda realized that she was foolish to confine the child to the house. Let children be children and navigate the world themselves. But that did not seem to be a wise decision either. One day Rama and Balarama were playing with other children, when one of them spotted Krishna eating dirt and promptly reported the matter to Yashoda, who took Krishna aside and asked him sternly, "Have you been eating mud?" Krishna shook his head. "Ask him to open his mouth!" insisted Balarama. "Yes, ask him to show his mouth," the rest of boys demanded. "Open your mouth, Krishna," Yashoda said firmly. As Krishna opened his mouth, Yashoda gasped at what she saw. Expecting to see a few pieces of mud inside the child's mouth, Yashoda instead saw the great cycle of the sky, the sweep of the stars, and the vast expanse of the earth. The eternal universe was inside the mouth of her little one. In it, Yashoda saw herself and her home. She was dumbstruck. The whole sight had her whirling in space and lost in time. "Oh God!" she thought, "Is this a dream?" What a fool she was! Here was her child carrying the whole

---

[7] Among Krishna's several names, the name "Damodara," meaning "one who is tied around the waist," originated from this incident.

universe within himself and she was worried about a few pieces of mud. Holding the precious boy in her hand, she whispered, "Son, who are you, really?" Then her vision faded, and she promptly forgot everything she had just witnessed. Meanwhile the boys, who gathered around her, were perplexed. Instead of scolding the child, she was hugging him. *These adults are weird*, they thought.

What Yashoda saw inside the child's mouth was the cosmic form of Vishnu known as Vishvarupa. At first Yashoda thought the child was simply lucky. But incident after incident—the fatigue during delivery that caused memory loss, the mother cow licking the child, the little girl locked in the chest, and the falling of the twin trees—all proved that Krishna was no ordinary child. Things seem to fall into place with an ease that suggested to her that his path has been prepared for him. Suddenly, it dawned upon Yashoda that what she was seeing were the footprints of God.

> *The robbed that smiles, steals something from the thief.*
> —WILLIAM SHAKESPEARE, 1564-1616

❀ ❀ ❀

5

Taming the Monstrous Serpent Kaliya

There seems no end to the extraordinary events that took place in Gokula where Krishna spent his childhood. There seems no end to the number of miraculous escapes the child had in his short years. Far away in Mathura, Kamsa was actively devising plans, in spite of the setbacks, to eliminate his prophesied killer. Worried about the safety of their children, Nanda and Yashoda—Krishna's foster parents—and other fellow cowherds relocated to Vrindavan, a picturesque town in the foothills of Mount Govardhana with the river Yamuna (also known as Kalindi) snaking through the forest. Vrindavan turned out to be a paradise with moderate weather that never became too warm in summer or too cold in winter. Both Balarama and Krishna loved the new town. One day, fascinated by the charm of the region, Krishna and his friends, unaccompanied by Balarama, made a long trek to the banks of Yamuna. The cowherds and cows were exhausted by the journey and drank deep from the water. Moments later they fell sick and collapsed lifeless on the bank. Little did they know the water in that area was extremely poisonous because that part of the river was the home to the gigantic, multi-headed serpent Kaliya.

That was not the only occasion when such calamity fell on the residents of Vrindavan. Every so often the inhabitants noticed a choking, toxic vapor rising from Yamuna. At these times, the monkeys stayed away, and occasionally a calf that wandered too close to the river died mysteriously. Kaliya has spread such a virulent poison in the waters that nothing could remain alive in that part of the river or its banks. Even the grass and trees had withered except for a Kadamba tree—which was once occupied by Kaliya's arch rival Garuda (the mount of Vishnu and the enemy of snakes). The mist and spray that arose from the waters had such a noxious effect that it killed the birds flying over the region.

Finding the lifeless form of the cows and cowherds, Krishna cast his glance at them. Miraculously they became alive as if they had woken from a deep slumber. Suddenly, he noticed unusual ripples in the rivers. *The serpent is lurking, and it's time to confront the reptile in its own home,* he thought. Resolutely, he climbed the Kadamba tree. From the top of the tree, he plunged into the water like an advanced open water diver, as his friends watched him with bated breath.

The big splash attracted the attention of the serpent, and it darted toward Krishna. Eyes swollen with rage and tongues flickering, the serpent emerged from the water and raised its cluster of heads menacingly at the intruder. The multiple heads of the reptile spanned so wide that they blocked the sun's rays. Hissing and spitting, the snake wrapped the child in its shiny black coils and dragged him down to the bottom of the river, where they wrestled and tussled. Holding its prey firmly, the snake bit Krishna several times only to realize that its deadly fangs made no impact on the little one.

On the banks, the cowherds swarmed around anxiously when they saw their beloved playmate disappear with Kaliya. They notified his parents. Yashoda and Nanda became distraught that Balarama had not accompanied Krishna that day. They had become accustomed to the pattern that whenever Krishna embarked on a new escapade, he left his elder brother behind. The family rushed to the scene accompanied by other cowherds. Seeing Krishna entangled with the serpent at the bottom of the river, Yashoda wanted to jump in and save him, but the *gopi*s thwarted her attempt.

Krishna confronts Kaliya

Meanwhile, on the river bed, the battle between Krishna and Kaliya raged on. It seemed Krishna was biding his time and waiting for the audience to build up before starting the real show. Finding Kaliya tiring at last, Krishna seized the moment to break free from the shackles and swam upwards. But the serpent followed him with its hoods raised threateningly, blowing toxic fumes through its nostrils. Krishna swam around the pool in circles evading his predator. Then in a swift moment, he jumped onto one of the snake's hoods. What happened next was beyond everyone's imagination. Taking out his flute from the waistband, Krishna began a gruesome dance on top of the serpent's hoods. Grooving to the music, he stamped on each of the hoods in succession. The hoods broke off, but were immediately replaced by new ones. The divine melody attracted the gods in the heavens. They came down to see the show. The sight was so spectacular that even the cowherds forgot their anxiety and were enraptured by the dance. As the music reached a crescendo, Krishna repeatedly struck Kaliya's umbrella of hoods with his heels. The serpent could no longer bear the beating. Its limbs dangled uselessly, and blood spurted from its mouth. With its body and spirit broken, Kaliya was humbled.

The serpent had a number of wives who saw their proud husband being battered. They reached out to Krishna and petitioned him to spare his life. Kaliya himself pleaded for mercy. "We serpents are ferocious and cruel because that's how we have been designed by you. You alone can help us with this ordeal. Our salvation and destruction are both in your hands." But Krishna was not satisfied by this apology. "You poisoned the pool and prevented other creatures from using it. Therefore, I banish you to the island of Ramanaka in the middle of the ocean." Saying so, Krishna placed his hands on Kaliya's heads and healed the monster and its menacing heads.

Originally, Kaliya had lived in Ramanaka along with Garuda. According to a legend, the locals provided offerings to the serpents on the first day of each month and a part of the offerings, in turn, was given to Garuda by the serpents. Pride, however, caught up with the serpents and Kaliya began thinking of himself superior to Garuda because of his lethal poison. He kept the offerings to himself and did not share them with Garuda. On learning this, Garuda became furious and attacked Kaliya, hitting him hard with his wings. Kaliya ran away and found shelter in a pool of the Kalindi from where Garuda was forbidden. (Garuda had previously stolen many fish from the river, so an enraged sage had cursed him with death if he were to enter the pool again.) This was the same pool Kaliya poisoned and made his home.

With Kaliya banished, the inhabitants of Vrindavan were liberated from the terrible scourge of the serpent. Grass started to grow and the forest crept back up to the banks to the river. As for the dwellers, they could once again bathe in the refreshing waters and drink to their contentment.

> *The ancient Indian philosopher Chanakya was once asked, "What is poison?" His reply: "Anything which is more than our necessity is poison, be it power, wealth, hunger, ego, greed, love, or ambition."*

6

Krishna Lifts Mount Govardhana

The summer had just ended, and the Indian monsoon was about to begin. That meant one thing: rain. For the residents of Vrindavan, rainfall—in the right amount—was crucial because their livelihood depended on cattle, which, in turn, needed green pastures for grazing. Lack of rainfall led to drought in the region and starved cattle to death. Lots of rain, on the other hand, caused floods, killing cattle and disrupting the habitat. To show their respect, the people of Vrindavan offered an annual sacrifice to appease Indra, the guardian of rains. When Nanda and fellow villagers were making arrangements for the sacrificial ritual, Krishna went up to them and said, "Let's not perform this ritual anymore!"

Nanda looked at his child in disbelief. "What? Don't say that, son. We should show our respect to the nature gods. Don't you know that Indra gives us the rains and our good fortune?" But Krishna shot back. "We have been worshipping Indra year after year. That's a mistake because Mount Govardhana is our true friend. He is the one who stops the rain clouds drifting over Vrindavan. He's one who gives us the rains. Besides, the mountain sustains a habitat that accommodates everyone. Think about it, father. Who gives us medicine in the form of magical herbs and plants? Who brings us clean water from the top? And who gives us grass for our cows so that they can produce milk? If someone deserves credit for this, then it should be Mount Govardhana. Not Indra!"

Nanda was brought up in the tradition of paying respect to ancient Vedic gods like Indra, Varuna, and Agni, but Krishna's words rang true. The cowherds who were privy to the conversation agreed with Krishna. After all, Indra is invisible in the heavens, whereas Govardhana is always present and can be seen from anywhere in Vrindavan. So they decided to worship Govardhana instead of Indra this time around. On the appointed day, plenty of butter, milk and sweets were prepared for the deity. Cattle adorned with garlands and anklets surrounded the mountain. But Nanda was apprehensive. He feared the shifting of loyalty might incur the wrath of Indra.

From the heavens, Indra saw the people of Vrindavan worshipping Govardhana instead of him. Livid, he summoned his troop of rainclouds to attack the cowherds, which he knew was their livelihood. The thunderclouds unleashed a terrible storm at Indra's behest. In a flash the horizon disappeared and the earth and sky became one. Buckets of rain came pelting down. The cowherds and cattle ran around aimlessly looking for shelter. The river started to overflow, and the trees wobbled in the waters. Buffeted by the fierce storm, the helpless cows stood trembling, some sheltering their calves under them. The relentless storm and rain threatened to destroy all of Vrindavan.

When Krishna saw the misery of the cowherds and their cattle, he knew it was the work of Indra. He wanted to protect those who trusted him. Then something unbelievable happened. With a strength borne out of divinity, Krishna uprooted the mountain with his hands and then held it aloft on one finger. Turning to the cowherds, he urged, "Bring your cattle and possessions and get under here. You can take shelter without fear of the mountain falling down." This act was a show of strength and utter disdain toward Indra in the heavens.

As instructed, the cowherds rushed under the mountain with their belongings and cattle. Inside, they felt safe from the storm with the mountain sheltering them like a giant umbrella. But Indra was not the type to give up without a fight. He was determined to make the cowherds come out and beg for mercy. The thunderstorm continued unabated and even grew in strength. *Krishna would get tired very soon*, thought Indra.

The storm raged on for seven days and seven nights and devastated the region. But Krishna did not tire. He held up the mountain the entire time. Indra, on the other hand, ran out of water. From the eighth day, the rainfall gradually lost its intensity and eventually came to a complete stop. The skies cleared and the last howl of the wind died in the distance.

Krishna holding Mount Govardhana aloft with his little finger

Indra was utterly humiliated. But he was quick to realize that only someone mightier than him would have been able to pull out this spectacle. He became deeply apologetic and begged for pardon. Until then the exceptional ability of the child was known only to a few. After this incident, the news spread far and wide. With Krishna holding Govardhana at his fingertips, the mountain became synonymous with Krishna.

This incident had a profound impact on the Hindu mythological landscape. It was history repeating itself. Just like Indra had ousted Varuna to become the king of heavens, Krishna had banished Indra to become the lord of the universe.[8] The new star would eclipse Indra in the years to come. This event underscored the fact that gods of natural phenomena, such as Indra, Varuna, and Agni, popularly known as *devas*, are only demigods and not true gods. They were relegated to their rightful place—that is, secondary to the supreme gods—after this incident. For that reason, not many temples dedicated to the demigods exist in India.

> *The Egyptians saw the sun and called him Ra, the Sun God. He rode across the sky in his chariot until it was time to sleep. Copernicus and Galileo proved otherwise, and poor Ra lost his divinity.*
>
> —ASHWIN SANGHI, 1969—

---

[8] Indra's ascendency to power is described in book 1 of this series.

7

Krishna Steals the Clothes of Gopis

It appears butter and other dairy products were not the only items Krishna had been stealing. He was found guilty of stealing girl's clothes including their undergarments. That was after the butter-stealing prankster of Gokula grew into a handsome young man at Vrindavan. Such was his grace and beauty that Krishna became a heartthrob among all the teen and tween girls. And when he played the flute standing under the shade of a tree, leaning against the bark with one leg crossed over the other, the man and the melody were utterly irresistible. The poor *gopi*s of Vrindavan fell head over heels in love with the flute maestro. Every fiber in their body longed for his companionship.

For Krishna, however, nothing had really changed. The childhood pranks of teasing the *gopi*s were followed up with adolescent pranks, but the situation had become overloaded with double entendre. An innocent child asking for milk was guileless, but an adolescent wanting to taste a *gopi's* wares had an unmistakable sexual connotation. Similarly the breaking of a *gopi's matki* or "pots containing milk products" also carried an equally undeniable sexual innuendo. Sometimes the *gopi*s complained to Yashoda about her son's behavior, but she dismissed them by saying he was still a child. The pranks continued unabated, and the most famous of them was when he stole the *gopis'* clothes while they bathed in the river. Let's visit the bath scene from the beginning.

Winter had just arrived in Vraj. During this season, it was a common practice among unmarried girls to observe a 41-day vow to appease goddess Katyayani[9] in the hope of obtaining a handsome groom. The *gopis* of Vraj were smitten by Krishna and prayed to the goddess to have him as their husband. As part of the vow, these girls would wake up at 3 a.m. in the morning and perform rituals. They would then head over to the river Yamuna in the bitter cold and take a bath at sunrise.

It was the final day of the vow. The *gopis* placed their clothes on the riverbank as usual, and entered the frigid waters where they played joyfully by splashing water against one another. On that day they were surprised to see Krishna, along with his friends, standing on the banks of the river and smiling at them teasingly. Suddenly the *gopis* became aware of their nudity. Staying in the water, they covered their faces with their hands and peeped at him through the fingers. To their surprise, they saw Krishna walk toward the riverbank, take their clothes, and climb a nearby Kadamba tree. From the tree, he hollered, "Come and get your belongings!" The *gopis* realized their clothes had been stolen. They begged Krishna to return them, which he agreed but on one condition—they would have to personally come and collect them.

Shivering in the cold water, the *gopis* had no choice but to ignore the shame and emerge from water. Embarrassed, each one came out with one hand covering her breasts and the other covering her crotch. Water dripped from their hair and body parts as they walked toward him. Having fulfilled his condition, the *gopis* asked for their clothes, but Krishna was not satisfied. "Since your girls swam naked in the water when under a vow, you have offended Varuna, the god of waters. Therefore, to expiate the sin, you must fold your hands and place them

---

[9] Katyayani is a form of goddess Durga, who is described in book 6 of this series.

KRISHNA STEALS THE CLOTHES OF GOPIS

Krishna steals clothes of gopis, 19*th* century painting by Raja Ravi Varma

above your heads." The *gopi*s had no choice. They did what they were told and were gratified to have their clothes back. Although the milkmaids were burning with embarrassment, they saw no lust in Krishna's eyes, only affection. Before he left, Krishna made amends for the prank with the promise that the following autumn he would spend the night with them on what would become the famous dance of divine love known as Rasa Lila.[10]

Modern day feminists use this incident and paint a picture of Krishna as a mischievous voyeur who took advantage of the vulnerabilities of his devotees. Was Krishna abusing his star power? There is no doubt the *gopi*s were deceived and robbed of their modesty. Most Hindus, however, consider this incident as an adolescent prank and nothing more. Even the *gopi*s held no grudge against Krishna, for they were happy to have a glimpse of their beloved let alone expose their youthful bodies to him. But to brand Krishna as a voyeur in spite of his stellar career as an avatar based on this incident will be unfair because he was the one who protected the modesty of Draupadi, the wife of the Pandavas. The Mahabharata relates that when the Pandava prince Yudhishthira lost everything in a game of dice, the Kaurava prince Dushasana dragged Draupadi into the assembly hall and tried to disrobe her in public. Unable to bear the humiliation, Draupadi prayed to Krishna. When Dushasana tried to undress Draupadi by unfurling the layers of her sari, it seemed to extend to infinity—thanks to Krishna's divine powers. An embarrassed Dushasana eventually gave up his efforts.[11]

But not everyone thought the stealing of clothes was a prank gone too far. The Vaishnavas believe that in asking the *gopi*s to overcome their shame and modesty, Krishna was teaching them the importance of total surrender or the very baring of soul. According to them, the eternal soul is in divine love with the Supreme and always longing to unite with it. Our human love is only a shadow of the divine love. If human love is the fragrance, then divine love is the flower. According to Vaishnavas, union with the divine will lead to eternal bliss and can be achieved only by total surrender.

---

[10] The dance is described in the next chapter.
[11] This story is described in detail in the Mahabharata section.

KRISHNA STEALS THE CLOTHES OF GOPIS

Modesty is a quality in a lover more praised by the women than liked.
—RICHARD BRINSLEY SHERIDAN, 1751–1816

8

Rasa Lila - The Dance of Divine Love

When autumn finally arrived in Vraj, the nights were soothing with gentle river breezes flowing by, drenched in the fragrance of jasmine flowers. On one enchanting evening, the forest began to glow in the reddish rays of the rising moon, creating the perfect setting for lovers and poets. Krishna took out his flute and began to play music. Then a strange thing happened. Upon hearing his enthralling music, the *gopi*s stopped what they were doing. They ran out of their homes in the direction of the music, forgetting their honor, husbands, and household duties. As promised, Krishna had come to spend the autumn nights with them. The Rasa Lila or "the Dance of Divine Love" was about to take place.

Hold on! But aren't Indian women known for their loyalty? Indeed, the Indian women are famous for their fidelity and stand on par with their Japanese counterparts. Every man cherishes the dream of spending their lifetime in the company of desi woman. Yet, the fiercely loyal women of Vraj could not resist the music emanating from Krishna's flute. The *gopi*s were obsessed with the flute player himself and would do anything to be with their lover. Panting with excitement, they met Krishna on the banks of Yamuna and sat down around him. The Rasa Lila began, sending the lovesick *gopi*s into ecstasies of delight, each one dancing with Krishna as if he was her sole lover. After some time, the minds of the *gopi*s were filled with pride. They thought they must have been especially beautiful to attract Krishna. Suddenly, their beloved lover vanished from sight. The light that illuminated the riverbank also disappeared with him.

With Krishna missing, the *gopi*s woke up from their trances and realized they were dancing foolishly without their hero. Many began to cry. Then one of them noticed that Radha was missing too. Radha was Krishna's childhood friend and especially dear to him. As the maidens went searching for Krishna, they found two sets of footprints in the sand. *Radha must have run off with Krishna,* thought the *gopi*s. At some distance, the two sets of footprints merged into one, but became deeper. *Krishna must have carried her from this point.* As they followed the trail, they found Radha slumped on the footpath alone. When she saw the *gopi*s, she gulped back tears, and sighed. She told them she and Krishna had walked together for some time until she asked him to carry him, and he had bent down to take her. Then the thought occurred to her how she could boast about her conquest to other *gopi*s. She would tell them Krishna was enchanted by her beauty and a prisoner of her love. *Indeed, she must be so special,* thought Radha, *for him to carry her on his shoulders.* As soon as pride asserted itself in her, Krishna disappeared leaving her alone in the forest.

Together with Radha, the *gopi*s went to the banks of Yamuna again. As darkness engulfed the land, they gave up their search. The *gopi*s gathered together and shouted "Krishna, Krishna," begging him to return. They sang together expressing their profound agony and intense longing for him. Suddenly, out of nowhere, Krishna emerged again in their midst. When they saw him, the *gopi*s felt as if their breaths had returned. They clung to him like bees to nectar, to not let him disappear again. The Rasa Lila commenced once again. The *gopi*s linked their arms together forming a great circle with Krishna in the middle. Each one of them circled him, singing and dancing. The rhythm of the steps grew quicker and the intimacy greater. By divine arrangement, Krishna danced with all the *gopi*s at the same time, yet each *gopi* thought he was dancing with her alone. Supreme love reached its height of fulfillment through joyous dancing and singing. The dance and its delights continued for six months and ended with the whole troupe bathing in the river. Thereafter, the *gopi*s returned to their homes only to find that no one knew that they had been away.

Rasa Lila painting, artist unknown

If you have been wondering about the significance of the Hare Krishnas singing, clapping, and dancing in the streets, they are only performing a variation of the Rasa Lila. The Chaitanya school of Vaishnavism, which provided the inspiration for the Hare Krishna movement, considers the divine love arising from the Rasa Lila as the purest form of bhakti. Furthermore, the Vaishnava devotees consider the portrayal of *gopi*s as the epitome of loving service and ideal devotion.[12]

---

[12] The Hare Krishnas are described in a later chapter.

The Rasa Lila comes to us from the ancient text Bhagavata Purana in five chapters entitled "Rasa Lila Panchadhyaya." Although the Rasa Lila is just a poem about young maidens joining their beloved to perform the circular dance of love, the love poem made a profound impact on the people of Vraj. It can be easily considered the "Song of Songs" from ancient India. On a spiritual level, the essence of Rasa Lila is the eternal soul's longing for union with Ultimate Reality in divine play or *lila*. Several Vaishnava sects single out the story of Rasa Lila claiming it to be the essence of all *lilas*.

The Rasa Lila took a significant long-term toll on Krishna. Many *gopi*s fell in love with him, and Krishna ended up with 16,108 wives and several children—something we'll discuss in another chapter. The dance also made a profound influence on the religion and culture of India. For thousands of years, poets and writers have continually narrated the story, often crafting new stories that expand on a particular theme of Rasa Lila. The circular dance was also the subject of pictorial adaptations and dance concerts from a variety of classical Indian dance schools—like kathak and Manipuri—in which artists have attempted to capture the essence and beauty of India's greatest love theme.[13]

> *Women are meant to be loved, not to be understood.*
>
> —OSCAR WILDE, 1854–1900

---

[13] The origin of Indian classical dances is described in book 5 of this series.

9

Krishna and Radha - A Pastoral Love Story

Did Krishna have a favorite lover among the *gopi*s? The Bhagavata Purana mentions the existence of Krishna's dearest consort in the Rasa Lila, but does not explicitly name her. It was Jayadeva Goswami, the renowned 12th century poet-cum-scholar from Bengal, who first identified her as Radha in his celebrated work Gita Govinda meaning "Song of Govinda," where Govinda is Krishna himself. Today Jayadeva is remembered for bringing the character of Radha into prominence, making her as large as Krishna himself. The Gita Govinda immortalized the love between Krishna and Radha though the work was published several centuries after the Bhagavata Purana was written.[14]

Significant differences exist between the Rasa Lilas of the Bhagavata Purana and Gita Govinda. In the Bhagavata Purana, the circular dance is between a group of heroines and Krishna, although special mention is given in one chapter to a favored *gopi*. In the Gita Govinda, the focus is on a single hero and heroine between whom a passionate romance develops.

---

[14] No one knows when the Bhagavata Purana came into existence. The oral tradition can be found as early as the fourth century CE while, according to scholars, the work was written between the seventh and ninth centuries CE.

KRISHNA AND THE LATER AVATARS OF VISHNU

While the older Rasa Lila takes place during autumn, the romance in Gita Govinda occurs during the spring season, and after the autumnal episode. Furthermore, the intensity of the love in the Gita Govinda is several notches higher than that of the Puranic version. On a Motion Pictures Association of America rating, if the Puranic version is rated "General Audience," then Jayadeva's version will be "Restricted."

The plot of Gita Govinda is surprisingly pedestrian. With just three characters—Krishna, Radha, and an unnamed Sakhi[15]—the story is about Krishna and Radha's love, estrangement, and reunion. One evening, Nanda is strolling in the forest along with Krishna, Radha, and many others when menacing storm clouds gather in the sky. A worried Krishna wants to go home, so Nanda asks the older Radha to accompany him. On their way, one thing leads to another and the two end up making love in an arbor on the banks of Yamuna.

After this incident, they go about their own separate ways. Meanwhile spring has arrived at Vraj, and along comes Kama, the god of love, with his bow-and-arrow, instilling passion in all creatures. Krishna is out in the forest celebrating the springtime festival of Vasant and recklessly dallying with the *gopi*s. Spring is also a cruel time for deserted lovers, for Radha remembers her first meeting with Krishna, its ecstasy and joy, and then the angst of separation. Struck by the shafts of Kama, Radha pines for Krishna and searches for him everywhere, but finds him playing the love dance with other pretty milkmaids. Deeply hurt, Radha walks away miffed only to weep reminiscing of the glorious love they shared in a previous Rasa Lila.

Sakhi informs Krishna about Radha's plight and implores him to meet her, but Krishna declines. Kama next takes aim at Krishna and romantically charges him with Radha's image. Krishna now finds other *gopi*s uninteresting. He searches for Radha, but is unable to find her in the dense forest and therefore heads toward the Yamuna. At the riverbank, Krishna meets Sakhi, who again informs him about the Radha's pitiful condition. "She is suffering in her separation from you and clings

---

[15] *Sakhi* is the generic term for a woman's female friend in many Indian languages.

Radha pining for Krishna

to you in fantasy." Krishna is touched by Radha's plight and asks Sakhi to bring Radha to the bower. Sakhi goes to Radha and describes the state of Krishna. "He has prepared a lotus bed and is anxiously waiting for you on the banks of Yamuna. When a leaf stirs or the wind whispers, he imagines it is you." She pleads with Radha to give up her bitterness and meet with Krishna, but Radha is unmoved.

One fine morning, Krishna arrives at Radha's abode, but she rejects him outright with derisive words. "Go away Krishna. Do not plead to me with your lies." Krishna tries to persuade her, but convinced of his infidelity, she retreats into a state of emotional paralysis for which there seems no cure. Radha's wrath abates over time. She's filled with remorse at the realization she has turned away the lord himself. Sakhi reminds her she must be prepared when Krishna comes for her. "When he is tender, you are rough. When he bends down in obeisance, you are unbending. Oh, Radha, do not turn him away. He is languishing for you."

Eventually Radha agrees to meet Krishna alone. When they meet, Radha's eyes overflow with tears of joy, and her friend leave them alone.

Krishna finds Radha irresistible. Her face resembles sea waves cresting in the presence of moon. Their deeply locked emotions break free. Ornaments dislodge from their place, and clothes desert Radha's body exposing her breasts and hips. In an arbor decorated with flower garlands, and on a makeshift bed made of Kadamba leaves, Krishna and Radha make furious love. The intensity of their longing for each other makes it appear as if the couple is at war. As if to avenge being neglected, Radha is on the offensive riding over him. The *maithuna* continues all night until dawn. In the morning, Radha asks Krishna to tidy up her disheveled hair and re-adorn her with ornaments. The enslaved lover, Krishna, who overcame the mightiest of the demons in combat, submits faithfully, utterly defeated by Radha's love.

Although the Gita Govinda was written in the 12th century, the first English translation of the poem was undertaken in 1792 by Sir William Jones,[16] the philologist well-known for his work linking Indo–European languages. Many scholars unanimously declared Gita Govinda to be a great piece of literary work. The poem was translated to many languages, and was considered one of the finest examples of Sanskrit poetry. According to Goethe, the 19th century German poet-cum-statesman, the remarkable feature of Gita Govinda was the "extremely varied motives by which an extremely simple subject is made endless." In his work, Jayadeva powerfully expresses the intensity of Radha's obsession with Krishna. Such is her fixation toward Krishna under the influence of Kama that she imagines pepper vines hugging trees, and bees kissing flowers. The cooing of cuckoo, for Radha, was nothing but an expression of sensual delight. The most famous verse of Gita Govinda is, however, Krishna's desperate appeal to Radha:

> *"My beloved, release me from Kama's poison*
> *by adorning my head with fresh buds of your feet."*

---

[16] While Sir William Jones was a linguistic prodigy, his father was a mathematician by the same name who is known for introducing the symbol π.

It is said that after Jayadeva wrote this line, he was appalled at his own impudence for asking a lover (Radha) to put her feet on the highest god's head. Promptly, he scratched these lines from the manuscript and went to bathe in a river. When Jayadeva returned, he was surprised to see not only did the deleted text remain in the manuscript but his wife had eaten her meal ahead of him, contrary to custom. Legend has it that while he was bathing, Krishna came to his house, restored the scratched lines from his text, partook of his food in the company of his wife, and promptly left. For Jayadeva, this was Krishna's own stamp of approval on his portrayal of the relationship between Radha and Krishna.

In the Gita Govinda, Krishna is the highest god, the prime manifestation of god incarnating in various forms. In fact, the poem attributes all incarnations to Krishna, not Vishnu—which contrasts with the Puranic view. Although the poem received critical acclaim, its blunt eroticism left many commentators unimpressed and occasionally livid. The 17th century Sanskrit scholar and poet Jagannatha Panditaraja did not mince words in his work *Rasagangadhara* while condemning Jayadeva and calling him "a rutting elephant describing the Gods inappropriately and bulldozing through propriety." Besides Jagannatha, many Indologists, whose Victorian sensibilities did not allow them to appreciate the poetry, also found the poem utterly distasteful.

You will be surprised to learn that Radha was already married when she fell in love with Krishna. In fact, some texts portray Radha as an older woman, while others as an aunt. Regardless, the Vaishnavas see her as the true spirit of a devotee yearning for god regardless of their situation. Radha is seen as "married" to social obligation while her soul seeks union and liberation with her true love. Followers of Vishnu endeavor to become like Radha, forever in love with Krishna, but occasionally separated from him. Although Radha's extramarital affair with Krishna goes against the social norms of those times, her unwavering love for Krishna and her willingness to risk her reputation is an example for her followers who aspire to be like her in devotion.

Radha-Krishna, the greatest divine love of all

The Gita Govinda became a favorite source of inspiration for Rajasthani and Pahari miniature painters.[17] The story also provided the impetus for producing many pictorial expressions from a single image, a technique commonly employed in miniature paintings. In these works, Radha is seen waiting in a forest grove for Krishna to return. In the northern and eastern parts of India, the bronze images of Krishna playing the flute that are enshrined in temples are often accompanied by images of Radha, who is worshipped as a goddess.

---

[17] Miniature paintings of ancient India are described in book 2 of this series.

KRISHNA AND RADHA - A PASTORAL LOVE STORY

A man is already halfway in love with any woman who listens to him.
—BRENDAN BEHAN, 1923–1964

10

Did Krishna Have Many Wives?

The biblical King Solomon is said to have had only one official wife despite having about 700 wives and a further 300 mistresses. That was considered okay in olden times when it was common for men to have multiple wives. Today monogamy is the norm, and we look at men having multiple wives as sexual predators—unless you happen to be a rich Middle Eastern oil sheikh, who usually have more than a dozen wives even though the Koran allows a maximum of just four wives at a time. That said, both Solomon and the Arab sheikhs pale in comparison to Krishna, for the flute maestro is said to have a whopping 16,108 wives.

In ancient Hindu societies, polygamy was the rule rather than the exception. History is replete with tales of emperors and kings having fleets of wives and even more children. Both Dasharatha and Vasudeva—Rama and Krishna's fathers—had multiple wives. A notable exception was Rama, who was married to only one wife throughout his life. With 16,108 wives, Krishna created a record of some sort and makes one wonder whether the purpose of his incarnation was to become a playboy and multiply the Yadava race. Far from it, Krishna became the husband of these wives because of extraordinary circumstances, as we'll learn shortly. He had eight principal queens: Rukmini, Satyabhama, Jambavati, Nagnajiti, Kalindi, Lakshmana (woman), Mitravinda, and Bhadra. Apart from these queens, Krishna had

16,100 junior queens. The biggest omission from his list of queens is Radha. Despite being Krishna's favorite lover, Radha was never married to Krishna.

Among his wives, Krishna loved his first wife Rukmini the most since she was loving, beautiful, and, above all, unassuming. The marriage between Krishna and Rukmini took place under strange circumstances. Rukmini grew up hearing stories of Krishna from childhood and vowed to marry only him. When she came off age, Rukmini's older brother wanted her to marry his friend Shishupala, the prince of a neighboring province and a relative of Krishna. On the day of *swayamvara*, Krishna had to abduct Rukmini as per her wish, and later he married her in Dvaraka.

Another girl pining for Krishna's love was Satyabhama, the only child of a Yadava chief. As a rich spoilt girl, she was the opposite of Rukmini. Feisty and argumentative, Satyabhama was known for her temper tantrums and initially had a low opinion of men. Her pride was humbled when she met Krishna, and was deeply attracted to him. Krishna came to know about her affection and fulfilled her desire but only after he had married another woman.

Satyabhama's father was the owner of the Syamantaka jewel, a gem with purportedly magical properties including bestowing wealth and prosperity on the possessor. When Syamantaka was lost, her father went livid and accused Krishna of stealing it since Krishna wanted the jewel to be presented to Ugrasena. Under strange circumstance, the gem came under the possession of Jambavan, the king of bears, who offered it to his daughter Jambavati.[18] To clear his name of any wrongdoing, Krishna went to meet Jambavan in his cave, but the bear mistook Krishna for an intruder and the two fought each other for many days. Eventually Jambavan realized that he was fighting with the lord, so to make amends for his imprudence, he presented both the jewel and his daughter to Krishna, who rejected the former but accepted the latter. The twice-married Krishna later married Satyabhama, consenting to her wish.

---

[18] Satyabhama's father had given the gem to his brother but he was killed by a lion during a hunting trip. The lion became fascinated by the shiny object and took the gem with it. The animal was later killed in an encounter with Jambavan, who then came in possession of the gem.

Emboldened by his three marriages, Krishna embarked on a wedding blitz and married five more times, mostly to princesses and each deeply in love with him. However, the biggest episode in Krishna's marital life was to happen thereafter. A mighty king called Narakasura became powerful through a boon and terrorized his neighboring provinces. He captured the nubile daughters of thousands of kings and confined them to prison. Not content with stealing the women, the demon went to heaven and helped himself to Aditi's earrings[19] and later filched Varuna's umbrella—both of which had magical properties. At the request of Indra, Krishna fought and defeated the demon along with his associates, and the stolen objects were returned to their rightful owners.[20] The young women were set free, but they collectively fell in love with their liberator and pleaded with Krishna to marry them en masse. What followed was one the greatest mass marriages in history where Krishna accepted all 16,100 of the women as his wives.[21]

With 16,108 women deeply in love with him, was Krishna the luckiest man on the planet? Not quite. Marrying many women is one thing, managing their marital needs, another. Why? That's because no two women are alike and each one has her own personality and biological clock. Dasharatha, the father of Rama, found it difficult to divide his love and attention equally among his three wives. Even rich oil sheikhs face problems not always related to wealth. For instance, one Arab sheikh found out to his dismay that all his 40 wives had gotten their period at the exact same time defying the laws of probability.

Krishna is said to have had occasional squabbles with his wives. One row was over a flower. Krishna and his wife Satyabhama were visiting Indra at his palace when she became utterly mesmerized by the fragrance of a flower from the Parijata tree. Used to getting her own way, Satyabhama

---

[19] Aditi is the mother of the *devas* (demigods). She's described in book 1 of this series.
[20] Hindus consider Satyabhama an incarnation of Mother Earth. She is also associated with the killing of Narakasura since his boon stipulated that he could only be slain by Mother Earth.
[21] Strictly speaking, Krishna had only eight principal queens or wives. For the remaining, Krishna acted as their protector and not as husband.

wanted the tree for herself to plant in her home in Dvaraka. So she asked Krishna to carry the tree. Knowing Satyabhama's uncompromising nature, Krishna uprooted the tree and placed it on his mount Garuda for transporting it to Dvaraka. Meanwhile, Indra came to know about this incident and became enraged. He confronted Krishna and promptly a fight ensued between the two. Indra had forgotten about his earlier encounter with Krishna at Mount Govardhana. Once again Indra proved that he was no match for Krishna. After the skirmish, both Krishna and Satyabhama returned to Dvaraka with their prized possession.

Back home, sage Narada assisted Satyabhama in planting the tree. The sage picked a spot close to the wall that separated Satyabhama's property from that of Rukmini's. The tree grew up but its branches spread over the wall into her neighbor's property. When it started flowering, the cornucopia of flowers carpeted Rukmini's garden even though Satyabhama watered the plant regularly. Satyabhama did not know that Narada had a soft spot for Rukmini, since he considered her to be the ideal Aryan wife.[22]

Narada was also behind another squabble between the two wives in the tale of Tulabhara, which is an ancient Hindu practice of weighing a person against an object. The sage held a contest between Rukmini and Satyabhama to determine whom Krishna loved most. Satyabhama was persuaded to outweigh Krishna with a measure of her wealth in gold and jewels. She loaded as much gold as possible on the scale, but Krishna remained heavier. When Rukmini's turn came, she placed a single Tulsi leaf on the scale and at once the balance tipped in her favor. For Krishna, love was more important than money. Rukmini's love and affection were superior to the material wealth of Satyabhama.

When you have a large family, how do you look after all the wives? Once Narada decided to find out how Krishna managed to keep so many wives happy at the same time and yet go about his life normally. For a celibate like Narada, the thought of having one wife itself seemed a burden

---

[22] The ideal Aryan wife is one who asks nothing, but gives everything to her husband. She finds the greatest happiness in the service of her husband.

let alone several wives. Accompanied by his veena, Narada paid a visit to Rukmini's abode, where he found Krishna slumbered on the swing bed with Rukmini massaging his feet. The couple seemed to be on cloud nine. The sage headed to the next house. At Satyabhama's palace, he founded Krishna and Satyabhama fully immersed in a game of dice, where Krishna appeared calm even though he was about to lose the game. *Krishna cannot be at Jambavati's house at this time*, thought Narada, as he rushed to her abode. At her palace, Narada, to his surprise, found both Krishna and Jambavati interlocked in *maithuna*. They did not seem to notice the sage's arrival. Narada pressed on and visited many more homes. At every place, he noticed that, just like a traditional husband, Krishna was always engaged in some activity or the other with his wives. Exhausted, Narada finally gave up his search. For Krishna, this was nothing unusual. He cloned himself to be with all his wives at the same time, just like he did with the *gopi*s during Rasa Lila.

A by-product of many alliances is the acquisition of many mothers-in-law. A large number of wives almost always lead to an even larger number of children. When Middle Eastern sheikhs are faced with big families, they often build elementary schools to educate their children. Krishna is said to have sired ten children from each of his queens.[23] That makes up a total of 161,080 children, enough to populate a small city. The dynamics of large families often creates an environment of mistrust and jealousy that leads to internal conflict and infighting, as many Arabian royal families have found out. Krishna was no exception, even with his ability to duplicate himself. Most of his children and grandchildren died because of bickering and infighting.

In a happy marriage it is the wife who provides the climate, the husband the landscape.

—GERALD BRENAN, 1894–1987

---

[23] Some texts state that Krishna had ten children each from his eight principal queens—which adds up to 80 children.

11

The Downfall of Kamsa

At this point, you might be wondering what happened to Krishna's arch nemesis, Kamsa? After hearing about the stupendous powers of Krishna, did you think Kamsa had a change of heart and met Krishna to tell him how much he loved his nephew and followed up with a confession that he had an ear infection at the time he heard the prophecy? Not a chance. Tyrants and dictators rarely accept defeat or accountability even if their life is on the line, and Kamsa was no exception. As the king of Mathura, he spent a lifetime scheming to destroy his prophesied killer. With all his plans ending in failure, Kamsa became desperate for success. Around this time, the sage Narada appeared before the king and told him everything that had happened, scene-by-scene, beginning with the exchange of embryos, and followed by the killing of Putana and numerous others.

Kamsa was dumbfounded. The shock slowly turned into anger as he brooded over the many plots he had devised to kill the boys. "No power can destroy me or my army," growled Kamsa. Anger spiraling out of control, he lashed out at the boys. "Balarama and Krishna are rogues who fooled the poor villagers with their antics. They don't stand a chance against my professional soldiers. Their bodies will be chopped into one thousand pieces and fed to the vultures."

KRISHNA AND THE LATER AVATARS OF VISHNU

He continued to think about how to get rid of Krishna and Balarama. *The boys are growing up. At this rate they will become invincible when they reach manhood. I must kill them before they gain full strength*, thought Kamsa. He arrested Krishna's parents—Vasudeva and Devaki— and put them in jail. He then decided upon a course of action. First, he would command the ferocious Keshi,[24] the demon who prowled around Vrindavan, to kill the boys in the woods. And if Keshi is not successful, like many demons before him, Kamsa had another plan. He would lure the boys to his trap by inviting them to a wrestling tournament. Many of his schemes went astray because they were attempted outside of Mathura. When the boys are in the capital, he would surround them with his military. He would pit them against the mightiest of his wrestlers and make it appear as if they were killed while participating in the competition.

The long-haired demon Keshi was at once summoned to hunt for "the boy with a peacock feather in his hair." Keshi was a vicious demon, known to be as quick as lightning. He nearly killed Indra in an encounter when the two fought over a girl called Devasena, who later became Kartikeya's wife. That happened when Indra was at the peak of his powers. This time Keshi took the form of a giant horse and galloped at a high speed, his hooves tearing into Earth. The crackling sound and the loud neighing terrified people and drove them away from their homes. Soon the equine homed in on its ultimate target—Krishna. Charging dangerously, the horse tried to trample Krishna with its hooves. But the demon underestimated the strength of its rival. The boy grabbed the animal by its legs and hurled it away at a great distance. Distressed at his fall, Keshi opened its mouth and lunged at its enemy. Krishna waited for the horse to approach him. He then thrust his arm down the throat of the stallion causing its body to swell. The horse inflated like a balloon and burst into smithereens.[25]

When Kamsa came to know about Keshi's fate, he became frantic. Although he knew that the demon was not a match for Krishna, he was

---

[24] Also referred to as Kesin.
[25] Krishna earned the epithet Keshava for slaying Keshi. Keshava also refers to Krishna's long unshorn hair.

unnerved by the ease with which Krishna had eliminated him. It was time to activate the master plan, the one he had meticulously plotted. *This time he would bring the boys to the capital. When the boys are in Mathura, he would personally supervise their demise*, thought Kamsa.

The head of his court, Akrura, was sent out as an emissary to invite the boys to a wrestling match during the grand bow festival, which was celebrated in honor of Shiva. Akrura was specifically chosen since he was one of the Yadava kin and a relative of Vasudeva. That way the cowherds of Vrindavan would not become suspicious. But Kamsa did not know that Akrura was a secret devotee of Krishna.

Akrura reached Vrindavan at dusk and saw Krishna herding the cows. He greeted Krishna effusively and was enthusiastically received in turn. As instructed, Akrura invited the brothers to Mathura for the wrestling tournament. The virtuous Akrura, however, could not hide the truth and told them about the monster in Mathura and his atrocities—his prosecution of the Yadavas, his secret police, and his sinister tyranny. He also revealed Kamsa's plan to kill the boys when they are in Mathura. Two wrestlers had been specially trained to finish them in a fight. Besides, a savage elephant had been stationed in the tournament arena to trample the boys.

After a brief pause, Akrura continued. "There is something else I must tell you that may change your lives." Addressing Krishna, he continued, "Yashoda is not your real mother, nor Nanda your father." Shock leapt into Krishna's eyes. Akrura then told him about the prophecy and everything that had happened. He also told him that their biological parents had been imprisoned by Kamsa. This was the first time the boys came to know about their real parents.

Both Balarama and Krishna were saddened to hear about their parent's plight and decided to accept the invitation. The *gopis* became inconsolable on learning that Krishna and Balarama were leaving Vrindavan. Nanda and Yashoda became concerned about their safety. At daybreak, Krishna and Balarama set off for Mathura along with Akrura in his chariot. When they approached the city precincts, they realized Mathura was no ordinary city. The roads were flanked by colossal mansions and magnificent gardens. The news of their arrival had reached before them. Having heard about Krishna's divine powers, women leant from their terraces and balconies to get a glimpse of the flute maestro. The boys reached the city, and then they sauntered through the roads of Mathura. They met with Kamsa's tailor, who made them new clothes. Further up, they saw the terrible sight of a hunchback called Kubja making her way to Kamsa's court. With one magical touch, Krishna straightened her crooked back, for which she was extremely grateful.[26]

Krishna and Balarama proceeded to the hall where the great bow of Shiva was laid. Many guards stood at the entrance to stop trespassers. But the guards were caught in a trance, as Krishna went past them nonchalantly and stopped in the middle of the hall where the bow was displayed. Bending down, he picked up the bow, and then with one casual pull snapped it into pieces much to the bewilderment of the spectators and guards. Until then no one was able to lift the bow let alone snap it. The cracking sound filled the skies. The guards came to their senses and at once surrounded Krishna and Balarama to arrest them, but the boys drove them away with the broken pieces of the bow. From afar, Kamsa heard the loud noise and realized the boys had arrived in town. That night he could not sleep a wink.

Early next morning, Kamsa gave orders for the commencement of the wrestling match. When the boys entered the arena, an irate elephant began to move its head up and down and came charging toward them. Unbeknownst to them, the keeper had incited the elephant to charge at Krishna. The pachyderm came running toward Krishna with its trunk raised high and caught hold of him. Somehow Krishna managed to wiggle out of its hold. The elephant turned around and tried to gore the boy, but Krishna moved out of the way, and the animal lost its balance. Its tusks hit the ground, pierced the earth, and got stuck. The elephant labored to extricate itself with all its might, but the tusks got broken. Without its

---

[26] This incident is described in detail in a later chapter in this book.

tusks, the elephant was no longer a force. Krishna and Balarama calmly took the tusks and paraded them around.

Meanwhile two wrestlers were waiting in the arena to confront Krishna and Balarama. These two men were the best wrestlers of Mathura and the veterans of many matches. Being a wrestler himself, Kamsa had personally selected them and supervised their training. They were given prior orders not to show any leniency to the boys from Vraj because of their tender ages.

The brothers clashed against the wrestlers—fist against fist, elbow against elbow, and chest against chest. Each wrestler tried to overpower the other in the midst of cheering and clapping by the spectators. At the outset it was apparent that the contest was unevenly matched. Adults were pitted against boys. Kamsa's wrestlers were thorough professionals, and grabbed the boys and threw them around. Some spectators began to walk out in protest. After being pounded and beaten, the brothers gradually gained confidence while the wrestlers became exhausted. Realizing this, Krishna picked one of them, spun him around, and dashed him to the ground. The crowd cheered at the sudden turn of events. Next Balarama slew the other with a deft blow of his hand. With the fall of the two wrestlers, another pair of gladiators came forward, followed by another, only to be slain by the boys.

Kamsa was in utter panic at the death of his powerful wrestlers. Months of careful planning had ended in failure. Terrified but still undaunted, he summoned his guards to bring Vasudeva and Devaki to the court, along with his own father, Ugrasena. They were ordered to be summarily executed. Krishna learned about Kamsa's orders and rushed to the court. There, eventually, he came face-to-face with Kamsa, his nemesis who had tormented him for many years. In true Kshatriya tradition, Kamsa charged at the unarmed boy with his sword raised. Like many others before him, Kamsa proved to be no match against the boy's incredible powers. He caught Kamsa by a clump of his hair and smashed him to the ground just like Kamsa had killed all of Devaki's children at birth. And there lay dead Kamsa, the mighty king of Mathura and the terror of the Yadavas.

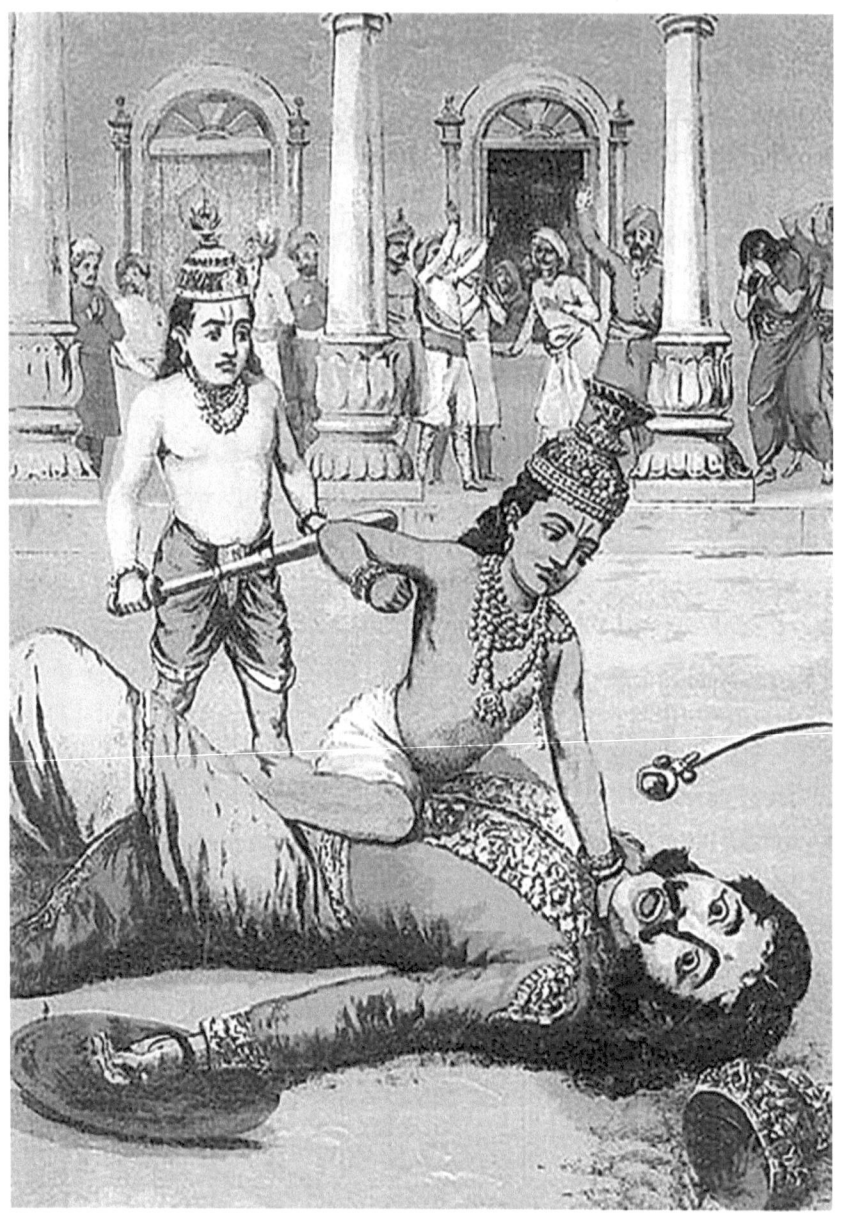

Krishna annihilates Kamsa, 19th century painting by Raja Ravi Varma

Krishna and Balarama at once released their parents from their shackles. Devaki and Vasudeva, overwhelmed by the scenes, stood before them deferentially, looking upon them as twin divinities rather than their own children. After some time, the parents forgot about their greatness and embraced them. When Devaki lamented about missing out on the parenting, Krishna suggested she hear all these stories from their foster parents.

After Kamsa's death, Ugrasena was reinstated as the king of Mathura. Abandoning the pastoral life and becoming a feudal prince, Krishna now entered the final phase of his life. With the main objective of his incarnation being achieved, Krishna was not yet ready to return to Vaikuntha, his true abode. Kamsa's allies remained at large—particularly Jarasandha—and wielded enough power to disturb the balance of good and evil.

The annihilation of Kamsa provided a rich source of inspiration not only to the artistic traditions of India, but also to Bollywood movie makers. The standard plot of brothers separated from family at birth and reunited at the end became a constant theme of Bollywood movies, particularly of the 70s and 80s.

Some cause happiness wherever they go; others whenever they go.
—OSCAR WILDE, 1854–1900

12

The Golden Touch That Healed a Hunchback

Krishna is said to accept anything given with love and affection by his devotees. It does not matter who gives the offering or how big or small it is. Says Krishna in the Bhagavad Gita, "If one offers me a leaf, a flower, fruit, or water with love and devotion, I will accept it." As a guest to Vidura,[27] Krishna was once offered an unusual item—a banana peel. That happened when Vidura's wife, a great devotee of Krishna, became so excited at serving the lord that she accidentally served him the banana peel instead of the fruit. Krishna accepted the peel and relished it with joy. But what if the offering is an invitation to *maithuna*? No problem. Krishna never refused love in any form when given with sincerity by a devotee. What if the offer comes from a high-class prostitute? No problem. Society may have its own taboos and stigmas, but for Krishna a royal or rabble is equal in devotional love.

The Bhagavata Purana states that when Krishna and Balarama were walking through the streets of Mathura prior to the wrestling match, they

---

[27] Vidura was a character in the Mahabharata and an uncle to both the Pandavas and Kauravas.

came across a young and beautiful hunchback maidservant of Kamsa called Kubja. Suffering from acute spine curvature, she was rolling along instead of walking, carrying sandal perfume to the court. The woman was a courtesan and her supplementary chores included preparing aromatic lotion for the court. On seeing her plight, Krishna asked in the gentlest of voices, "O beautiful one, would you be kind enough to give us the fragrant ointment you are carrying?" The woman was thunderstruck. No one had said anything kind about her appearance. Mesmerized by Krishna's words, she replied, "I shall certainly share with you some, for no one ever spoke to me in such glowing kindness." Saying so, she bent down to get some paste, but struggled to lift herself up. It was then that she felt Krishna's finger beneath her chin. A hand then rested on her hump while his foot pressed down her toes. As Krishna lifted her up, Kubja realized that for the first time she stood tall and straight. The hump that had made her suffer for years was gone.

Her heart overflowing with love, Kubja anointed the paste all over Krishna until he begged her to stop. But Kubja felt she should do more to the person who got rid of her deformity. She grabbed Krishna's garments with both hands and whispered to him shamelessly, "Come to my house tonight. I will show you the delights of Mathura." Balarama, standing next to Krishna, disapprovingly looked at this young woman soliciting his brother in broad daylight. "Certainly, but after I finish the job for which I have come," spoke Krishna, for he never refused love in any form when given with sincerity by a devotee.

Krishna kept his word to Kubja after annihilating Kamsa. Since Kubja had nothing else to offer, he accepted the offer with as much joy as he had accepted rice flakes or banana peel. Hindus believe that Kubja is the reincarnation of the apsara Tilottama who attained liberation after the embrace of Krishna.

THE GOLDEN TOUCH THAT HEALED A HUNCHBACK

Krishna cures Kubja of her hump, artist unknown

13

Krishna - The Lord of Dvaraka

If you thought Dwarka and its variant Dvaraka refer to the same place, you are mostly right but not hundred percent so. Careful writers maintain a distinction between the two. Strictly speaking, Dwarka is a corruption of the word *dvaraka*, which in Sanskrit means "door to heaven." Today, Dwarka refers to the existing modern-day city on the western coast of the Indian state of Gujarat. A member of the holy Char Dham, Dwarka is home to the Dwarkadhish Temple and an important pilgrimage center for the Hindus. On the contrary, Dvaraka is the ancient island kingdom of Krishna that is non-existent in today's political maps. After Krishna's time, floods wiped out the island and it was submerged into the Arabian Sea. But not everything of Dvaraka was washed away. Hindus believe the island Bet Dwarka, which is 3 km off the coast of Gujarat, is a remnant of the original Dvaraka.

How did the butter thief of Gokula and the darling of *gopi*s become the lord of Dvaraka?[28] After Kamsa was killed, Krishna was hailed as the liberator of the Yadavas. But even after Kamsa's death, the allies of Kamsa controlled the neighboring territories of Mathura. Among them, Jarasandha, the king of Magadha, was the most powerful ruler of the

---

[28] Unlike Rama, Krishna was never anointed as a king. That is because Ugrasena, who died after Krishna, was restored to the throne after Kamsa's death. Krishna was, however, the leading prince and the lord of Dvaraka for all practical purposes.

region. The legend of his birth is akin to that of Rama, the seventh avatar of Vishnu. Jarasandha's father was childless for a long time. The king went to the forest and performed devotional services for a sage. The sage was pleased by his services and gave him a blessed mango to give to his wife. But the sage did not know the king had two wives. Not to displease either wife, the king cut the mango into two equal halves and gave a half to each. The wives became pregnant and each gave birth to half a child. The king became horrified at the sight of his lifeless infants and dumped their bodies in a forest. A *rakshasi* called Jara found the bodies while foraging for food and put the halves in a basket and carried it home. But, inside the basket, the halves bonded into single baby boy. Hearing the cries, the demon took the baby to the elated king, who rewarded her suitably and named the child Jarasandha[29] in her honor. The bonded joint in the child's body, however, would become his weakness and was later exploited by Krishna.

Despite being born with a fused spine, Jarasandha was a formidable warrior who became the king of Magadha. He was politically shrewd and entered into a strategic alliance with Kamsa and neighboring rulers of the region. His two daughters were married off to Kamsa even though Kamsa was a cruel ruler. In return, Jarasandha got protection from enemy attacks. After the death of Kamsa, however, the daughters returned to their father and pleaded with him to avenge the death of their husband in typical Kshatriya tradition. Jarasandha swore to raze the town of Mathura and exterminate the Yadava race. The time was ripe for such an attack since the Yadavas were scattered during the rule of Kamsa. Jarasandha gathered a large army and reached the outskirts of Mathura. Despite being outnumbered, Krishna and Balarama organized a fighting force to repel Jarasandha's attacks. Jarasandha retreated on that occasion, but returned to attack again and again. It is said that Jarasandha attacked Mathura 17 times and was defeated every time by Krishna and Balarama.

With success evading him, Jarasandha became desperate like his predecessor Kamsa. He sought the help of the mighty Kalayavana, a fierce invader

---

[29] Meaning the one joined together by Jara.

of foreign origin. Together they marched with their troops on both flanks of Mathura. With the threat of attack looming on two fronts, Krishna devised a ruse. He pretended to flee from the war and lured Kalayavana into the cave where the great king Muchukunda, a forefather of Rama, was in perennial slumber. The king was the bearer of a strange boon that gave him the power to destroy anyone who disturbed his sleep. Inside the cave, Kalayavana mistakenly kicked the king and woke him up. Kalayavana was instantly charred to death with the fire born from the king's anger.

The relentless battles and loss of lives, however, took a toll on both Krishna and Balarama. They decided to build a new capital that would be away from the neighboring kingdoms and easier to defend. Krishna summoned Vishwakarma, the divine architect of the demigods. Vishwakarma wanted to reclaim some land from the sea, and needed the blessings of Varuna, the god of oceans. So Krishna worshipped Varuna, who gave him the necessary land in which the magnificent city of Dvaraka[30] was commissioned. (Varuna also took the island back after Krishna's time.) The Yadavas were transported to the new island city. Their enemies could not launch an attack as Dvaraka (like Lanka) was surrounded by sea on all sides.

With a military base established in Dvaraka, Krishna was ready to make his move against his foes. For that he sought the assistance of his cousins, the Pandavas.[31] Krishna persuaded Yudhishthira to conduct the Rajasuya sacrifice, which was a symbolic acknowledgement of the Pandava sovereignty. Krishna, however, warned that the sacrifice could only be conducted after Jarasandha was vanquished because he was capable of challenging the might of the Pandavas. About the same time, Jarasandha was planning to become the emperor of the region. Being a Shiva devotee, Jarasandha wanted to appease Shiva by performing a yajna with 100 human heads. For that he had imprisoned 95 kings, and was on his way to capture five more.

---

[30] Some scriptures record that Dvaraka was built on the sunken ruins of a kingdom, which itself was built on the ruins of another kingdom.
[31] The Pandavas were the children of Kunti, the sister of Vasudeva.

To stop Jarasandha's yajna, Krishna played an elaborate ruse. Disguised as Brahmins, the trio—Krishna, Arjuna, and Bhima—arrived at the fortress of Jarasandha. They knew that holy men had immediate access to the king, while ordinary people had to wait many days for entry. Jarasandha met with the Brahmins and enquired about their antecedents. Krishna told him bluntly that they were his enemies. The king was given a choice to pick any one of them for a wrestling match. Jarasandha did not choose Krishna since he believed Krishna was from the cowherd community and beneath himself. He also rejected Arjuna for he considered him a weakling because of his ordinary physique. Instead, he chose the hefty Bhima.

Bhima and Jarasandha, both equally matched, fought for days and neither succumbed to the other's blows. Bhima was younger and stronger but he could not take Jarasandha's life. Many times Bhima felt that he had nearly killed his opponent but Jarasandha kept coming back. On the 16th night of the battle, a debilitated Bhima looked at Krishna askingly. Krishna picked up a twig from the floor, broke it in two halves and threw the halves in opposite directions. Taking the cue from Krishna, Bhima fought with renewed vigor. He threw Jarasandha to the ground, held his legs and split his body in two. He then threw the left half to the right side and the right half to the left so that the two halves could not join. And that sealed the fate of Jarasandha. Krishna crowned the king's son as the ruler of Magadha. All the imprisoned kings were freed. Elated, they swore their loyalty to Krishna, thus guaranteeing their support for the Rajasuya sacrifice.

Like many Shiva devotees, Jarasandha is a villain in Hindu mythology, although he is not in the same league as Kamsa or Ravana. Jarasandha destroyed Mathura and tormented Krishna for many years until Krishna was forced to seek refuge in Dvaraka. Despite being a baddie, he is a popular figure in Jain mythology, particularly in Jain Mahabharata, where the battle is not between Kauravas and Pandavas, but between Krishna and Jarasandha.[32]

---

[32] The Jain Mahabharata can be found in Harivamsa Purana of Jinasena—which should not be confused with its namesake, the addendum to the Mahabharata.

14

The Eternal Bond of True Friendship

One loyal friend is worth ten thousand relatives.

—EURIPIDES

Once Krishna and Arjuna were travelling through a forest disguised as ordinary travelers when they came across a Brahmin single-mindedly focused on sharpening his sword. Surprised by the Brahmin's actions, Arjuna enquired, "O Brahmin, why are you resorting to violence when you should be concentrating on priestly duties?" Swift came the reply, "There is no *paapa* (sin) in killing to defend the dignity of my lord, Krishna. You see, three people have treated him badly. One is that rascal called Sudama, who allowed my lord to clean his feet and forced him to eat unclean rice flakes. The second is the sage Narada, who keeps on muttering my lord's names incessantly and disturbing his sleep. The third is that fellow Arjuna, who insisted that my lord take the menial job of being his charioteer." Saying this, the Brahmin looked up at his guests only to find his weary travelers had vanished from sight without a trace.

KRISHNA AND THE LATER AVATARS OF VISHNU

Krishna and Kuchela

While Narada and Arjuna are household names, not much is known about Sudama, who is the subject of this chapter. A Brahmin by caste, Sudama was a close childhood friend of Krishna. He came from a poor family unlike Krishna, who was from a royal clan. Despite the difference in social standing, an intimate friendship developed between the two when they were young. Like most classmates, they lost contact over time, and destiny took them to different directions. While Krishna became the lord of Dvaraka, Sudama ended up as an impoverished villager, living a life of complete austerity and devotion. Because Sudama wore tattered clothes, he was often called Kuchela.

With the passage of time, Kuchela's financial situation deteriorated to such an extent that the family did not have the means to meet the basic necessities of life. But the lack of material wealth did not affect Kuchela, for he was a true devotee dedicated to spiritual practice. His wife, however, could not bear the financial strain anymore. Unable to stand the sight of her children starving, she urged her husband to ask his childhood friend for a small favor. But Kuchela reprimanded her at the thought of begging for material wealth.

His wife continued to drum the idea into his head. Eventually, Kuchela agreed to meet Krishna, but more so on the prospect of meeting his old friend than asking for a favor. He cautioned his wife not to get her hopes high since it was unlikely Krishna would remember him. Kuchela did not have anything substantial to offer to his friend as a gift, yet he was adamant not to go empty handed. He remembered Krishna used to love rice flakes when he was a child.

Early next day, Kuchela started his journey to Dvaraka. As he was leaving, his wife handed him a bundle of rice flakes, which he tied to the end of his shawl. Kuchela set off on foot. It took him several days to reach Krishna's place. When he approached the city, his anxiety increased with every passing minute. He wondered whether he would be able to get past the gate. *The palace guards would not entertain a penniless haggard wandering into their premises*, thought Kuchela.

Once in Dvaraka, Kuchela was dazzled by the sight of the golden turrets of the palace shining in the sun. The old Brahmin felt lost and lonely and was about to return home when something caught his eye. From far he saw Krishna walk down the palace steps and head in his direction. On recognizing Kuchela, Krishna ran up to him and embraced him warmly. "Where were you all these years?" exclaimed Krishna. Before Kuchela could say anything, Krishna had grabbed him by his shoulder and escorted him to the palace. They went upstairs to his room, where they sat together on Krishna's favorite swing bed. As they exchanged pleasantries, Krishna's wife Rukmini entered carrying a container of aromatic water. Krishna washed Kuchela's tired feet with the water. Kuchela was speechless. Never in his dreams had he expected a reception of this kind.

At the palace, everyone was astonished to see Krishna treating an emaciated Brahmin with tenderness. For Krishna, it didn't matter. Together they reminisced about the happy days of their youth. Noticing a small bundle tied to Kuchela's shawl, Krishna leaned forward and grabbed it. "My dear friend let me see what you have brought for me!" While Kuchela looked down in embarrassment, Krishna opened the bundle and glanced at the contents. "O rice flakes! My favorite food! How thoughtful of you to bring something I love the most!" Without any prompting, Krishna downed a fistful of the stuff into his mouth. Eating with relish, he was about to go for another helping when Rukmini caught his hand. "Another handful will be too much. One is enough to last a lifetime."

Kuchela did not quite comprehend what Rukmini said, but nevertheless, he was overjoyed because Krishna loved his simple gift. After spending the night at the palace, Kuchela got up early the next morning. Bidding goodbye to Krishna, he trudged back on the road to his house. As he neared home, he wondered what he was going to tell his wife. She would be furious that he went all the way and did not even mention his financial situation to Krishna. When he reached the spot where his old house stood, he was stunned to see a mansion in its place surrounded by gardens and lakes. "Did someone raze my house and built a mansion while I was away?" wondered Kuchela. Suddenly he became worried about his family.

At that moment, the door of the mansion opened and a lovely woman walked down the steps. When she got closer, Kuchela realized she was his own wife in new clothes. "Krishna has saved us from our misery," said his wife cheerfully. "But I didn't ask him anything," confessed Kuchela. "Well, I suppose he understood our problems. Soon after you left, our old house fell down, and this one came up in its place filled with fine food, clothes, and piles of gold coins. We will never have to starve again." Kuchela shook his head and closed his eyes. A friend in need is a friend indeed, but Krishna had been an extraordinary friend. It was then that Kuchela realized why Rukmini had stopped Krishna from eating more rice flakes. All his wealth had come from one fistful of rice. Nothing more was needed.

Although Kuchela was a simple Brahmin without many wants and needs, he taught mankind a timeless lesson. It is not the size of the gift, but the size of the heart that matters the most. The tiniest morsel given with a big heart is more precious than the grandest feast given out of pride.

When it is dark enough, you can see the stars.
—CHARLES A. BEARD, 1874–1948

15

Dvaraka - The Atlantis of the East

It's the early 2000s. A team of oceanographers trawled the murky Arabian Sea in the Gulf of Khambhat to measure levels of marine pollution. They were stunned to see regularly spaced stone buildings buried in the sand under the sea. On closer inspection they found the ruins to be submerged about 40 meters beneath the sea and strung across a nine-kilometer-long stretch of what was once a river. Little did the oceanographers realize that their chance discovery would revolutionize Indian history because the site lies in the vicinity of the legendary city of Dvaraka, the Atlantis of the East. Until then, the existence of Dvaraka was a matter of legends and myths. Dvaraka, or Krishna's city, is held dear by millions of Hindus and is mentioned in many texts including the Mahabharata and the Bhagavata, Skanda, and Vishnu Puranas.

Dvaraka is not the only lost city in the world. History abounds with stories of land masses or cities that have disappeared under unique circumstances. Most famous of them was Atlantis, an idyllic city created by the Greek philosopher Plato in 360 BCE. Atlantis was deemed to be inhabited by a utopian society, but in due course people became greedy and morally corrupt. Because the residents turned to immoral pursuits, the gods punished them with one terrible night of fire and an earthquake that caused Atlantis to sink into the sea.

Is Dvaraka entirely mythical like Atlantis? Hindu scriptures say that after the death of Kamsa, the city of Mathura repeatedly came under the attack of Jarasandha, the tyrant king of Magadha. The persistent battles led Krishna to shift his capital to the western coast of India and far from these invaders. One version of the scriptures say Krishna was brought to the island by the giant bird Garuda, the mount of Vishnu. Another version says the island city was specially built for Krishna by the divine architect Vishwakarma, who incidentally had provided palatial accommodation to many celestials including Indra and Kubera.

With the passing away of Krishna and his clan, Arjuna went to Dvaraka to bring the rest of Krishna's grandchildren and Yadavas to safety. Shortly thereafter, Dvaraka was flooded and the city was submerged. The following lines from the Mahabharata highlight the terrible ending of Dvaraka:

> *The sea, which has been beating against the shores,*
> *suddenly broke the boundary imposed by nature.*
> *It rushed into the beautiful city,*
> *and swallowed everything in its path.*
> *I saw the grand buildings submerge one by one,*
> *In just a few moments it was all over.*
> *The sea had now become as placid as a lake,*
> *There was no trace of the city anymore,*
> *Dvaraka was just a name; just a memory.*

So much for mythology, but is there any support for the existence of Dvaraka in other sources? In this context, the epics Mahabharata and Ramayana cannot be entirely characterized as mythology since they belong to the category of Hindu texts known as *itihasa* meaning history;

the criterion being the writer of the story has himself witnessed the story. Yet history and mythology are so deeply intertwined in the Mahabharata that it becomes difficult, even for the best of minds, to separate fact from fiction. That's because the text became affected with embellishments and additions over thousands of years. But myths rarely appear out of the blue. Bruce Masse, an environmental archaeologist at Los Alamos National Laboratory, California, says, "Myths are largely event-based in that they are triggered to a large part by an event, or combination of events, that catastrophically impact society ... Then these myths provide a window upon those events that can be recovered, retrieved and even dated."

The west coast of Gujarat was the traditional land of the Yadavas, the clan of Krishna. The modern coastal town Dwarka is in Gujarat and is often identified with Dvaraka. Both Dwarka[33] and the nearby island Bet Dwarka, which is 3 km off the coast of Gujarat, are famous pilgrim centers. Because of the importance of Dwarka, underwater archeologists and marine scientists have been routinely scanning this region and searching for artifacts buried in the ocean floor. These underwater expeditions were never easy and undertaken only during low tides, between the months of November and February. At other times of the year, the waters are known to be treacherous with strong currents and rip tides. Furthermore, excavations are possible only on sunny days when the sea is relatively calm.

Excavations completed outside modern Dwarka in the 80s gave some indication of the existence of an ancient city. The most significant discovery was the unearthing of seven temples, each built on top of the other. Encouraged by these findings, a team of archaeologists and divers from National Institute of Ocean Technology (NIOT) and Archaeological Survey of India, under the guidance of eminent archaeologist S. R. Rao,[34]

---

[33] Dwaraka is one of the Char Dham or top four pilgrimage sites.
[34] Dr. S.R. Rao is considered the grand-father of Indian archaeology and is also credited with the discovery of a number of Indus Valley sites including the port city of Lothal in Gujarat.

conducted several underwater expeditions along the coast of Dwarka and Bet Dwarka. Between 1987 and 1990, Rao discovered two underwater settlements—one near Dwarka and the other off Bet Dwarka. He also identified the well-fortified township of an ancient city extending more than half a mile from the shore. The township was built in six sectors along the banks of a river, just how Dvaraka is described in the scriptures. The city's walls were erected on boulders confirming that the land was reclaimed from the sea. In fact the layout of the submerged city was so identical to Dvaraka as described in ancient texts that Rao wrote in this book, "The discovery ... sets to rest the doubts expressed by historians about the historicity of the Mahabharata and the very existence of Dvaraka city."

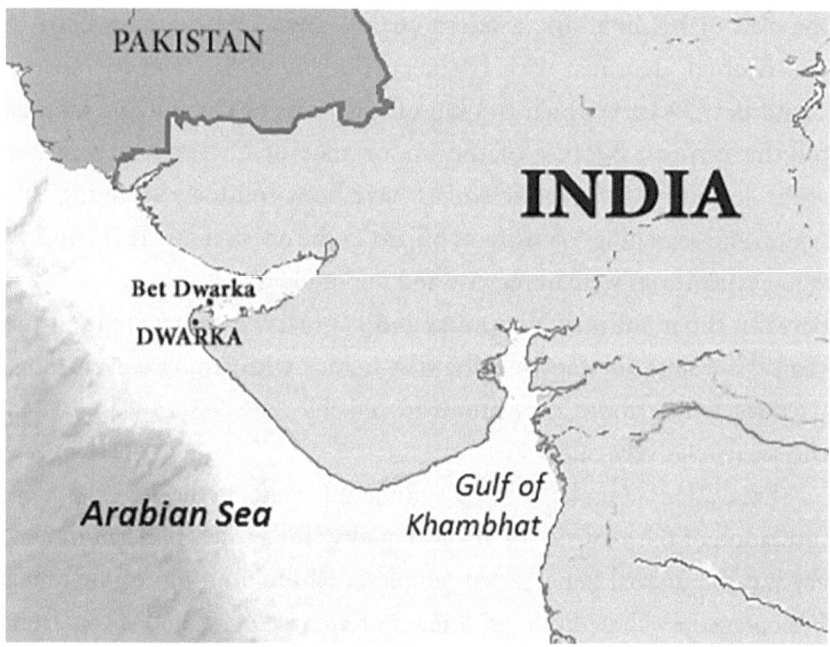

Location of Dwarka and Bet Dwarka

The next breakthrough was the one we described at the beginning of this chapter—the discovery of a sunken city by a team of oceanographers from NIOT in the Gulf of Khambhat.[35] The submerged city had structures that resembled a public bath, a large granary, a citadel, and a drainage system. A row of rectangular basements was also found in the vicinity that looked like the foundation of homesteads. The discovery was followed up by another investigation that included dredging to excavate objects and solar scans to detect structures. Over 2000 artifacts were picked up by the NIOT team in this round. The items included carved wood, polished stone tools, broken pottery, beads, sculpture, and human teeth. Carbon dating of a wooden sample revealed a bombshell—that the site was nearly 9,500 years old. Until then it was believed that first cities of the world appeared in the Sumer Valley (in Mesopotamia) around 3000 BCE.

Indian culture is a mishmash of many roots. Two of the most important ones can be found in the Indus Valley Civilization and the Vedic culture even though certain practices are common in both cultures. Western scholars have dated the Indus Valley Civilization to around 2500 BCE. Likewise they have created this notion that the Vedic period supposedly began in 1500 BCE through Aryan migration. The ruins from the Gulf of Khambhat, such as the public bath and granary, show similarities to those found at other Indus Valley sites. (This is not surprising since the Indus site Lothal, a port city, is located at the head of the Gulf of Khambhat.) However, ruins found by S.R. Rao in other parts of the region, such Dwarka and Bet Dwarka, indicate a Vedic origin in which the epics Ramayana and Mahabharata are based. The discovery of a 9,500-year-old sunken city, however, contradicts all the prevailing theories and threatens to push back the dates of India's earliest civilization by at least 5000 years.

The discovery created headlines around the globe. Archeologists from many countries scrambled to the scene where the ruins were being examined. Some voiced their concerns regarding the NIOT findings. Many items identified as artifacts (man-made) were actually geo-facts (objects of natural origin). The archeologists also frowned upon the process used to recover the items. The use of dredging, instead of controlled excavation,

---

[35] The Gulf of Khambhat is also known as Gulf of Cambay.

may allow errant artifacts to be collected. The claim of the city being 9,500-year-old did not stand up to scrutiny as the only item that was carbon dated was a piece of wood. According to them, the discovery of an ancient piece of wood did not imply the discovery of an ancient civilization. In fact wood pieces are scattered throughout the ocean floor.

Not every foreign archeologist subscribes to this view. Tom Higham of the University of Oxford's Radiocarbon Accelerator Unit says submerged wood is often well-preserved and should be relatively straightforward to carbon date. "I don't see how you could get it grossly wrong," he says. "In the past, it has been said that you shouldn't pin all your interpretations on a date from one sample. But that's not so true these days. And dating a sample that's between 5000 and 10,000 years old is pretty easy."

The above discussion highlights some of the difficulties with underwater archeology. Smaller items can easily move around during tides and cannot be pinpointed to a site. Larger items, like structures, remain stationary, but do not lend themselves to carbon dating. Only materials that have been part of a living organism can be carbon dated. That means objects like stones, metal, or pottery cannot be directly dated unless some organic material is embedded as residue. Furthermore, samples may be contaminated by other carbon containing materials, like soil that surrounds these objects.

Yet there is little doubt that these collections represent an exciting breakthrough in underwater archeology. The findings at Dwarka, Bet Dwarka, and in the Gulf of Khambhat underscore that fact that this area was once part of a larger civilization. Before these discoveries, some scholars were of the view that Mahabharata was just a myth and to search for the remains of an ancient city was a futile enterprise. Others believed that the Battle of Kurukshetra was a family feud that was exaggerated into a stupendous war. For Hindus, the excavations are a national heritage and a symbol of pride. The uncovering of these evidences demonstrates that Krishna was more likely to be a historical figure than a mythical ruler who ruled the kingdom of Dvaraka. More importantly, the discovery of sunken cities attests that the Mahabharata cannot be dismissed as a myth and has some historical basis to it.

16

Chaitanya Mahaprabhu - The Dancing Saint

Dance is the hidden language of the soul of the body.

—MARTHA GRAHAM, 1894–1991

Traffic comes to a crawl at a busy road in New York as a handful of strangely-clad men and women enter the sidewalk holding drums and hand cymbals. They walk along the street, singing and dancing oblivious to the traffic. Among them are women dressed in bright saris and men in saffron or white often with clean shaven heads except for a topknot. The unmistakable spectacle of the Hare Krishnas is a familiar sight to many Americans, as is their commitment to lifelong celibacy and vegetarianism. The movement, which came to the USA only in the 60s, was originally inspired by Chaitanya, the 16th century dancing saint who is believed to be an incarnation of Krishna.

Hare Krishnas singing at a street in Moscow, Russia.

Chaitanya was born in 1486 at a place called Mayapur near Kolkata, the capital of the Indian state of West Bengal. At the time of Chaitanya's birth, his mother consulted an astrologer, who foretold that she would give birth to an extraordinary child. Soon a son was born but only after an unusually long gestation period of 11 months. He was the second son born to conservative parents, and between this child and his older brother, eight daughters were born of which not one survived. The parents were overjoyed and named him Vishwambara. Friends and relatives, however, preferred to call him Nimai since he was born under a Neem tree. Both these names did not stick for long.

The boy soon picked up another name. Because he was fair in appearance compared to other kids, his neighbors called him Gauranga. Mischievous and playful, the fair-skinned Gauranga took a liking to the blue-skinned Krishna and was particularly fond of singing hymns about him. It is said that his first mystical experience occurred when he was only nine, at the time of Upanayana, the Hindu sacred thread ceremony. The child collapsed during the recitation of Gayatri Mantra and his body began to shine radiantly. His distressed mother heard a voice coming from the child that said, "I am leaving the body of your son, but I will return. Look after your son in my absence." This event led many to believe that young Gauranga had a divine calling to worship god.

From an early age, Gauranga proved to be a gifted child, mastering Sanskrit and rhetoric beyond his age. His intellectual zeal astonished everyone but only worried his parents. Excessive learning had made his older brother an eccentric, who became a monk and renounced the world at a young age. Biographers and hymnologists unequivocally describe Gauranga as a brilliant scholar and a master of traditional learning. When he was a student, he wrote a small grammar book followed by a commentary on the philosophy of Nyaya, one of the darshanas of Hinduism.[36] After his father's death, Gauranga established his own school where he is said to have further honed his rhetorical skills by scoring debating victories over philosophers much older than him. Within a short period, his fame as a debater became so well known that many

---

[36] Darshanas refer to the six systems of Hindu philosophy.

philosophers of his time began to fear his presence and refused to debate with him.

At the age of 22, Gauranga's life would change forever. To pay homage to his deceased father, Gauranga went on a pilgrimage to Gaya, a place considered holy by both Hindus and Buddhists. Buddha attained Nirvana under a Bodhi tree centuries ago at Gaya. For Hindus, Vishnu's footprints, aka Vishnupada, can be found here. Legend has it that the asura Gaya, after performing severe austerities, obtained a boon that allowed him to bestow moksha to anyone at his will. After many immoral people were granted mokshas, Vishnu put an end to this practice by stomping on the asura, pushing him beneath the surface of earth. The basalt markings seen at the Vishnupada temple in Gaya are believed to be Vishnu's footprints. Over the years the site became famous for the ritual of Shraaddha where Hindus offer oblations to their forefathers. It is said that upon seeing the footprints of Vishnu, Gauranga became ecstatic and his body began to tremble uncontrollably. A voice reportedly told him, "You are the chosen one to spread the message of love and devotion in the world."

Among the pilgrims present at the temple was a monk called Ishvar Puri, a Vaishnava leader of the Madhava sect. Puri realized that Gauranga was no ordinary soul and initiated him to the worship of Krishna. Thereafter, Gauranga returned home but as a changed man. He was no longer the unrivalled debater or the staunch grammarian. Instead, there stood a man constantly chanting the mantra, "Hare Krishna, Hare Krishna, Krishna Krishna Hare Hare," and longing for Krishna's presence.[37] The stories of Radha's love affair with Krishna formed the backdrop of Gauranga's intense devotion. Shortly thereafter, Gauranga closed his school and spent the rest of his life devoted to *sankirtanas*[38] or

---

[37] The Hare Krishna mantra is a Vaishnava mantra and is recited as follows: Hare Krishna Hare Krishna, Krishna Krishna Hare Hare, Hare Rama Hare Rama, Rama Rama Hare Hare.

[38] *Kirtana* is a song that glorifies god. *Sankirtana* is the singing of *kirtana*s in small groups.

the choral singing of the lord's names—which would later become the hallmark of the Gaudiya Vaishnava school.

About a year later Gauranga renounced the world and joined an ashram, where he was officially given the name Chaitanya, "one who awakens god in others." His followers, however, referred to him as Krishna Chaitanya or Chaitanya Mahaprabhu. For the next few years, Chaitanya traveled throughout India chanting the monikers of Krishna and attracting a throng of devotees. Soon he became the leader of the local Vaishnavas of the Gauda region (present day regions of Bengal/Bangladesh) drawing large numbers to his sect. Not only the common people, but even the esteemed philosophers of that time were attracted to his fold. The success of Chaitanya's bhakti movement, however, created envy within the Brahmin community. They complained to the local magistrate, a Muslim by the name of Kazi, about the noise levels and community disturbances caused by congregational singing. Kazi took the matter assiduously and sent constables who disrupted the *sankirtana* and broke some of the devotee's drums. Hosting *sankirtana*s at homes was summarily banned. But nothing could stop Chaitanya from spreading his love for his lord. He organized a peaceful procession of a hundred thousand men who went around with harmoniums, mridangas, and *khartal*s, dancing to the chant "Hare Krishna, Hare Krishna." The huge procession went past the streets of Mayapur and finally reached Kazi's mansion chanting the name of Krishna.

On seeing the massive crowd assembled outside, Kazi initially hid inside his residence. However, after realizing the nonviolent nature of the demonstration, he came outside and appeared before the crowd. Kazi was impressed by the peaceful nature of the devotees and had lengthy discussion about the nature of *kirtana*. At the end, Kazi himself fell at Chaitanya's feet and became a follower of the bhakti movement. The victory without any bloodshed raised the morale of the Vaishnavas, many of whom believed that some spiritual force must have been behind it. For the same reason, Chaitanya is considered the pioneer of the civil disobedience movement—which was later adopted by Gandhi during the Indian independence movement.

Chaitanya eventually settled in the city of Puri in Odisha, where he lived the rest of his years in seclusion. He spent his time advising disciples and worshipping the local temple deity Jagannath (Vishnu), whom he regarded as Krishna himself. Among his disciples, Rupa Goswami and Sanatana Goswami—two among the famous "Six Goswamis of Vrindavan"—became central figures in the systematic development of the Gaudiya Vaishnava philosophy. Chaitanya is believed to have died in 1533, but his death is shrouded in mystery. It is said that Chaitanya merged with the statue of Jagannath and disappeared completely. Other accounts state that he either died of septic fever caused by an injury or drowned in a nearby river in a state of religious ecstasy.

As the founder of Gaudiya Vaishnavism, Chaitanya embodied Krishna himself. Krishna became Chaitanya to experience his longing for Radha, his beloved concert whom Chaitanya imagined himself to be. For his followers, Chaitanya was conceived as Krishna and Radha in the same body. A great saint of this period asked Chaitanya why he preferred *sankirtana* over scholarship. According to Chaitanya, the Kali Yuga—the present age (the dark age of Hinduism)—is not suited for spiritual attainment through knowledge because of the short duration. In this age infinite love is superior to infinite knowledge. For Chaitanya, bhakti was the purest path to reach god, for it was attainable by anyone regardless of their social status or spiritual purity. One of the blights of the caste system was it excluded lower classes from many things including spiritual practice. But bhakti broke down the caste barriers and reached out to both Hindus and non-Hindus of all colors and class.

Chaitanya left no writings of his own except for a series of verses known as *Siksastaka*. However, his writings inspired the creation of many secondary works that expound his principles and philosophy. Following Chaitanya's death, the Gaudiya Vaishnava tradition flourished in northeastern India, but over time it was divided into many branches. In the early 60s, a charismatic retired pharmacist from Bengal called A.C. Bhaktivedanta Prabhupada—a descendant of Chaitanya—renounced his family life and brought the Gaudiya philosophy to the shores of

West by founding the International Society for Krishna Consciousness (ISKON), also known as the Hare Krishna movement. The Hare Krishnas permeated into the society and became part of the culture of most countries. With more than 400 temples all over the world, ISKON is known worldwide, but more than one million adherents call themselves Hare Krishnas—thanks to the dancing saint Chaitanya Mahaprabhu.

ISKON Temple at Mayapur, West Bengal, India

17

A Thousand-Year-Old Stotra of Krishna

Stotra means song of praise. One such popular *stotra* of Krishna called *Achutha ashtakam* has been servicing the devotional demands of devotees for more than a thousand years. Credited to Adi Shankara, the eighth century founder of Advaita Vedanta, the song, composed in Sanskrit, encapsulates the life and times of Krishna (Vishnu) by invoking his description and names, thereby conjuring the many myths surrounding his persona. Over the years, many artists have rendered the song, but few so with the melody and rhythm of M.G. Sreekumar,[39] the playback singer from Kerala who turned this sleepy bhajan into a sensational *stotra*.

Below you will find the lyrics of the song followed by their meaning. In them you will find the many names of Krishna. Question: How many of them can you link to a myth? My favorite name for Krishna—Pitambara—was somehow overlooked by Adi Shankara. For those readers who are musically inclined, do not forget to checkout this song on YouTube.

---

[39] Undoubtedly, others singers have also done justice to the song. However, I thought Sreekumar did an outstanding job of lifting this song from oblivion to stratospheric heights. It is a strange coincidence that Sreekumar, like this author, hails from the state of Kerala.

KRISHNA AND THE LATER AVATARS OF VISHNU

Achutham Keshavam Rama Narayanam
Krishna Damodaram Vasudevam Hari
Sridharam Madhavam Gopika Vallabham
Janaki Nayakam Ramachandram Bhaje

Salute you O Achutha (the infallible), Keshava (one with beautiful hair and the vanquisher of demon Keshi), Rama, the incarnation of Narayana (Vishnu)

Salute you O Krishna (the dark one), Damodara (one who was tied around the waist by his mother), Vasudeva[40] (son of Vasudeva and another name for Krishna), Hari (one who forgives sins)

Salute you O Sridhara (one who bears Sri [Lakshmi] on his chest), Madhava (consort of Lakshmi), Gopika Vallabha (the beloved of the *gopi*s)

Salute you O Janaki Nayakam (the lord of Janaki [Sita]), Ramachandram (Rama, the avatar of Vishnu)

Achutham Keshavam Satyabhama Dhavam
Madhavam Sridharam Radhika Radhitam |
Indira Mandiram Chetasa Sundaram
Devaki Nandanam Nandajam Sandadhe

Salute you O Achutha (the infallible), Keshava (one with beautiful hair and the vanquisher of demon Keshi), Satyabhama Dhavam (the lord of Satyabhama)

Salute you O Madhava (consort of Lakshmi), Sridhara (one who bears Sri [Lakshmi] on his chest), Radhika Radhikam (one who was worshipped by Radha).

Salute you O Indira Mandiram (temple of splendor [Lakshmi]), Chetasa Sundaram (Splendor of Magnificence)

---

[40] Strictly speaking, Krishna is Vasudeva Junior while the father of Krishna is Vasudeva Senior.

Salute you O Devaki Nandam (son of Devaki), Nandajam Sandhadhe (foster child of Nanda)

Vishnuve Jishnuve Shangkhine Chakrine
Rukmini Ragini Janaki Janaye
Vallabhi Vallabha Architha Atmane
Kamsa Vidhvamsine Vamzine Te Namah

Salute you O Vishnu (the all-pervading one), Jishnuve (the ever victorious one), Shangkhine (one who holds the conch-shell), Chakrine (one who holds the chakra [discus])
Salute you O Rukimi Ragini (one who is dear to Rukmini), Janaki Janaye (one who has Janaki [Sita] as his wife)
Salute you O Vallabhi Vallabha (beloved of Radha [Vallabhi]), Architha Atmane (one who is the offering of the hearts)
Salute you O Kamsa Vidhvamsine (one who destroyed Kamsa), Vamzine Te Namah (the flute player)

Krishna Govinda He Rama Narayana
Sripathi Vasudeva Ajita Sri Nidhe
Achutha Ananta He Madhava Adhoksaja
Dvaraka Nayaka Draupadi Rakshaka

Salute you O Krishna (the dark one), Govinda[41] (protector of cows), Rama, the incarnation of Narayana (Vishnu)
Salute you O Sripathi (Consort of Sri [Lakshmi]), Vasudeva Ajita (the unconquerable Vasudeva [Krishna II], Sri Nidhe (the storehouse of Sri [Laskhmi])
Salute you O Achutha (the infallible), Ananda he (the blissful one), Madhava (consort of Sri [Laskhmi]), Adokshaja (one who can be know only through Agamas)

---

[41] Govinda has many meanings like protector of cows, protector of land, lord of the Vedas, and so on.

Salute you O Dvaraka Nayaka (the lord of Dvaraka), Draupadi Rakshaka (the savior of Draupadi)

Rakshasa Kshobhita Sitaya Shobhito
Dandakaranya Bhu Punyata Karanah
Lakshmane Anvito Vanara Sevito
[A]gastya Sampujito Raghava Patu Maam

Salute you O Rakshasa Kshobhita (the one who enraged the Rakshasas [Rama]), Sitaya Shobhito (one who is adorned by Sita)

Salute you O Dandakaranya Bhu Punyata Karanah (the one who was the cause of purification of Dandaka forest),

Salute you O Lakshmane Anvito (one who was attended by Lakshmana), Vanara Sevito (one who was served by monkeys)

Salute you O Agastya Sampujito (one who was worshipped by sage Agastya), Raghava Patu Maam (protect me Raghava [descendent of Raghu, an ancestor of Rama])

Dhenuka Arishtaka Anista Krod Dvesiha
Keshiha Kamsa Hrd Vamshika Vadaka
Putana Kopaka Sura Ja Khelano
Balagopalaka Patu Maam Sarvada

Salute you O Dhenuka Arishtaka Anista Krod Devisha (the one who repelled the cruel attacks of demons Dhenuka and Arishtaka)

Salute you O Keshiha Kamsa (and Keshi and Kamsa) Hrd Vamshika Vadaka (the one who played soulful tunes on his flute),

Salute you O Putana Kopaka Sura Ja Khelano (one who overcame the anger of Putana, who assumed the form of Devi to poison Krishna)

Salute you O Balagopalaka Patu Maam Sarvada (Protect me young cowherd [Balagopala] by protecting me from dangers, just as you thwarted the attacks of many demons)

Vidyud Udyota Vat Prasphurad Vasasam
Pravrd Ambhoda Vat Prolasad Vigraham
Vanyaya Malaya Shobhito arahsthalam
Lohita Anghri Dvayam Varija Aksam Bhaje

Salute you O Vidyud Udyota Vat Prasphurad Vasasam (the one whose garments shine like lightning in the sky)

Salute you O Pravrd Ambhoda Vat Prolasad Vigraham (the one whose beautiful form are like the movement of clouds during rainy season)

Salute you O Vanyaya Malaya (Garland of Wild Flowers) Shobhito Arahsthalam (Adorned on your chest)

Salute you O Lohita Anghri Dvayam Varija Aksam Bhaje (pair of feet glows in red and whose eyes are like lotus)

Kunjitah Kuntala Bhrajamana Ananam
Ratna Maulim Lasat Kandalam Gandaye
Hara Keyuurakam Kangkana Projvalam
Kingkini Manjulam Shyamalam Tam Bhaje

Salute You O Kunjitah Kuntala Bhrajamana Ananam (one who possesses lovely locks of curly hair over his gleaming face)

Salute You O Ratna Maulim Lasat Kandalam Gandaye (one whose face is adorned with a gem and shining earrings)

Salute You O Hara Keyuurakam Kangkana Projvalam (one whose arms and waist are decorated with shining bracelets)

Salute You O Kingkini Manjulam Shyamalam Tam Bhaje (one who bears tiny bells over his dark body that make melodious sounds)

Achutha ashtakam Yah Pathed Istadam
Premata Pratyaham Purusah Saspraham
Vrtatah Sundaram Kartr Vishvambharas
Tasya Vashyo Hari Rajayate Satvaram

Whoever recites *Achutha ashtakam* as an offering to Ishta (god)
With devotion and pines for Purusha (the Supreme Being),
Achutha Shasthakam is always encircling the Supreme Being,
And will reach the abode of Hari (Vishnu) by his will.

Oh, you heard a different version of *Achutha ashtakam*? Such is the popularity of this song that devotees have either chopped the lyrics or even adapted them for deities other than Krishna. For instance, a popular North Indian version, dedicated to Krishna, goes by slightly jumbled lyrics of "Achutham Keshavam Krishna Damodaram ..."

Hope you enjoyed the song. According to music aficionados, if you are unmoved by the song, then music is not your cup of tea.

MAHABHARATA

18

The Greatest Epic of All

Study without desire spoils the memory,
and it retains nothing that it takes in.

—LEONARDO DA VINCI, 1452–1519

Back in the late 80s, India's public broadcaster Doordarshan began telecasting episodes of the epic Ramayana on a weekly basis. Until then, it was thought that secular India had no time for religious serials. The result was unprecedented. The serial created not only a TV revolution, but a record for being the most watched program. Less than six months after the last episode of Ramayana was broadcast, Doordarshan tried to repeat its success by telecasting the longer Mahabharata to mythology-weary Indian viewers. History has proven ample times that when you try to repeat the formula of success, the result is often the opposite. In this case the result was even more stunning. The new serial beat Ramayana in terms of viewership and became the most watched program ever. Such was the popularity of the show that BBC broadcast the serial. It was also dubbed in Tamil, Telugu, and Indonesian. According to Ravi Chopra, director of the original TV serial Mahabharata, the success of these serials tells a lot about the Indian culture. "No other country in the world has its values so deeply and permanently entrenched in its mythology."

With more than 100,000 two-line stanzas, the Mahabharata holds the record for being the longest poem in the world. It is eight times longer than Homer's Iliad and Odyssey put together, and nearly three times as long as the Judeo–Christian Bible. The name "Mahabharata" means "great Bharatas," referring to emperor Bharata,[42] an early ancestor to both the Pandavas and Kauravas. It is based on an 18-day war between two feuding families—the Pandavas and the Kauravas—that happened some time in ancient India. The battle was fought at Kurukshetra, a place close to present-day New Delhi. For that reason, the battle is often referred to as the Battle of Kurukshetra or Kurukshetra War.

The epic is attributed to Veda Vyasa, who himself has a cameo in the epic. Legend has it that the story was dictated by Vyasa to his divine scribe Ganesha, who wrote it down using his single tusk. Since the Mahabharata belongs to the category of smriti (remembered) Hindu texts, no one knows the date of composition. Oral versions could have been going around for hundreds of years. Most scholars, however, place the written version to be anywhere between 300 BCE and 300 CE. The epic, however, denotes 3102 BCE as the year of the battle. The specific date was likely chosen since it marks the beginning of the Kali Yuga, the darkest of the four ages of Hinduism. Because the epic contributed to a precipitous plunge in ethical standards, the Puranas considered it the beginning of the dark ages. The Mahabharata may be a relic of the past, but for millions of Hindus throughout the world it is a "living" epic, as can be seen by its popularity on TV.

The Mahabharata consists of 18 *parvas* (books), each of which is divided into many chapters. Among the books, the sixth is the renowned

---

[42] The emperor Bharata of Mahabharata is the son of Shakuntala and unrelated to King Bharata of Ramayana where Bharata is a step brother of Rama. The story of emperor Bharata is described in detail later in this book.

Bhagavad Gita, which contains 700 two-line stanzas in itself. You would be surprised to learn that the original Mahabharata was called *Jaya* and was only a tenth of its present size. Yet *Jaya* contained the core of the Mahabharata, including the Bhagavad Gita. The work was later expanded by two of Vyasa's disciples, creating the Mahabharata as we know it today. During the expansion, the title changed from *Jaya* to *Vijaya*, then to *Bharata*, and eventually to Mahabharata.

The Mahabharata is not entirely about the Battle of Kurukshetra. It is littered with entertaining tales from many aspects of life. However, the main story is about a family feud between two sets of cousin brothers—the Pandavas (consisting of five brothers) and the Kauravas (consisting of 100 brothers). Raised in the forest, the Pandavas value virtue and respect. Among them the most skilled in warfare is Arjuna, the archer par excellence. Unlike their cousins, the Kauravas grew up in the comfort of the palace and are corrupt and cynical. They are led by their oldest brother Duryodhana, who is second only to Ravana in depravity. While the Pandavas were growing up in the forest, unbeknown to them their cousin Krishna was roaming in another part of the forest. The cousins met for the first time during an archery contest at the *swayamvara* of Draupadi, who would later become the shared wife of all five Pandava brothers.

The Mahabharata is said to be a mixture of fact and fiction but simplicity is not one of them. If the storyline of Ramayana is simple and straightforward, then Mahabharata is complex with a myriad of intriguing characters. While the Ramayana has clear role models—Rama as king, Sita as wife, Lakshmana as brother, Hanuman as loyal friend—there are no role models in the Mahabharata. Even a single hero is hard to find. Krishna plays a key role, so do Arjuna and his older brother Yudhishthira. There are, however, many less-than-perfect role models. For instance, Yudhishthira is the ideal king, but has a weakness for gambling and ends up losing his family and kingdom. Arjuna is daring in battle but employs underhand tactics at war. Krishna is a noble friend to both warring parties but seen to be driving the battle to its terrible end.

Despite the complexity of the plot, the Mahabharata has been the inspiration for many books, a super-hit TV series, and countless movies, plays and folk songs in many Indian languages and foreign ones. In the next several chapters, we'll look at the plots and intrigues leading up to the Battle of Kurukshetra. The Mahabharata begins with King Shantanu's attraction for the goddess Ganga, who makes her appearance in human form on the banks of a river to fulfill a heavenly curse. The king's reckless passion plants the seed of sibling rivalry which consumes the characters in the epic and ultimately results in the destruction of the entire Kuru[43] tribe.

---
[43] The Kurus are the ancestors to both the Pandavas and Kauravas.

19

Ganga Kills Her Own Children

Bhishma, the one who bestowed on us the Vishnu Sahasranama on his deathbed, is undoubtedly one of the most powerful characters of the Mahabharata. Yet the significance of his role was simply overlooked or little understood for ages. Why? Maybe he was overshadowed by the star power of Arjuna and Krishna. Or maybe he supported the evil Kauravas and was on the losing side of the war. The national broadcast of the Mahabharata in the late 80s, however, changed that perception and made the relatively less known character of Bhishma into a memorable grandsire. Although he is respected for his ethics and fairness throughout the epic, Bhishma is immortalized for his selflessness and the sacrifices he made for his family.

Bhishma's birth took place under unique circumstances. At the time, Shantanu was the king of Hastinapura. He was known to be brave and virtuous with an exceptional eye for feminine beauty. Once the king went hunting and stopped by the banks of a river to quench his thirst. There he saw a divine maiden called Ganga whose beauty was so alluring that he kept gazing at her and forgot about this thirst. Smitten by her, the king wanted to fast track the introductions and courtship. "Who are you O beautiful one, a goddess or an apsara? Whoever you are, I, the king of Hastinapura, have fallen in love with you. Allow me to marry you and take you to my abode." Ganga consented but on one condition. "I will, but promise me never to question my actions however disagreeable they might be." Without a moment's hesitation, the king granted her request. Together as husband and wife, they headed to Hastinapura.

At the palace, Shantanu was overjoyed with his new wife's modest ways, gentle manner, and her concern for his comforts. In due course, Ganga gave birth to a son. There was no celebration because as soon as the child was born, she threw the newborn into the river. Shantanu was appalled, but he said nothing remembering the condition of their marriage. As the years went by, Ganga gave birth to six more children. Each one of them was drowned in the same way much to the anguish of the king. Shortly thereafter, the eighth child was born. As Ganga made her usual walk to the riverside to cast away the child, Shantanu could not remain silent. "Stop! You cruel woman! Let this poor child live! Who are you really and why are you murdering your own children?"

Surprisingly, Ganga remained calm. "You have broken your promise, King. Therefore, it's time for me to leave. I am goddess Ganga, and the children I had killed were the seven Vasus.[44] They were cursed to be reborn as humans for stealing sage Vasishtha's cow. At their request, I agreed to be their mother and tried to keep their stay on earth as short as possible. Because of your intervention, I could not save the last one. The eight Vasu—your son—will live on earth, but lead a terrible life because of the curse. For now, I shall take him with me to train him to be the best warrior. I shall return him to you when he's ready."

With these words, Ganga vanished with her son leaving Shantanu lonely and despondent. The eighth son thus survived and would later become one of the most important characters in the Mahabharata. He was called Devavrata, but later became known as Bhishma for his ultimate sacrifice—which is a remarkable story described in another chapter.

---

[44] The attendants of Indra, the Vasus are gods representing natural phenomena over which they have control. Their names and functions are Apa (water), Dhruva (polestar), Soma (moon), Dhara (earth), Anila (wind), Anala (fire), Prabhasa (dawn), and Pratusa (light). Like many things in Hindu mythology, the name and functions are not consistent and vary with texts, such as the Mahabharata or the Bhagavad Gita.

Shantanu stops Ganga from killing her eighth child,
19th century painting by Raja Ravi Varma

Although the meeting of Shantanu and Ganga at the banks of river Ganga and their subsequent marriage may appear to be sheer coincidence, Shantanu was predestined to meet and marry the river goddess as a punishment for a heavenly indiscretion in his past life. In his earlier life, Shantanu was the pious king called Mahabhisha. For the merits earned during his lifetime, Mahabhisha was granted entry to heaven where he enjoyed the music of Gandharvas and the dance of apsaras. Goddess Ganga was once paying a visit at Indra's court when a strong wind blew and lifted her garment exposing her ample breasts. All the celestials assembled in the court looked down out of respect except Mahabhisha who kept feasting his eyes on her. Indra was insulted by the king's manners and put a curse on Mahabhisha that he will return to earth. Ganga was not spared for she seemed to have enjoyed the king's undivided attention. She was ordered to travel to earth and return only after breaking Mahabhisha's heart.

20

The Ultimate Sacrifice of Bhishma

After Ganga took away his only son, Shantanu fought loneliness and depression not by resorting to fast food, alcoholism, or drugs, but by immersing himself in the affairs of the state. The people of Hastinapura loved their king, but they were also worried. The king had no wife to beget sons let alone a successor.

In another part of the forest, another king became exhausted while hunting and took rest under the shade of a tree. There he dreamt about his young wife and experienced a moment of profound joy, which led to the involuntary release of seminal seeds. The resourceful king collected the seeds, wrapped them in a leaf, and gave it to an eagle with instructions to deliver the packet to his wife so that she could bear a child. On its way, the eagle was attacked by a rival eagle since it did not have distribution rights in that territory. The packet fell into a river where it was swallowed by a fish, who really was an apsara under curse. Some days later, the fish was caught by a fisherman, who, to his disbelief, found in its belly two babies: a boy and a girl. The fisherman promptly took the twin babies to the king. The king gladly accepted the boy.[45] The girl had an awful fish stench, so she was rejected. Luckily for the girl, she was

---

[45] The boy grew up to become King Matsya who founded the Matsya kingdom.

adopted by the chief of fishermen, who named her Satyavati and raised her as his own child.

When Satyavati came of age, she worked as a conductor helping her father ferry people across the river. Once she had the occasion of ferrying sage Parashara, who became infatuated with the attractive conductor despite the fish stink. The sage asked her consent to perform *maithuna* together in the middle of the river. "No, not in this broad daylight where people can see us," protested Satyavati. "Besides, if I lose my virginity, no one will marry me." But Parashara was no ordinary sage. He had illusory powers and problem-solving skills beyond the capability of ordinary sages. Using his mystical powers, the sage drew a cloud of mist over the ferry pacifying her anxiety. Midstream the boat rocked several times in the calm waters transmitting ripples to the shores. Out of the union was born the child prodigy, Krishna Dvaipayana, who later became known as Vyasa, one of the greatest seers of Hinduism and the one who compiled the Vedas, Mahabharata, and other sacred books. In return for her favors, the sage restored her virginity. He also relieved Satyavati of her fish stink. "From now on, your body will exude fragrance that men will find utterly irresistible." Satyavati was ecstatic and basked in the afterglow of good fortune.

Sixteen years after his wife and child left him, the lonely Shantanu went out for a stroll one day along the banks of the river Ganga. There he noticed a handsome lad shooting arrows at the river and trying to break the flow of water. The turbulent river seemed to accommodate his actions. The lovely form of goddess Ganga suddenly emerged and announced, "O King, this is our son Devavrata, whom I am returning to you, as promised. Having learned archery from Parashurama, the Vedas from Vasishtha, and political science from Brihaspati, your son is the most skilled in the art of warfare and matters of the state." Saying so, Ganga disappeared once again. Although Ganga left him for good, Shantanu's joy knew no bounds on getting back his son. "Devavrata will be installed as the crown prince immediately," declared Shantanu exuberantly to his ministers.

THE ULTIMATE SACRIFICE OF BHISHMA

The people of Hastinapura rejoiced with the coming of an heir to the throne. There was happiness and prosperity for several years. Shantanu saw an able and sensible king-in-the-making in his son Devavrata. Another occasion and another trip took Shantanu through the forest to the banks of the river Yamuna where he found the air curiously filled with divine fragrance. He dismounted from his chariot and walked along the banks to discover the source of this sweet scent. The trail led to a stone bench on which was seated an enchanting beauty with black eyes. Shantanu approached her gently and enquired, "Who are you and what are you doing here?" The woman was taken in by the sudden appearance of the king. "I am Satyavati, daughter of the fisherman chief. I ferry people across the river."

Shantanu was struck by her beauty, friendliness, and intoxicating fragrance. Suddenly he realized that he was in love again. The king did not waste any more time. "As the king of Hastinapura, may I seek your hand in marriage?" Satyavati looked down blushing. She couldn't believe a poor girl like her would be sought after by the king. "If you have my father's permission, I consent." On hearing this, Shantanu proceeded to meet her father and seek his blessings.

The chief was delighted to hear Shantanu's proposal for marriage. However he was worried about Satyavati's future. "O King, it is indeed an honor to have you as my daughter's husband, for I couldn't possibly have found a more worthy husband for her. However, my daughter's welfare is of utmost importance to me. I shall agree to the marriage provided you promise that none other than my daughter's children shall succeed you to the throne." Shantanu was taken aback by the chief's demand. If he agreed to the precondition, it would be unfair to Devavrata, who had already been made the crown prince and heir apparent. Torn between duty and desire, Shantanu mounted his chariot without uttering a word and went back to Hastinapura, where he spent the next several days in solitary confinement—which did not escape the eye of his ministers or his son.

Devavrata realized that his father was a victim of love. He felt sorry for his father, who had suffered at the hands of Ganga and lost seven

Shantanu woos Satyavati, 19*th* century painting by Raja Ravi Varma

children. His father then spent the next 16 years in despair waiting for his son to come back. Devavrata did not have the heart to make his father suffer any more. So he told the chief, "For the sake of my father, I hereby take a vow. If your daughter marries my father, I shall renounce my claim to the throne." But the chief was not satisfied. "Prince, the vow you had taken in the presence of elders is praiseworthy. However, I have my doubts regarding the children you may sire. Although you have relinquished your right to the throne, they have a legitimate right to it, don't they?" On hearing this, Devavrata replied, "I have already relinquished my right to the throne. I shall now settle the matter of my children. From today, I will remain a celibate until death."

From the sky, the gods and sages, impressed by Devavrata's ultimate sacrifice, showered flowers on his head chanting, "Bhishma" meaning "the one who has taken a terrible vow." From then on, he became known by that name. Bhishma then escorted Satyavati, addressing her as mother, to the palace much to the disbelief of Shantanu. The couple was married shortly after. For his ultimate sacrifice, the gods rewarded Bhishma with the power to choose the time of his own death.

Back at the wharf, the chief was happy that he was able to negotiate the best deal for his daughter. Little did he realize that his onerous conditions for marriage would boomerang and inadvertently sow the seeds of one of the bloodiest battles in the history of ancient India.

21

The Birth of Pandavas and Kauravas

Sometimes even the best laid plans go crook. "Everybody has a plan until they get punched in the mouth," says Mike Tyson, the bad boy of boxing. In the Mahabharata, the chief of fishermen obtained the best bargain for his daughter, Satyavati. He made Bhishma, the king's eldest son, relinquish his right to the throne. He then went overboard by making Bhishma take a vow of celibacy thereby ensuring only his daughter's sons could inherit the throne. Despite the chief's best efforts at securing the future of his grandsons, fate had a different road map. Several years later, Satyavati had to grovel at Bhishma's feet to renege his vow and father children to save the future of the dynasty—which is the subject of this chapter.

By this time you may think that King Shantanu went childless with his new fisherwoman-turned-queen Satyavati. Not quite. In fact their alliance led to the birth of two sons, Chitrangada and Vichitravirya. After Shantanu's death, the hot-headed Chitrangada ascended the throne. His reign did not last long. He was killed during a battle with a Gandharva. With his brother's death, Vichitravirya was crowned king. He turned out to be an inept monarch and Bhishma had to rule the kingdom as his regent. Despite being an eligible bachelor, Vichitravirya was not the type who would set a woman's pulse racing at the *swayamavaras*. So the onus fell on Bhishma to find a suitable princess as a bride for him.

Around this time, the king of Kashi had arranged a *swayamvara* for his three daughters, Amba, Ambika, and Ambalika. No invitation was extended to Vichitravirya. Bhishma took this as an insult. On the day of the *swayamvara*, Bhishma rode to Kashi in a chariot and abducted the three sisters. The guests assembled at the arena tried to stop Bhishma, but they were no match for him.

When Bhishma returned to Hastinapura with his abductees, he learned that one of the sisters, Amba, was already in love with another prince. Out of respect, Bhishma allowed Amba to leave. The lover, however, rejected Amba on the grounds that her virginity was suspect since she was abducted by another man. Nowhere to turn to, Amba went back to Hastinapura. She begged Bhishma to marry her because he was the one responsible for her plight. But Bhishma reminded Amba of his vow of celibacy. Enraged, Amba sought the assistance of Parashurama, who was Bhishma's teacher. Parashurama initially pleaded with Bhishma, then threatened him, and finally fought with Bhishma for days over the issue. But Bhishma's determination was firm. A crestfallen Amba then retreated to the forest and undertook severe penance. She was reborn as the man-woman Shikhandi, who was eventually responsible for Bhishma's death in the Battle of Kurukshetra. (We describe this story in a later chapter.)

At Hastinapura, Vichitravirya married both Ambika and Ambalika at the same time to increase his chances of obtaining progeny, but, alas, it turned out to be match made in hell. He died leaving the two widows childless. Fearing the dynasty might become extinct without any children, Satyavati made use of *niyoga*, a time-honored custom where a widow could request her dead husband's nearest relative to father a child. Satyavati appealed to Bhishma to make her widowed daughters-in-law pregnant forgetting the fact that it was her own father who made Bhishma take a vow of celibacy. Bhishma remained steadfast to his vow.

THE BIRTH OF PANDAVAS AND KAURAVAS

Satyavati then summoned her elder son Vyasa to assume the role of husband. Born out of wedlock, Vyasa was a hermit practicing austerities in the forest. Living in the forest for many years took its toll and he was anything but attractive. He had matted locks, a beard that reached to his ankles, and a body odor that made people within a radius of one kilometer squirm. When the sage engaged in *maithuna* with Ambika, she became horrified by his looks and shut her eyes in fright. Consequently she gave birth to a blind son named Dhritarashtra. When Ambalika encountered the sage, she found him equally revolting and turned pale. She delivered a pale-complexioned son named Pandu. Since both the babies were less than perfect, Satyavati urged Ambika to again try to become pregnant. But Ambika could not bear the thought of another intimate encounter with the sage. She sent her maidservant in her place. The maidservant performed her duty cheerfully and gave birth to a flawless boy named Vidura—who later became a key character in the Mahabharata.

The three sons were brought up by Bhishma, who acted as a regent until they grew up. It was ironical that Bhishma, who was made to take a vow of celibacy, had to raise the children of someone other than himself. When the sons came off age, the younger Pandu assumed the throne of Hastinapura. The older Dhritarashtra was disqualified from kingship because he was blind. Pandu's reign, however, was short-lived. During a hunting trip, Pandu mistakenly shot dead a Brahmin and his wife engaged in *maithuna* thinking they were a pair of mating deer. The Brahmin cursed Pandu that he would also meet with a similar fate if he were to engage in *maithuna*. To avoid an untimely death, Pandu restrained himself from performing *maithuna* anymore. He retired to the Himalayas along with his two wives, Kunti and Madri. In Pandu's absence, Dhritarashtra became the caretaker king.

Since Pandu could not sire children, he became concerned about the absence of a successor to this throne. Kunti reminded him of a mantra bestowed on her by the sage Durvasa as a reward for her devotional service. With the mantra, she could invoke any god and bear his child. After

Pandu persuaded Kunti to invoke the mantra on his behalf, Kunti gave birth to three sons—Yudhishthira, Bhima, and Arjuna—fathered by the gods Yama (Dharma), Vayu, and Indra respectively. Pleased by the size of her brood, Kunti did not want to invoke any more gods because of the fear of being labeled a whore. On Pandu's advice, she taught the mantra to Madri, who invoked the Ashvin twins and gave birth to twins—Nakula and Sahadeva. Together the five sons of Pandu were thereafter called the Pandavas.

Meanwhile the blind Dhritarashtra married Gandhari after Pandu had left for the forest. When Gandhari learned about her husband's blindness, she decided to cover her eyes with a blindfold for the rest of her life, joining him in the world of darkness. After an abnormally long gestation period of two years, Gandhari gave birth to a ball of flesh. She was distraught that she had delivered a lifeless form and summoned Vyasa to the court. On the advice of Vyasa, the ball was split into 101 parts and then placed in jars of ghee—which incubated into hundred sons and a daughter.[46] These hundred sons became known as the Kauravas from the name of the renowned king Kuru. Although Kuru was the common ancestor for both branches of the family, only the hundred sons of Dhritarashtra were called Kauravas. Prominent among the Kauravas were the first two sons—Duryodhana and Dushasana.

One beautiful spring day, when the tree frogs were chirping, the streams were gurgling, and butterflies were flapping, Pandu had a surge of adrenaline. He tried to impose his will on the resisting Madri and died in her arms. A broken-hearted Madri leaped into the funeral pyre of Pandu, leaving Kunti behind to raise the five boys single-handedly.

As you may have noticed, the author Vyasa makes his appearance in the epic as the slovenly sage. Although Mahabharata is known for many things, rarely is Vyasa's penchant for saga and humor mentioned.

---

[46] The daughter was called Dushala. Dhritarashtra also fathered a son called Yuyutsu through his maid. Yuyutsu fought on the side of the Pandavas in the Kurukshetra War.

THE BIRTH OF PANDAVAS AND KAURAVAS

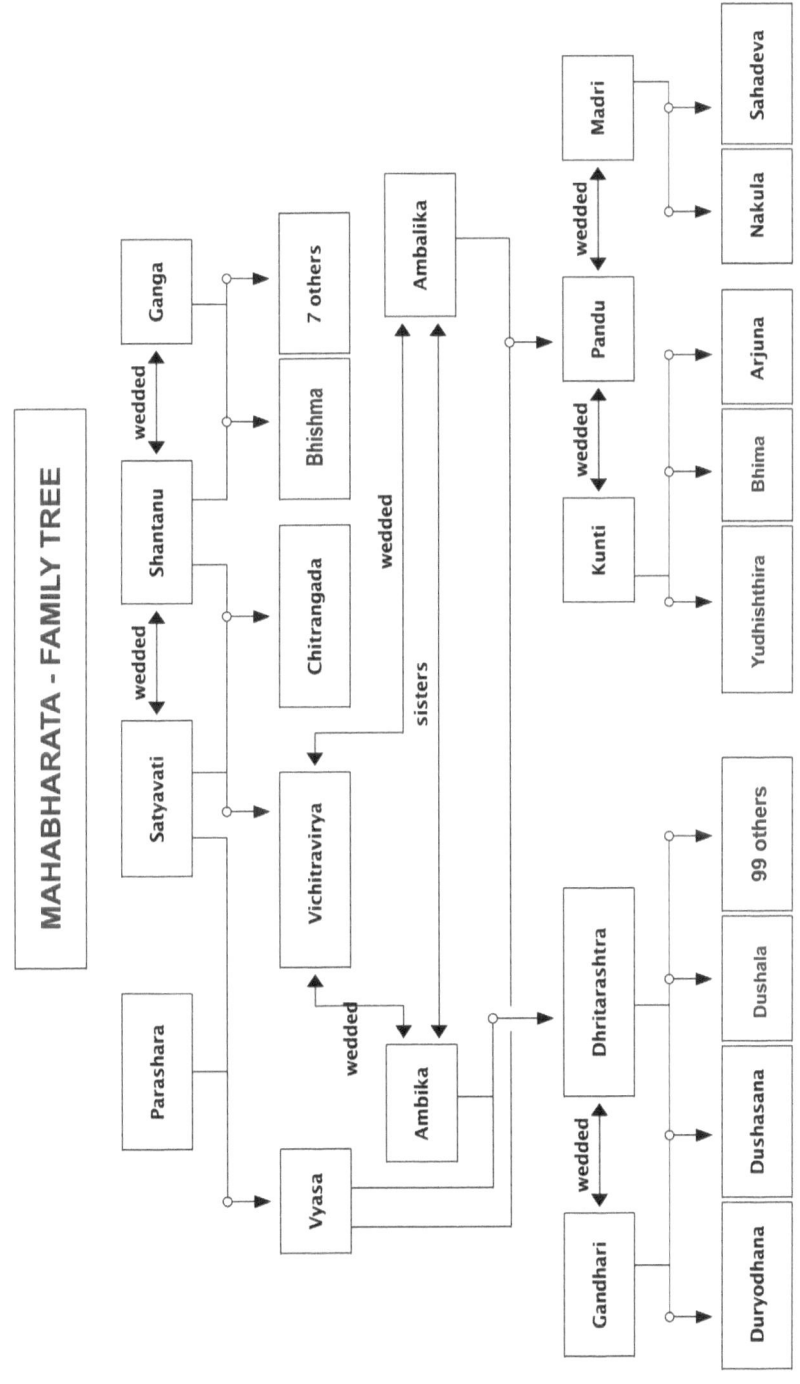

22

Feuding Cousins

Sudden death often triggers a traumatic experience in a family. One harrowing experience following the death of a family member is relocation. The Pandavas faced this ordeal after the death of their father Pandu. They gave up their forest life and returned to Hastinapura. At the palace, the Pandavas were welcomed enthusiastically by their relatives and cousins. Dhritarashtra became their guardian and treated them with respect and on par with his sons. He entrusted them to the old warrior Bhishma, who brought up the children under his supervision. The cousins grew up together in typical boyish rivalry.

Among the Pandavas, Yudhishthira was the most honest and level-headed. Bhima was the strongest but a bully. Physically bigger than the other children, he delighted in tormenting his Kaurava cousins. He would hold them under water until they ran out of breath or pick them up and throw them onto the ground. When they tried to escape him by climbing trees, he would shake the trees until they fell down like ripe fruit. The Kauravas hated him from infancy. Bhima's younger brother, Arjuna beat everyone in archery. He was a great warrior, yet very humane. The youngest two of the Pandavas, Nakula and Sahadeva, were the best horsemen on the field.

Despite all the children receiving equal attention and training, the Pandavas excelled the Kauravas in all fields, particularly martial arts. Consequently the Kauravas became jealous of their cousins, and Duryodhana, in particular, regarded the Pandavas as arch rivals. While Bhima's persistent bullying annoyed him to no extent, Duryodhana was more concerned that Yudhishthira might succeed him to the throne. About this time king Dhritarashtra made plans for the succession and formally designated Yudhishthira as the heir apparent since he was the oldest of all children. After the nomination, Duryodhana's hatred for the Pandavas became even more intense. He believed he should have been the heir apparent because he was the eldest son of a ruling king, even though the king was acting in a caretaker capacity.

As the princes continued their education, the rivalry between Pandavas and Kauravas became more pronounced. About this time, a Brahmin called Drona appeared at the court and demonstrated great skills in weapons. He was appointed the martial instructor of the boys. Of all the students that received training under Drona, Arjuna emerged as the most talented in the use of weapons, exceeding even Drona's own son.

A tournament was organized to mark the graduation of the Kuru princes. The Pandavas, particularly Arjuna, excelled throughout the tournament displaying superior skills much to the discontent of the Kauravas. This was followed by a single combat with clubs between Duryodhana and Bhima. But the fight became so serious that Drona had to separate them. At this point, a man called Karna stepped forward from the spectators and performed all the breathtaking feats Arjuna had demonstrated. He then challenged Arjuna to a single combat much to the delight of Duryodhana. No one knew anything about this unknown combatant except Kunti, who fainted in the gallery upon seeing him.

Karna's challenge was rejected because princes could only fight princes, and Karna was allegedly a charioteer's son. But Duryodhana, jealous of Arjuna's successes, was determined to give Karna the chance of defeating a Pandava. He persuaded his father and conferred the kingdom of Anga on Karna on the spot. When Karna's charioteer father congratulated his son on becoming a king, Bhima taunted Karna over his low lineage. The single combat between Arjuna and Karna never materialized as the sun went down and the tournament was closed. Neither Karna nor the Pandavas knew then that Karna was actually the elder brother of the Pandavas since he was the abandoned first son of Kunti whom she conceived before she married Pandu. (We will revisit this story later in this book.)

The rift between the Pandavas and Kauravas widened and took a sinister turn. When Yudhishthira came of age to succeed the throne of Hastinapura, Duryodhana hatched a plan to wipe out the Pandavas. Until then Dhritarashtra treated his nephews with kindness and would hear nothing about the plot. Duryodhana's constant persuasion, however, changed his mind and he began to offer a sympathetic ear to his son's arguments. Aware of Bhima's love for food, the Kauravas offered Bhima sweets laced with poison. They then bound him and threw him into a river. But the poison only fortified Bhima, who broke the bonds and swam to safety.

Duryodhana next convinced his father to persuade the Pandavas to spend a year at the beautiful city of Varanavata where a great Shiva festival was planned to take place. Secretly, Duryodhana had built a house of inflammable lac for the Pandavas to occupy during their stay. His plan was to set fire to the house and kill them when they were asleep. Fortunately for the Pandavas, they were warned in time by their uncle Vidura, the younger brother of Pandu and Dhritarashtra. When the house was being set to fire, the Pandavas had already escaped through a secret tunnel leading to the forest. For a while, the Pandavas decided to hide in the forest disguised at Brahmins and let Dhritarashtra and the Kauravas believe they were dead. Dhritarashtra and his sons wore funereal garments and performed impressive obsequies near a river mourning the death of their dear cousins.

Although the Pandavas managed to escape unscathed, they were shaken by this attempt on their lives. They realized that the family feud had taken an ugly turn. While in the forest, the Pandavas learned about the *swayamvara* of Draupadi, daughter of King Drupada of the Panchala dynasty. Draupadi was a great beauty and princes from many distant kingdoms had come to win her hand in marriage. Disguised as Brahmins, the Pandavas came to the *swayamvara*. Krishna and Balarama were also present at the *swayamvara*. It was the first time the Pandavas met their cousin Krishna, for Kunti was Vasudeva's sister.

Like others, Drupada was disheartened to learn that Arjuna had died in the house fire with the other Pandavas. He had wanted Arjuna to marry his daughter. However, he still wished to marry his daughter to a good archer. Hence the *swayamvara* involved an archery contest in which the suitors had to not only string a heavy bow, but shoot and pierce the eye of a golden fish by looking at its reflection. This was an extremely difficult task by all means. One after the other, the princes came to the arena to display their skill. Some could barely lift the bow, while none succeeded in hitting the target. Karna, now the king of Anga, stepped forward and lifted the bow. Instantly Draupadi protested that she would never marry the son of a charioteer.

When all the princes failed the test, Drupada invited the Brahmins to take part in the contest. To the astonishment of all, a Brahmin came forward, lifted the bow, and shot an arrow straight at the fish's eye. Everyone assembled in the hall was impressed by his strength and precision. Both Drupada and Draupadi were overjoyed and the king acknowledged him the victor. The assembled princes protested that the winner was a Brahmin in a contest meant for warriors. A melee ensued and the Pandavas joined in the scuffle and drove away the fuming princes. At the end, the Brahmin revealed his true identity as Arjuna, to the great delight of Drupada.

When the Pandavas returned home, Arjuna proudly announced to their mother, "Look, what we have won today!" Kunti was praying, but before she realized, she responded, "Whatever it is, share among all of you." Since Kunti was highly respected and her word was the law, Draupadi became the shared wife of the five brothers. King Drupada objected to the marriage, but later he yielded. Impotency among Kshatriya kings was rampant at that time, so having multiple options to obtain an heir was prudent. But then although polygamy was a common practice among ancient Hindus, polyandry was not. The arrangement was that

Draupadi would spend a year with each husband in turn.[47] Despite having five husbands, Draupadi had the greatest liking for Arjuna. Later when Arjuna married Krishna's sister Subhadra, whom he carried by force with Krishna's permission, Draupadi was struck with jealousy.

Arjuna aims at the target at Draupadi's swayamvara, artist unknown

Now allied with the powerful Panchala dynasty, the Pandavas discarded their disguises publicly. However Karna and Duryodhana had seen through their disguises and recognized Arjuna and Bhima at the *swayamvara*. Back in Hastinapura, the Kauravas once again thought of a plan to get rid of their cousins. Karna wanted to dispose the Pandavas in open warfare, while Duryodhana advanced a plot of turning the Pandava brothers among themselves. But Drona rejected both plans and suggested the rights of the Pandavas be recognized by dividing the kingdom into two. Since Krishna and Drupada were aligned to the Pandavas, Dhritarashtra did not want any confrontation. So he took Drona's advice and gave a

---

[47] Draupadi became the mother of five sons, one each from each Pandava brother.

vast tract of jungle territory bordering the river Yamuna to the Pandavas. But in a short time, the Pandavas cleared the forest and developed the land by building irrigation channels. From the developed land, they built the magnificent and opulent capital called Indraprastha (close to today's Delhi) and crowned Yudhishthira as the king. Men of all ranks flocked to the city and made it their new home.

With the Pandavas and Kauravas ruling their own kingdoms, you think peace and friendship returned to the region? Far from it, the success of Indraprastha made the Kauravas, particularly Duryodhana, even more jealous of his cousins.

> *You have enemies? Good. That means you've stood up for something, sometime in your life.*
>
> —WINSTON CHURCHILL, 1874-1965

23

The Deadly Game of Dice

Nobody has ever bet enough on a winning horse.

—PROVERB

Throughout its history India has been blessed with rulers of exceptional merit. One among them was Akbar the Great, the Mughal emperor who conquered most of North India and yet practiced religious tolerance. Others include Ashoka the Great and Kanishka the Great. As the son of Dharma (Yama), Yudhishthira was a just ruler who unflinchingly adhered to dharma. Yet the epithet "Yudhishthira the Great" is not associated with the oldest son of Pandu. Why? Despite being an embodiment of fairness, Yudhishthira had one weakness—a penchant for gambling, which the Kauravas exploited to their advantage, as we shall see in this chapter. The consequences were sweeping and led to a bloody war.

As the nascent king of Indraprastha, now a fabulous glittering city, Yudhishthira began to have dreams of an empire and set out to perform the Rajasuya sacrifice that would establish him as the emperor of the world. Armies were dispatched across four corners of the world to obtain tributes from other rulers. The non-complaint king Jarasandha was defeated with the help of Krishna. (This was described in an earlier chapter.) At the Rajasuya sacrifice, Krishna was the chief guest. The kings at the ceremony lavished Yudhishthira with numerous gifts. Among the guests was Duryodhana, who could not help but notice the prosperity the Pandavas had brought to Indraprastha. The city with its beautiful orchards, busy river ports, and vibrant markets looked impeccable. On invitation, Duryodhana took a tour of their palace. The opulence and the intricate designs on the structures amazed him. He encountered a crystal floor in the hall, but mistaking it to be a pool of water Duryodhana drew up his garments only to realize his folly. Another time, he confused a pool for a crystal floor and fell into the water. On seeing Duryodhana floundering in the pool, Draupadi mocked Duryodhana by calling him the blind son of blind parents without realizing that no one is more dangerous than one who has been humiliated. Later, Duryodhana walked into a closed crystal door thinking it open only to bang and hurt his head while embarrassing himself even more.

Humiliated, Duryodhana returned to Hastinapura. Back at his own palace, he kept brooding over the prosperity of the Pandavas. He regarded his cousins as freeloaders who came from the forest with the sole purpose of appropriating the entitlements of the Kauravas. Now they had accumulated vast amount of wealth through the Rajasuya sacrifice. His mind wandered over to the gaffes he had committed at the palace and the snickers and guffaws of the Pandavas. The thought of Draupadi's insensitive remark made him livid. He swore he would avenge this insult.

Duryodhana approached his uncle Shakuni with the proposal that the Kauravas should declare war against the Pandavas and take back the kingdom given to them. But the wily Shakuni had a better plan. He hatched a plot with Duryodhana to exploit Yudhishthira's one weakness—love for a good game of dice. If the Kauravas could beat the Pandavas in this game, Duryodhana would achieve by peaceful means what he wanted to accomplish by war. Initially Dhritarashtra opposed the idea, but his love for his eldest son made him waver and eventually consent to the plan.

When Duryodhana invited Yudhishthira for a friendly game of dice, he could not pass up the opportunity. Everyone gathered in the assembly hall to watch the match. The spectators included Bhishma, Drona, Vidura, and Dhritarashtra. In the course of the game, Yudhishthira lost steadily—cattle, sheep, jewels, gold, chariots, horses—yet he persisted, convinced that luck would turn his way. As the game continued, the stakes got bigger—palaces, territories, entire kingdoms—and Yudhishthira lost everything.

Why did Yudhishthira lose heavily? The game pitted two players against each other. Each player had to throw the dice and move the pawns on the game board in accordance with the outcome. A player needed both luck and skill to win. Yudhishthira represented the five Pandava brothers. The Kauravas enlisted the help of their uncle Shakuni to play for them. Unknown to the Pandavas, Shakuni was a sophisticated cheat at dice. With a loaded dice and expert sleight of hand, Shakuni had the odds stacked in his favor. He had altered the face of dice so that certain outcomes were more likely to occur. Further, he used his index finger and thumb to control the roll thereby favoring certain outcomes. As Yudhishthira kept losing, the Pandavas suspected the dice was loaded. But being amateurs, the brothers were unable to prove any foul play. Meanwhile, Yudhishthira became restless with successive defeats and could not be persuaded to stop. In the end, with nothing left to wager, a desperate Yudhishthira staked each of his four brothers as slaves, then himself, and finally, their wife Draupadi. He lost them all.

As Duryodhana, Karna, Shakuni, and the remaining sons of Dhritarashtra celebrated the occasion, the elders Drona, Bhishma, Vidura, and even Dhritarashtra were outraged to see what was happening. A triumphant Duryodhana ordered his brother Dushasana to strip off the royal garments from the Pandavas. They were now slaves who were not entitled to wear regal clothes. When the Pandavas disrobed their upper garments, Duryodhana commanded Dushasana to bring Draupadi to the assembled court. "She is our slave. Take off her clothes and expose this shameless creature to the court." Dushasana stormed to Draupadi's quarters and found her sitting with her hair untied. He grabbed her by her long hair and dragged her into the assembly hall. When Dushasana stopped in front of the gathered assembly, Draupadi stood up and challenged the Kauravas, "How can someone who has lost himself wager someone else in a game?" The assembly hall fell silent, as no one knew the answer to the question.

To provoke the Pandavas, Duryodhana bared his thighs and beckoned Draupadi to sit on them. Bhima became infuriated and swore that he would smash Duryodhana's thighs. Meanwhile, Dushasana tugged at Draupadi's sari, attempting to disrobe her in front of everyone. Draupadi clutched herself in desperation as her body spun around several times. She became dizzy and her eyes lost focus. Crying out of desperation, she prayed, "O Krishna, where are you? Save me from this humiliation!" Bhima became livid on seeing Draupadi's agony and swore one day he would rip the heart of Dushasana and drink his blood. And then, a miracle happened. The more Dushasana tried to unfurl the sari, the more cloth it revealed. The sari seemed to extend to infinity. Having piled up a big heap, Dushasana pulled faster, and faster. With no end in sight, he eventually gave up out of exhaustion.

Everyone present in the hall witnessed the divine intervention. The howling of the jackals and the braying of the asses could be heard foreboding the destruction of the race. Until this time, Dhritarashtra was a silent spectator from the sidelines. He knew his sons had won by cheating and decided it was time to end the madness. "Stop!" he cried. "Release the empress immediately!" Calling Yudhishthira and Draupadi to his side, the blind king apologized and asked for forgiveness for what his sons had done.

Fortunately for the Pandavas, Indraprastha was rightfully restored to its owners. Although fond of his eldest son, the vacillating Dhritarashtra took the courageous step of putting an end to the insanity perhaps because of a sense of fairness and the epic dire tones adopted by elders such as Drona, Bhishma, and Vidura. Even the blind man had his doubts about the legality of the wager.

THE DEADLY GAME OF DICE

Dushasana disrobing Draupadi, unknown artist

There is a very easy way to return from a casino with a small fortune; go there with a large one.

—JACK YELTON, 1921–1999

24

The Declaration of War

Those who can win a war well can rarely make a good peace, and those who could make a good peace would never have won the war.

—WINSTON CHURCHILL, 1874–1965

After the high-stake game of dice between the Pandavas and Kauravas ended in a disaster, you would think the Pandavas would never venture into gambling let alone play another game of dice, right? In fact the opposite happened. That's because the incident only firmed Duryodhana's resolve for vengeance. When Duryodhana learned that the Pandavas had returned to Indraprastha, he reprimanded his father for interfering with his plans. Duryodhana could not believe that his father had let the Pandavas off after he had them by the scruff of their necks. He scoffed at Dhritarashtra's scruples and complained that through his generosity, the king had inadvertently strengthened the Pandavas again.

Restless, Duryodhana sat down and devised another plan. He knew the Pandavas respected his father more than any of the Kauravas. So he pleaded with his father to invite the Pandavas again for another game of dice. The blind man, his mind oscillating like a pendulum, agreed because he did not want to upset his son again. This time there would be just one game. Whoever lost would go into exile to the forest for 13 years and pass the 13th year unrecognized in a city. Should they be recognized in the 13th year, they would have to go into exile again for another 13 years.

When the invitation for another game of dice came from Dhritarashtra, Yudhishthira could not turn down the offer. He had utmost respect for the king. Once again, he played and lost to the Kauravas, Shakuni again playing a pivotal role for the hosts. This time there was no intervention from Dhritarashtra. The outcome of the game was declared valid and legal. Duryodhana could barely wipe the smile off his face having had the opportunity to get his hands on Indraprastha. Drona and Vidura were despondent and felt the Kuru race was doomed. The Pandavas and their wife, Draupadi, along with some followers, set off to the forest. Kunti wanted to join them too, but Yudhishthira refused. He did not want Kunti to go through the hardships of forest life again. But Kunti refused to stay at the palace, so she went to live with Vidura.

The Pandavas wanted to get as far away from Hastinapura as possible. During the course of the exile they stayed in many places. They met leaders of many tribes and kings sympathetic to their cause. Over the years, their bitterness toward their cousins softened. But Draupadi sought revenge. She could never forget the humiliation she suffered at the palace.

Soon the 12 years of life in the wilderness came to an end and the 13th year of the exile arrived. Since the Pandavas had to spend the last year incognito, they came to the court of King Virata in various disguises, each befitting to his stature. Yudhishthira became an advisor to the king, Bhima, a cook at the royal kitchen, Arjuna a eunuch, Sahadeva a cowherd, and Nakula a horse trainer. Draupadi became the attendant of the queen, but she had a hard time concealing her identity because she was too beautiful. Most of the year passed uneventfully; however, toward the end of the year, Draupadi's beauty caught the eye of Kichaka, the queen's brother and commander-in-chief of Virata's army. He found her irresistible and attempted to seduce her. Draupadi rejected his advances and pleaded with him to stay away from her as she was a low-caste woman. But Kichaka continued to pursue her regardless. The job of protecting Draupadi's honor fell on Bhima. He took a break from the kitchen duties and beat the commander to a pulp.

Meanwhile, in Hastinapura, Duryodhana, realizing this was the 13th year of exile, sent out his spies in all directions to find the Pandavas. He wanted them to track his cousins' whereabouts so that the exile could be extended for another 13 years. After an extensive search, the spies came back and reported they could not locate the Pandavas. Duryodhana was not pleased and asked them to redouble their efforts. The news of Kichaka's death sent shock waves in Hastinapura since he was a formidable warrior. Duryodhana began to suspect that the Pandavas were hiding at Virata's palace. He commanded his army, along with his allies, to attack Virata's kingdom from both sides. Their efforts, however, proved to be in vain. They were repelled by Virata's forces, who were assisted by the Pandava brothers in the absence of Kichaka. Meanwhile, the period of 13 years of exile had expired. The Pandavas were no longer required to live incognito. When the Pandavas disclosed their identity to the king, he was delighted. Nevertheless he apologized for treating them as servants. He offered his daughter in marriage to Arjuna, who declined the offer himself, but accepted her as a daughter-in-law for his son, Abhimanyu.

Finally, after spending the last year of the 13-year exile incognito successfully, the Pandavas returned to Hastinapura. They made a request for peace and their share of the kingdom. During this time, Duryodhana had made alliances and fortified his army. Emboldened by the strength of his military, he took the request as a sign of weakness and refused to make any concessions. As a last resort, Yudhishthira relinquished his right to the kingdom, and instead asked for just five villages—one for each of the five brothers. Such was the vindictiveness of Duryodhana that he declared he would not give even the tiniest bit of land, not even that which could fit on the tip of a needle.

Having exhausted all options, Yudhishthira was left with no other choice than combat. He pronounced war against the Kauravas. Both sides began frantic negotiations with friends, families, relatives, and kings to get them to fight on their side. More and more kings signed up until the entire region became entrapped in the family conflict. Bhishma, Drona, and Karna took the side of the Kauravas because of their dharma even though they knew their cause was unjust. Kunti attempted to prevent her eldest son Karna from fighting on the side of Kauravas, battling against her five other sons. But the revelation that he was the sixth Pandava came too late, for he owed allegiance to Duryodhana for supporting him and making him a king. However, he promised that he would not harm any of the Pandava brothers except Arjuna. Krishna was the only one who did not choose a side. He declared that since both the Pandavas and Kauravas were his relatives, he could not afford to pick a side. However, he made them an offer: one side could have his armies, and the other side could have him, in a non-combat role, as an advisor. "Whoever of you —Arjuna or Duryodhana—shows up first tomorrow morning at my house will have the first choice."

Before the break of dawn the next day, Duryodhana came rushing to Krishna's abode and sat nervously at the head of Krishna's bed, waiting for him to wake up. Arjuna, on the other hand, got up at his usual time and proceeded to Krishna's house, where he stood humbly by the foot of Krishna's bed. When Krishna woke up, he first saw Arjuna standing near his feet even though Duryodhana got there first. "My army or me?" asked Krishna to Arjuna, who instantly replied, "I choose you, lord." Thinking Arjuna to be the greatest fool on earth, Duryodhana walked away a happy man knowing that he had all the military might of Krishna at his command.

And the stage was set for the Battle of Kurukshetra between the Kauravas and the Pandavas.

Nothing has more strength than dire necessity.

—EURIPIDES

25

The Rules of War

Peace is the virtue of civilization. War is its crime.

—VICTOR HUGO, 1802–1885

It is early morning on the day of war. Arjuna asks his newly appointed charioteer Krishna to take him to the center of battlefield so that he can have a good look at the armies. Seeing the soldiers lined up for battle, the ever-valiant Arjuna becomes mentally paralyzed and surrenders his bow. He is unable to bear the thought that many of his family members and friends may perish in the war even though he is convinced he is on the side of dharma. Krishna comes to his aid and enters into a long conversation with him. Krishna tells him that the purpose of life is fulfilling duty (dharma) and action (karma) even if the consequences are tragic.[48] While Arjuna's utmost concern was about the lives of his near and dear ones, much less was discussed about the plight of bystanders, children, workers,

---

[48] This discourse is found in the Bhagavad Gita.

and civilians who are not fighting the war. What happens to thousands of those innocents trapped in the war zones for no fault of theirs?

Today, the Geneva Convention protects individuals not fighting in an armed conflict. Established in the 19th century, the Geneva Convention lists out the rules of the war (among other things) and dictates what can or cannot be done during an armed conflict. Did any such framework of rules exist in ancient times? An early instance of such rules can be found in the Mahabharata. Hindus often refer to the Kurukshetra War as *dharma-yudha* meaning "righteous war." The war was fought according to certain rules of knightly etiquette. Below we list some of these rules:

- Fighting should take place only in daylight. (A daily ceasefire after dusk.)
- Anyone leaving the battlefield or sitting in yoga posture is exempt from attack.
- No warrior may strike an animal not considered a direct threat.
- The lives of women, prisoners of war, and farmers are sacred

Also in the Mahabharata you find one of the earliest examples of the rule of proportionality; i.e. equals fight equals.

- Horsemen are prohibited from attacking foot soldiers.
- Mounted warriors should fight only other mounted warriors.
- Warriors on chariots should fight only those on chariots.
- No warrior may injure another who has surrendered or is disarmed.
- Warriors must not engage in any unfair warfare.

Thus, in the Mahabharata, we find provisions existed for treatment of injured soldiers.

Yet, rules are meaningless without enforcement. While rules are created by elites on high moral grounds, enforcing them in a conflict situation is not easy, as signatories to the Geneva Convention have found out. At the UN Security Council, for instance, all the five veto-holding permanent members must agree to conduct an investigation of breach or refer a case to court or impose sanctions. Most often one of these countries has a vested interest in the conflict and therefore an agreement is hard to reach.

As it turned out, Kurukshetra War was no different. Although the rules for knightly behavior were established prior to the war, these rules broke down gradually as the war turned ugly, and the perpetrators included Drona, Arjuna, and Krishna. In fact, during the last days of the battle, the rules were entirely forsaken, which resulted in Drona's son, Ashwatthama, committing the gravest atrocity.

Never think that war, no matter how necessary, nor how justified, is not a crime.

—ERNEST HEMINGWAY, 1899–1961

26

The Dynamics of the War

After Arjuna's mental meltdown, the Pandavas and the Kauravas braced for battle on the wide plains of Kurukshetra. Yudhishthira was on the western side of the plains, seated in a chariot and leading his troops. On the opposite end, at the center of his army, Duryodhana appeared, riding an elephant. An unexpected thing then happened. Yudhishthira stopped his chariot, dismounted, and walked unarmed toward the Kaurava army. The king of dharma wanted to seek the blessings of Bhishma and Drona prior to the fight. This was akin to Indian soldiers seeking the blessings of Pakistani Generals before a border skirmish. What was Yudhishthira thinking?

I mention this incident not to highlight Yudhishthira's obsession with dharma and protocols; rather to emphasize a salient feature of the Mahabharata—its vast scope that covers many vicissitudes of life. The Mahabharata is said to contain all the contradictions of life—dignity and mutiny, life and strife, agony and joy. Hindus believe there is nothing in human life that does not have a place in the epic. Two of the greatest compositions came into existence during the Kurukshetra War. At the outset, Arjuna's moral meltdown led to the creation of the Bhagavad Gita. Likewise, the Vishnu Sahasranama or "thousand names of Vishnu" was delivered by Bhishma when he was on his deathbed.[49] Oh, in case you are wondering, both Bhishma and Drona gave their blessings to Yudhishthira to fight against them—which made Duryodhana wonder whether his senior commander's allegiance lay elsewhere.

In the following chapters, we cover the major events of each day of the war. That raises a valid question: how can we confirm the truth about the war and ascertain it is not a Kaurava or a Pandava version of events? History tells us that war reports are often controversial and each side will claim victory using obscure stats. For instance, back in 1965 Pakistan secretly sent 30,000 armed men into the Indian-administered Kashmir to incite an insurgency and annex Kashmir from India. Although the plan was thwarted by the Indian army, Pakistan claims to-this-day that they won the war despite not gaining a single inch of new territory.

The events of the battle were reported by the war correspondent Sanjaya, a charioteer by profession and a minister to Dhritarashtra. The blind king wanted someone like a modern-day roving reporter, who would provide him instant updates from the battlefield. He turned to the sage Vyasa, who, in turn, bestowed upon his disciple, Sanjaya, the power of *divya-drishti* or "divine glimpse." Through these powers, Sanjaya was able to perceive events without being physically present on the battlefield. As the official commentator of Mahabharata, Sanjaya not only provided Dhritarashtra an unvarnished account of the war, but narrated the entire Bhagavad Gita to the king even as the conversation between Arjuna and Krishna was happening miles away.

Although the Kurukshetra War is remembered as the clash between Pandavas and Kaurava, it was not just a battle between five brothers and hundred brothers. While Arjuna and Bhima featured prominently in the war and inflicted a heavy toll on the enemy, the hundred sons of Dhritarashtra did not make a significant impact by themselves. In fact, most of the major accomplishments on the Kaurava side came with the help of their allies. As we discussed earlier, friends, relatives, and family

---

[49] The Vishnu Sahasranama is described in book 2 of this series.

members became embroiled in the feud. At that time North India was a conglomeration of small kingdoms and many such kingdoms participated as allies of the two rival groups. King Drupada, the ruler of the powerful kingdom of Panchala, and his family were aligned to the Pandavas because his daughter Draupadi was the shared wife of the Pandavas. Another king that came to the aid of Pandavas was Virata, the king of the Matsya, who provided shelter to the Pandavas during their last year of exile. Meanwhile, the kingdom of Gandhara, with its strong links to the Kauravas, naturally became their ally. The Gandhara prince Shakuni, often regarded as the mastermind of the Kurukshetra War, was a councilor to Duryodhana.

Krishna offered to be Arjuna's charioteer, but his army fought on the Kaurava side. Kritavarma was one such army chieftain of Krishna who fought for the Kauravas because of Krishna's orders. But not everyone obeyed Krishna's orders. A warrior called Satyaki did not listen to Krishna and fought for the Pandavas. Another king who fought for the Kauravas was Shalya, a renowned warrior and the ruler of the Madra kingdom. The word *shalya* means "pointed weapon" in Sanskrit but in recent times has acquired the connotation of "nuisance." For instance, back in 2017 Prime Minister Narendra Modi of India labeled his critics of economic policies as *shalya*. A steady and calm fighter, Shalya was the brother of Madri, the second wife of Pandu. Being related to the Pandavas, Shalya was sympathetic to the Pandavas and was heading to fight on their side with his army. On the way, he took part in a grand feast that was offered to his troops. Shalya assumed it was Yudhishthira's welcoming party and granted a boon to the host. He was shocked to learn that the feast was, in fact, organized by Duryodhana, who promptly asked him to fight for the Kauravas. Being a man of honor, Shalya obliged without protest.

Unlike Shalya, Jayadratha, the king of Sindhu, lent his support to the Kauravas willingly. He was married to Dushala, the only sister of the hundred Kaurava brothers. Jayadratha's hatred for the Pandavas went back to the time when the Pandavas were in exile. Once Jayadratha met Draupadi in the forest and was smitten by her beauty. Although she was married to the Pandava brothers, Jayadratha attempted to woo her. When his attempts failed, he tried to abduct her only to be pursued by the Pandavas. Jayadratha was promptly caught, but the Pandavas spared his life. Since then, Jayadratha was longing for retribution. Overall, 11 battalions fought on the side of the Kauravas; and seven on the side of Pandavas. Balarama remained neutral and refused to take sides. While the Pandavas had soldiers numbering about 1.5 million, Kauravas had even more—2.4 million.

Were all participants equally motivated for the war? Not really. Although tensions had been simmering for many years, the dynamics of hatred were deep-seated and nothing short of the India-Pakistan rivalry or the Israeli-Palestinian conflicts or US Republican-Democratic party battles. The five Pandavas and the hundred sons of Dhritarashtra through this wife Gandhari were clear on their loyalties. The blind king had sired a 101st son called Yuyutsu through his maid, but that lovechild hated Duryodhana's evil schemes and switched his loyalty to the Pandavas before the war. He became the only Kaurava to fight on the side of the Pandavas. The elders Drona, Kripa, and Bhishma were against the war, but considered it their dharma to fight for the Kauravas. While Karna hated both Arjuna and Draupadi with a vengeance and was grateful to Duryodhana for anointing him as king, Shikhandi (Amba) spent an entire lifetime seeking revenge against Bhishma for tainting her honor. Meanwhile Bhima could never forgive the humiliation Draupadi suffered at the hands of Duryodhana and Dushasana. And the rivalry between Drona and Drupada went back to their childhood. (We will discuss these conflicts in detail in the upcoming chapters.)

Even though the Mahabharata is about an ancient conflict, it was not like soldiers lined up on either side of a hill and started attacking each other at the blow of a whistle. In fact, warfare was quite sophisticated and the epic mentions many *vyuha*s, or battle formations, used by the commanders of each side. These intricate arrangements of troop were designed not only to prevent the enemy from penetrating, but also to make it difficult for the enemy to extricate once it got in. These formations were

THE DYNAMICS OF THE WAR

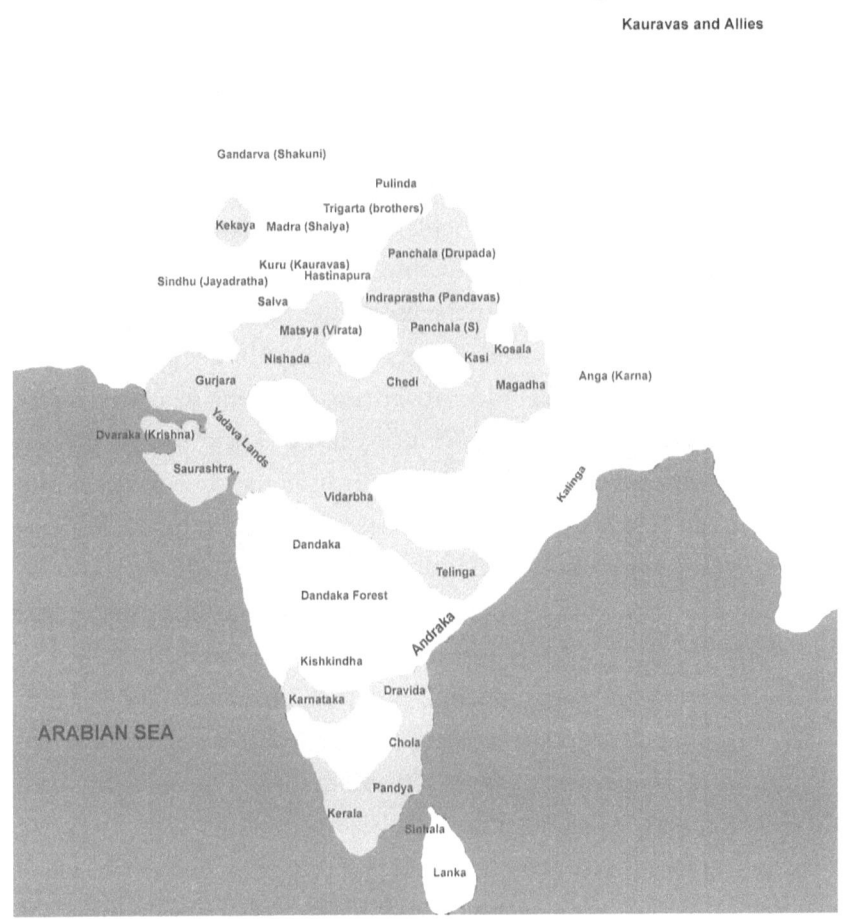

India during the Mahabharata times

dynamic and continuously adapted to the situation. For instance, if one section of the *vyuha* was taking huge casualties, the formation restructured itself to defend that section. Although it was a commander's duty to choose and execute the most appropriate *vyuha*, it required tremendous skill to prevail, as it was proved later.

Some key formations in the war include the crocodile (*makara*), eagle (*garuda*), and wheel (*chakra*). The crocodile formation was deployed by both the Pandavas and Kauravas on different days of the war. Certain formations operated in pairs. For example, when Kauravas chose the heron (*krauncha*) formation, the Pandavas went for the Garuda since the eagle is a natural predator of the heron. It is said that Yudhishthira opted for *suchimukha* (needle-shape) *vyuha* on the first day after seeing the bigger army of the Kauravas advancing. In a needle-shaped formation soldiers are arranged in a long line. It is a defensive approach and well suited to situations where a smaller army fights a larger one. Arjuna differed with his brother and chose an aggressive, three-fold formation known as *vajra* (diamond) but it produced little success. The most widely recognized *vyuha* is the *chakra vyuha*, which trapped young Abhimanyu leading to this death. Abhimanyu was the warrior son of Arjuna who was taught how to penetrate the formation. But he did not know how to get out of the labyrinth because his father did not have the time to teach him that technique. Consequently the boy became encircled by the Kaurava stalwarts and was brutally killed inside the wheel formation.

The weapons used were not just bow-and-arrows, discuses, spears, and maces. A variety of sophisticated weapons are cited in the text of which some were released by hand, others by machines, and a handful by invoking a mantra. The Mahabharata mentions several celestial weapons or *astras* that were released by incantation. One weapon called the *Brahma Astra*, which manifests the head of Brahma, is said to wield enormous power. Even more powerful is the *Brahmashira Astra*, which manifests the four heads of Brahma and is capable of consuming the whole world. While the invocation of a mantra can unleash a celestial weapon of immense power, the inability to remember a mantra could also lead to one's downfall. The death of Karna is attributed to his inability to remember an incantation because of a curse. When Arjuna was fighting Karna, a wheel from Karna's chariot became entrapped in mud. Karna tried to invoke the mantra from his stationary chariot, but his memory deserted him. He was forced to descend from the chariot and was shot by Arjuna.

If you know the enemy and know yourself, you need not fear the result of a hundred battles. If you know yourself but not the enemy, for every victory gained you will also suffer a defeat. If you know neither the enemy nor yourself, you will succumb in every battle.

—SUN TZU (CHINESE GENERAL), 544–496 BCE

27

Fierce Fighting Breaks Out at War

In the next few chapters, we describe the significant events from the battlefield of the 18-day Kurukshetra War or the battle for Hastinapura. Although the term Pandavas mean the five Pandava brothers, here we use it occasionally to refer to the Pandava army—those fighting on the side of Pandavas. The same goes for Kauravas. First time readers may be overwhelmed by the plethora of characters, not to mention the constant confusion between Bhima (Pandava) and Bhishma (Kuru preceptor). This chapter highlights events from day one to four of the war.

The fall of Bhishma or the death of Abhimanyu is often considered the turning point of the war. Often overlooked are the key moments that lead up to the turning points. These critical moments may appear in many forms, such as an angry outburst from a coach to his player or a gentle tap on a student's shoulder by his teacher. These teaching moments make you realize that you need to make a shift and respond differently. Such a critical moment in the Kurukshetra War happened on the ninth day when Krishna grabbed a broken chariot wheel from the battlefield and charged toward Bhishma menacingly. Although Krishna's gesture was merely symbolic, it was a pivotal moment in the war. Until then Arjuna was waging the war half-heartedly and he saw Bhishma as his preceptor, not an enemy. Krishna's dramatic act, however, transformed the Pandavas' collective thinking and, subsequently, the course of the war. Let's go back to the events from day one of the war.

Despite being inspired by Krishna in the morning, Arjuna could not translate his words into on-field success on the first day. Bhishma was the commander-in-chief of the Kauravas, while the relatively younger Dhrishtadyumna performed the same role for the Pandavas. Dhrishtadyumna had been chosen since a major part of the Pandava army was made up of divisions from Panchala. The Mahabharata says Dhrishtadyumna, along with his twin sister Draupadi, was born out of a yajna, organized by King Drupada. That was because Drupada once humiliated his childhood friend Drona for being stuck in poverty, and this led to bad blood between the two. When Drona became the teacher of the Kuru princes, he organized a small army to attack Drupada. Not only did he defeat the king, Drona took half of his kingdom as well. Drupada wanted vengeance, so he decided to perform a yajna that would give him a son capable of killing Drona. The result was Dhrishtadyumna. Despite being his prophesied killer, Drona accepted Dhrishtadyumna as his student and trained him in warfare. At the Kurukshetra War, however, the young and inexperienced Dhrishtadyumna was no match for the war hardy Bhishma.

The first day of the war witnessed the oldest warrior pitted against the youngest. Arjuna's son Abhimanyu became a hero for putting up a brave fight against Bhishma, who complimented the young lad for his fighting skills. When Bhima pressed Abhimanyu in combat, Virata, Uttara (Virata's son), Dhrishtadyumna, and Bhima came to his defense. Uttara had learned warfare from Arjuna during the Pandavas' sojourn at Virata's palace in the last year of their exile. Uttara had been Arjuna's charioteer when the Kauravas attacked Matsya. With his confidence level sky-high, Uttara challenged Bhishma. But Shalya reminded everyone why he could be a nuisance to any side. He dealt the first major blow of the day by killing Uttara with a lance. Watching the fate of his brother, Shveta, the elder brother of Uttara, became infuriated and turned his fury on Bhishma. Shveta, however, proved no match for the grandsire and was killed in a sword fight. Thus the Pandavas fared badly on day one. While Bhishma was at his destructive best, Arjuna seemed to hold back. Yudhishthira was despondent at the death of Virata's sons on the first day itself. Within the Pandava camp, there was an atmosphere of dejection as the realization struck that this was not going to be a cake walk.

After the initial setback, Pandavas became desperate to inflict some losses on the enemy. They realized that they need to strengthen their defenses and protect key military personnel since any further losses would be extremely demotivating. The Pandavas did not have to wait too long—thanks to Bhima, who dealt blow-after-blow on the Kaurava army. In the morning, Arjuna confronted Bhishma with a rain of arrows. Both were equally matched in strength, but at some point Bhishma hit Krishna with an arrow. That upset Arjuna. Meanwhile, Dhrishtadyumna had a fierce encounter with Drona. The Kaurava stalwarts were proving their mettle and Dhrishtadyumna soon lost his charioteer and horses. Luckily, Bhima came to the commander-in-chief's rescue. Duryodhana chose this moment to send the Kalinga army after Bhima—which turned out to be a bad decision. The Kalingas were a warrior clan on the eastern part of what is now modern India. Duryodhana was married to the Kalinga king's daughter,[50] whom he abducted at a *swayamvara* with his friend Karna. The arrival of the Kalinga army only strengthened Bhima's resolve. The giant went on a spree destroying enemy chariots, killing elephants, and slaying soldiers. Bhishma tried to stop Bhima's rampage and began gaining on Bhima. Seeing Bhima falter, Satyaki lent support to him.[51]

---

[50] Although Duryodhana is often compared to Ravana as ancient India's greatest villain, Duryodhana was not known as a womanizer. He had only one wife called Bhanumati.

[51] Satyaki was a warrior from Krishna's army. He defied Krishna's orders and fought for the Pandavas.

He penetrated Bhishma's defense and killed his charioteer. Without a charioteer, Bhishma became stranded and was forced to flee.

By now a pattern had emerged. When the Kauravas isolated a key Pandava, other Pandavas came to his support. Likewise, when the Pandavas separated a Kaurava fighter, other Kauravas rallied to his defense. To gain an upper hand, the two sides tried out different war formations. On the third day, the Kauravas chose the eagle formation, with Bhishma leading the front and Duryodhana defending the rear. The Pandavas opted for the crescent or half-moon formation and were led by the Pandava brothers. On that day the Gandhara forces, led by Shakuni, attacked the Pandavas but in vain. They were defeated by Satyaki, Abhimanyu, and Ghatotkacha. For those who don't know, Ghatotkacha was the gigantic son of Bhima from his demon wife. He was so named because his head was hairless and shaped like a pot. Ghatotkacha was an expert at sorcery, a skill that would become useful in later days. Both Ghatotkacha and Bhima went after Duryodhana from the rear. For the Kauravas, Bhima and Ghatotkacha were like twin Bhimas coming after them. Soon an arrow hit Duryodhana making him faint in his chariot. The charioteer, however, drove him out of danger. Duryodhana was upset by the ordeal, and in his typical fashion, accused Bhishma of favoring the Pandavas. Duryodhana was mad that Bhishma had not killed a key Pandava by now and broken their morale. Later in the day, Bhishma launched a tremendous attack on the Pandavas. Krishna prodded Arjuna to respond, but Arjuna was full of respect for Bhishma and did not retaliate.

Day four of the battle belonged to Bhima. The Kauravas targeted Bhima and sent a large force of elephants after him. Bhima attacked the elephants with his mace, making them run back and cause a stampede among the Kauravas. Bhima then attacked Duryodhana and nearly killed him. The Kauravas struck back immediately. Bhima became dazed after being hit by an arrow and had to sit down in his chariot. Ghatotkacha came to guard his father. After Bhima recovered, the two of them went on an onslaught. Such was the devastation caused by Bhima with the assistance of his son that eight of Duryodhana's brothers were single-handedly killed by Bhima. Thus, the Pandavas celebrated a huge victory on day four, while the Kauravas were downcast. Duryodhana started having doubts about his army. He grilled Bhishma why the superior forces of the Kauravas could not prevail against the Pandavas. Bhishma advised Duryodhana to seek truce, but that was not something Duryodhana was prepared to listen.

After the conclusion of the fourth day, no side seemed to demonstrate any superior strength. Although the Pandavas were routed on the first day, they regrouped and strengthened their defense avoiding further steep losses. Among the Pandavas, Bhima, Abhimanyu and Ghatotkacha had shown their prowess. Bhima, in particular, was unstoppable and he inflicted many casualties among the Kauravas. Yet, not all Pandavas were primed for battle. Arjuna seemed to have reservations about competing against the old stalwarts Bhishma and Drona—which became a cause of concern for the Pandavas.

For the Kauravas, both Bhishma and Drona dominated the battlefield and no Pandava came close to defeating them. Duryodhana was erratic and showed his wretched skill in archery despite being skilled in mace fighting. Further his constant nagging and finger pointing only aggravated Bhishma and Drona particularly when they were doing their best in the battlefield. The veterans were fighting for the sake of dharma, shunning Duryodhana's illegal tactics.

For the Pandavas, Bhishma has become a formidable opponent. They realized that they had to eliminate Bhishma. Drona was also proving to be equally difficult despite his age. Another concern was the depth of the Kaurava military. Their best archer, Karna, has not even entered the battlefield so far. Thus, the Pandavas were deeply worried despite their recent success in the battlefield.

Older men declare war. But it is the youth that must fight and die.
—HERBERT HOOVER, 1874–1964

28

Raging Krishna Charges at Bhishma

This chapter highlights some of the critical events from day five to nine of the Kurukshetra War.

The fifth day saw a number of tactical moves in the battlefield. In one move, Duryodhana employed Bhishma to attack the Pandavas relentlessly. When the Pandavas suffered at his hands, Arjuna came to their defense and countered Bhishma. Duryodhana then sent thousands of troops to attack Arjuna, but they were killed by him instead. In his typical fashion, Duryodhana complained to Drona about the weakness of the Kaurava attacks and asked him to attack the Pandavas from another front.

In another tactical move, Drona attacked Satyaki—which was negated by Bhima coming to Satyaki's aid. Bhishma, Drona, and Shalya then combined forces and tried to isolate Bhima. The Pandavas employed a positional play by bringing in Shikhandi to support Bhima. The grandsire turned away saying he would not fight with a woman. Shikhandi was Amba reborn as a son to King Drupada. Despite the gender change, Bhishma saw Shikhandi as Amba, whom he had abducted from a *swayamvara* decades ago.

KRISHNA AND THE LATER AVATARS OF VISHNU

The biggest tragedy of the day was yet to strike. Bhurishravas, a prince of a minor kingdom supporting the Kauravas, attacked Satyaki's sons. Satyaki tried to protect them but his efforts were in vain. Not only were all his sons killed, Satyaki himself came under the direct attack of Bhurishravas. Luckily, Satyaki was saved by Bhima. Before he left the battlefield for the day, Satyaki swore vengeance on Bhurishravas for killing his sons.

Day six brought in more slaughter. Bhima fought with 13 of the Kaurava brothers and killed them all with his mace. Soon he became encircled by the Kauravas, but Dhrishtadyumna came to his rescue. Duryodhana and his army attacked the two Pandavas. Now Yudhishthira came with a larger force to support Bhima. With the army behind him, Bhima turned into his overpowering self and defeated Duryodhana, who fell unconscious and had to be carried away by his brother-in-law Jayadratha. Dhrishtadyumna, however, did not have the same success. Drona attacked Dhrishtadyumna's horses and shattered his chariot. However, Dhrishtadyumna managed to escape by taking refuge in Abhimanyu's chariot.

In spite of his age, Bhishma proved his mettle on day seven of the war. He attacked Abhimanyu, and the young man had to be rescued by his father. The Pandavas retaliated by surrounding Bhishma and rained arrows on him. But Bhishma held his own against them. On another side of the battlefield, Bhima let loose his mace again. His tally of Kaurava brothers reached 26. Further away, Virata and Drona were engaged in a fierce struggle for supremacy. After a long battle, Drona defeated Virata. Although Virata was unscathed in the encounter, his third son was killed. Virata had now lost three sons to the war. He still had another son fighting for the Pandavas. By now it has become a standard practice for Duryodhana to whine at the end of the day. He bemoaned the loss of his brothers to Bhishma, who told him that warriors should expect to die when going to war. Duryodhana was not pleased with this response and sent his brother Dushasana to ask Bhishma to step down and let Karna take up the leadership. The grandsire refused flatly.

RAGING KRISHNA CHARGES AT BHISHMA

As you may have noticed, Karna has not entered the war yet. That's because a verbal brawl broke out between Karna and Bhishma on the eve of the war. Karna had bragged that he would slaughter all five Pandavas single-handedly. But Bhishma ridiculed Karna and called him a fool to think he was better than Arjuna. Karna was offended at Bhishma's remark and refused to take part in the battle as long as Bhishma was in command. He did not want to fight under someone who doubted his ability.

Arjuna's son Iravan[52] had tremendous success on the eighth day of the war. (Iravan was Arjuna's son born from a Naga princess when the Pandavas were in exile.) He single-handedly killed five brothers of Shakuni. Unfortunately, Iravan died in an encounter with a rakshasa warrior. Arjuna was sunk in gloom at the news of his son's death. Meanwhile, Bhima went on a killing spree bringing down another 16 of the Kaurava brothers taking his tally to 42. Like Bhima, his son Ghatotkacha also attacked the Kauravas unremittingly. Duryodhana tried to stop the giant and nearly got killed, thanks to a last-minute rescue act by Drona. That night, Duryodhana taunted Bhishma for his lack of vigor even though he was responsible for many Pandava casualties. The grandsire ignored the insults and continued to do his duty.

On the ninth day Abhimanyu avenged his brother's death by killing the rakshasa warrior who had killed Iravan. Maybe because of Duryodhana's pep talk, Bhishma came out with renewed vigor and went on a rampage. His weapons burned up the Pandava army, and none seemed capable of stopping him. Krishna realized something had to be done to halt Bhishma, for the Pandavas were dying by the thousands. He asked Arjuna to stop Bhishma. Arjuna promptly released a shower of arrows at Bhishma, but his faint-hearted attempt did not pose any serious threat. Krishna became frustrated with Arjuna. His lackadaisical attempts at fighting with Bhishma were not only causing needless deaths in the Pandava army but were unnecessarily prolonging the war. Exasperated, Krishna got out of the chariot and charged toward Bhishma holding a

---

[52] Iravan is also known as Iravat and Iravant.

broken chariot wheel in his hand. On seeing Krishna approach him, Bhishma was stunned and he put down his weapons. Meanwhile, Arjuna rushed toward Krishna and reminded him of his vow to not wield a weapon in the war. By then Arjuna had realized the reason for Krishna's frustration. He promised Krishna that there would be no letup in the next encounter.

Krishna charges menacingly at Bhishma, wall sculpture

The war had raged on for nine days, and hundreds of soldiers had died on both sides. Not only a decisive victory had eluded either side, but the leaders of the Pandavas and Kauravas remained largely unscathed. The Pandavas had realized that as long as Bhishma remained alive, they had little chance of victory. Bhishma had to go, but the Pandavas did not know how.

> *What is essential in war is victory, not prolonged operations.*
> —SUN TZU (CHINESE GENERAL), 544–496 BCE

29

The Downfall of Bhishma

Day ten was a turning point in the war. It was the day when one side gained ascendency in a bitterly fought battle. This chapter describes the significant events from day ten of the Kurukshetra War.

On the tenth morning Krishna devised a ploy to trap Bhishma. He had realized that Bhishma could not be beaten in combat either single-handedly or collectively. But only the downfall of Bhishma would give the Pandavas the dominance they were seeking. Krishna had observed that Bhishma refused to retaliate against Shikhandi because he considered Shikhandi to be a woman. The plan therefore was to pit Shikhandi against Bhishma and then take on the grandsire when he was not fighting.

As fighting resumed on day ten, Krishna steered Arjuna's chariot toward Bhishma. Other Kauravas came to thwart his passage, but Krishna pressed on. Mounted on the chariot was Shikhandi, whom Arjuna was using as a shield. Seeing Shikhandi, Bhishma, predictably, lowered his bow and did not offer the slightest of resistance. Arjuna seized the opportunity and sent a barrage of arrows at Bhishma. Everyone watched in disbelief as the arrows pierced through the war veteran's body even though he was in armor. Many arrows got stuck on his body, and one in his heart. Bhishma was thrown off his chariot, and a bed of arrows supported his body on the ground. Mortally wounded and resting on the bed of arrows, Bhishma asked for water. Arjuna shot an arrow into the ground. Water sprang forth. "Ganga has come to quench her son's thirst," said those who had gathered around the wounded warrior.

Bhishma's last moments on a bed of arrows, artist unknown

Both sides stopped fighting since Bhishma was the great patriarch of the Kuru clan and revered by all. He was admired for his vow to not only relinquish his right to the throne but also remain a lifelong celibate. Arjuna dismounted from the chariot and went up to Bhishma. Finding Bhishma's head tilted downward and unsupported, Arjuna struck three arrows in the ground, creating a headrest for the dying man. Meanwhile, Karna rushed to the battlefield on hearing about the attack on Bhishma. He approached Bhishma and asked for his blessing despite having had differences with him in the past. Bhishma advised him to not join the battle, but Karna shook his head. He had struck a strong bond with Duryodhana and had no choice but to continue.

Despite being mortally wounded, Bhishma survived for 58 days. He was one of the few still alive after the battle had ended. Bhishma had received a boon that allowed him to choose the time of his death. He kept himself alive so that he could die on the auspicious day of Uttarayana, the day the sun begins its northern phase, and thus attain liberation.

It is worth mentioning that there is another version of how Bhishma's death was orchestrated. According to this version, Krishna advised the Pandavas the previous night to seek Bhishma's advice on how to end the stalemate. When the Pandavas led by Yudhishthira met Bhishma in the night, they told him that he was the obstacle in their path to victory. Because Bhishma loved the Pandavas, he hinted that he would lay down his arms if he were to encounter a woman in the battlefield.

In this version, Bhishma performed yet another selfless act before his death—sacrificing his own life for the sake of dharma.

Your right is to action alone; never to its fruits at any time.
Never should the fruits of action be your motive; never let there be attachment to inaction in you.

—KRISHNA IN BHAGAVAD GITA 2.47

30

Abhimanyu Is Trapped in the Chakra Vyuha

This chapter describes the significant events from day 11 to day 13 of the Kurukshetra War.

After the fall of Bhishma, the Kaurava camp was not only demoralized but aghast at the tactics employed by the Pandavas that led to his downfall. They gathered at the battle camp to discuss future tactics. The conversation shifted to the question of who would be the new commander-in-chief. With Bhishma gone, the stage was set for Karna to enter the battlefield. Speculation was rife that he would be the next commander-in-chief. But when Duryodhana announced that Drona would be the next commander-in-chief, many Kauravas were surprised. *Maybe Duryodhana did not want to offend Drona,* they thought.

After the loss of Bhishma, the Kauravas badly needed a win to lift their morale. So Duryodhana asked Drona to capture Yudhishthira alive. Although Yudhishthira was not in the same league as Bhishma in military skills, he was the eldest brother of the Pandavas and widely respected despite his addiction to gambling. As a staunch defender of dharma, he had a unifying effect among the Pandavas. *If Yudhishthira was captured, the Pandavas would fall into complete disarray without a leader,* thought Duryodhana. Secretly, Duryodhana harbored hopes of having another gambling match with Yudhishthira and reversing his losses incurred in the war.

The Pandavas were supercharged going to battle on day 11. As expected, Karna entered the battlefield and wreaked havoc, as he had gloated. Krishna steered his chariot away from Karna because he did not want Arjuna to engage with Karna early on. Other Pandavas needed Arjuna's assistance. Meanwhile, Drona tried to corner Yudhishthira but he escaped on a horse. Shalya had a bad day. First, he was defeated by his nephew Nakula, though he managed to escape. Next, he battled with Bhima and was again defeated. In the meantime, Drona made another attempt to capture Yudhishthira, but this time Arjuna backed him up and Drona was forced to retreat. At the end of the day, Drona realized that as long as Bhima was able to swing his mace with gay abandon and Arjuna was protecting Yudhishthira, there was no hope of capturing Yudhishthira, dead or alive.

On day 12, Drona planned to draw Arjuna out and then isolate Yudhishthira. The Trigarta brothers were dispatched to attack Arjuna. The Trigartas were allies of Duryodhana and sworn enemies of King Virata, so they fought on the side of the Kauravas. Unfortunately, the Trigarta brothers were no match for Arjuna, and all four were killed. Meanwhile, news of Duryodhana's master plan to capture Yudhishthira reached the Pandavas. They guarded Yudhishthira from all sides keeping him safe. Once again, the day ended with Drona failing to capture Yudhishthira. Unfortunately on that day, Virata lost his fourth and last son, who was killed in an encounter with Drona.

By the 13th day, Drona was utterly frustrated at his inability to harm a single Pandava, let alone capture Yudhishthira. He realized that Krishna was keeping Arjuna away from Karna and setting him up for a later encounter. Drona thought he could use his rival's tactic to his advantage.

He organized his troops in a *chakra vyuha* or a concentric circles formation. The plan was designed to ensnare Yudhishthira. Drona knew only Krishna and Arjuna knew how to breach the circular maze. So he brought Karna into the formation so that the Kauravas did not have to worry about Krishna and Arjuna. And it worked. Finding himself trapped in the *chakra vyuha*, Yudhishthira hollered for help. Unable to locate his father, Abhimanyu, who also got trapped with Yudhishthira, came to Yudhishthira's rescue. He broke open the *vyuha* and penetrated all seven rings of the concentric circles. Suddenly, the lad found himself surrounded by Drona, Karna, Duryodhana, Ashwatthama, Dushasana, Jayadratha, and other Kauravas. Sensing danger, Abhimanyu wanted to get out of the *vyuha* but he did not know how. Although Abhimanyu was taught to breach the *chakra vyuha,* he did not know how to escape it once trapped—his father did not have the time to teach him. From afar, Pandavas came to know about Abhimanyu's plight. But the Kauravas formed a tight outer ring and prevented the Pandavas from entering the formation.

But Abhimanyu was not the type to panic and seek mercy. One of the most heroic moments of the battle then unfolded. In a tremendous display of courage, Abhimanyu fended off the entire Kaurava army, who had ganged up on him. First Duryodhana and then Dushasana fought with him. Both had to beat a hasty retreat. Several soldiers came forward to confront Abhimanyu, but he beat them all. The Kauravas realized Abhimanyu could not be conquered in a fair fight, so they circled him and slowly disarmed him. Karna came from behind and broke his bow. Soon his sword and spear were gone. Stripped off his weapons, Abhimanyu was unable to mount a challenge. Like a wounded deer fending off a pack of hungry jackals, he picked up a chariot wheel from the ground to defend himself. Before he could raise it as a shield, the wheel was broken into a thousand fragments. From behind, Dushasana's son hit Abhimanyu with a mace that sent him reeling to the ground. Abhimanyu never recovered from the blow. Before he could try to get up, Jayadratha crept up from behind and smashed his skull with a mace. And as if that wasn't enough, Dushasana's son pounced on the fallen body and cut it into pieces. Yudhishthira could only watch from afar, as monstrous atrocities were committed on his nephew.

Yudhishthira blamed himself for the death of Abhimanyu. That evening utter silence greeted the Pandava camp. Arjuna was devastated on hearing the news of Abhimanyu's death. Seeking revenge on Jayadratha, he swore to slay him by sunset the next day or set himself on fire. The so-called righteous war has been overtaken by untoward events. It had taken a vicious, ugly turn.

> *In peace, sons bury their fathers. In war, fathers bury their sons.*
> —HERODOTUS

31

Krishna Conjures an Eclipse

This chapter describes the significant events on day 14 of the war. This was the day when the battle went into overtime.

The death of his heroic son Abhimanyu made the war personal for Arjuna. He blamed Jayadratha for Abhimanyu's cruel death and took an oath to kill him by sunset the next day. If he failed to fulfill his vow, Arjuna was prepared to end his life by jumping into a pyre. By now the codes of warfare were rapidly breaking down. A major escalation had occurred when the Pandavas circumvented the rules of knightly etiquette by using Shikhandi in the battlefield to take down Bhishma. The Kauravas retaliated with the ruthless slaying of unarmed Abhimanyu, one of the most flagrant violations of war rules until then. As the 14th day dawned, both sides faced the grim prospect of an increasing likelihood of such underhand tactics becoming the norm rather than the exception.

Meanwhile, news of Arjuna's vow to kill Jayadratha by sunset or set himself on fire reached the Kauravas. In olden times, men of honor walked the talk. Jayadratha became frightened and wanted to quit fighting. Drona, however, assured him of full protection even if that meant keeping him in hiding. At dawn on the 14th day, Drona put Jayadratha at the rear end of the army surrounded by other soldiers and hidden from the Pandavas. Predictably Arjuna confronted the Kauravas looking for Jayadratha. Attacking aggressively, he tried to get past the Kaurava army by releasing hundreds of arrows and crushing the chariots and weapons of the Kaurava army. Yet, he could not locate Jayadratha.

Just then Arjuna saw Bhurishravas attacking Satyaki and bringing him to the ground. Satyaki remained motionless for some time. Seeing Satyaki's plight, Arjuna turned his focus toward Bhurishravas. He sent a hail of arrows at Bhurishravas that severed one of his arms. Wounded, Bhurishravas sat down on the ground in a yoga position. Meanwhile, Satyaki came to his senses. Seeing an unarmed Bhurishravas, he picked up his sword and swung at Bhurishravas beheading him. With that act, Satyaki had avenged the death of his sons. But that savage act drew deep condemnation since it was against the code of conduct to kill anyone in a yoga position. This became one of the controversial episodes of the war and would haunt Satyaki for years.

Meanwhile, Arjuna returned to search for Jayadratha. As the sun raced westward across the sky, Arjuna realized time was his enemy. Drona had packed soldiers in the middle and rear and Arjuna found it increasingly difficult to penetrate the Kaurava formation. And then Krishna played a trick. He held his divine hand to conceal the sun. Suddenly, darkness enveloped the region and the Kauravas thought that the sun had set. As the Kauravas celebrated, Jayadratha emerged out of hiding. In the darkness Arjuna could hear his unmistakable peel of laughter. With careful aim and utmost concentration, Arjuna let loose his arrow aimed at Jayadratha. Such was the fury of a man intent to avenge his beloved son that the arrow found its mark even in the dark. As the arrow neatly detached Jayadratha's head from his body, Krishna uncovered the sun. From darkness, the battlefield was filled with the blaze of the setting sun. Krishna had used his divine powers to create an eclipse to help Arjuna fulfill his vow.

But the danger was not over. Jayadratha's father had obtained a strange boon that stipulated whoever felled his son's head to the ground would perish. To prevent this from happening, Krishna used his divine powers again to propel the arrow carrying Jayadratha's severed head like a missile in the sky. After flying through the atmosphere the arrow landed on Jayadratha's father's lap. Alarmed, the old man jumped up on seeing his son's head and the head rolled down from his lap to the ground. The conditions for the boon were now satisfied. Instantly, the father's head imploded into smithereens—as dictated by the curse.

So furious was Drona at Krishna's ruse that he refused to stop fighting for the day. He was particularly irate that Krishna had tricked everyone into believing that day was night. The rules of the war were suspended and the battle continued after dusk with the aid of torches. The darkness favored Ghatotkacha. Being a half-rakshasa, his strength increased with nightfall. With his long, sharp teeth and claws, he looked formidable at night and had the Kauravas running for cover. Drona countered the move by pitting a powerful Kaurava rakshasa against Ghatotkacha. The full-rakshasa waddled like a porcupine and rushed at the half-rakshasa with great force. They pushed, shoved, and stabbed each other like sumo wrestlers until Ghatotkacha pinned down his opponent to the ground. He grabbed his neck with both hands and choked him to death.

Drona became frustrated on hearing Ghatotkacha had killed the rakshasa. Nothing worked for the Kauravas that day. They did not make any significant gains even with the extension of battle hours. Desperate, Drona called on Karna to finish off Ghatotkacha at any cost. Karna was caught in a quandary whether to use his powerful weapon against Ghatotkacha. He has been reserving the celestial spear against his arch rival Arjuna since it could only be used once. The weapon was gifted to him by Indra for his generosity. When Duryodhana invaded kingdoms with Karna by his side, Indra became worried about Karna's invincibility in battle and wanted to protect his own son Arjuna. He knew Karna's strength lay in his golden armor and earrings. So Indra approached Karna disguised as a priest and asked for his armor and earrings as alms. When Karna handed them over, Indra was so pleased that, in return, he presented Karna with a celestial spear, one with deadly accuracy but limited to a single use.

After Drona's repeated pleas, Karna decided to use his celestial weapon and discharged it toward Ghatotkacha. On sighting the weapon, Ghatotkacha charged toward it like a rhinoceros, but the weapon was too strong and pierced through his heart, bringing the giant down and also crushing several Kaurava soldiers as he fell. The Pandavas were shocked to hear about the loss of Ghatotkacha. Bhima went into a rage. But they were also relieved to hear that Karna's potent weapon could no longer be used. As the night continued, fatigue overtook soldiers and they became tired to the bone. They decided to leave the battlefield for the rest of the night.

> *All warfare is based on deception.*
> —SUN TZU (CHINESE GENERAL), 544–496 BCE

32

Rumor Leads to Drona's Undoing

This chapter describes the significant events on day 15 of the Kurukshetra War.

An unwritten rule of war says never reveal your weakness to your enemy. If you hate cockroaches, for instance, and your enemy knows it, then please expect to be bombarded with cockroaches. Unbeknown to the Kauravas, they had entered the war with a disadvantage because the weaknesses of the war veterans were glaringly obvious to their former students. In an early chapter, we learned how Bhishma became a victim of his own foible. In this chapter, we will see how Drona, like Bhishma, succumbed to this own shortcoming.

On the 15th day, Drona came to the battle with vigor despite having had a long day on the battlefield the previous day. He was deadly and inflicted multiple casualties among the Pandavas. He killed Virata after a prolonged encounter. Having lost four princes and their king in the war, the Matsya kingdom was now left without an heir. Drona next fought with his childhood enemy, Drupada, and killed him too. Devastated, Dhrishtadyumna came charging angrily at Drona only to be pushed back by him. Arjuna was dispatched to stop Drona. But the preceptor was fighting with utter disregard for his own life, and even Arjuna found it difficult to penetrate his defenses.

With Drona at the helm, the Kauravas became a potent force once again. The loss of Bhishma on the tenth day was compensated by Karna. The Pandavas needed another big scalp to tilt the war in their favor, and Drona was proving too difficult to overcome. Arjuna realized that Drona, like Bhishma, could only be defeated with his guard down. But that was not an easy task to accomplish against a seasoned veteran of many battles and the guru of many princes.

With the help of Krishna, the Pandavas devised a plan to trap Drona. They knew Drona loved his only son Ashwatthama dearly. He was born after Drona undertook severe penance to please Shiva. For Drona, no love was greater than his love for his son. During a lull in fighting, the Pandavas surrounded Drona and Bhima broke the news that Ashwatthama was dead. At first Drona ignored him. He looked around for Ashwatthama, but could not find him anywhere. The doubt slowly turned into anxiety. He looked to Yudhishthira for confirmation. He knew if there is one person in the world he could trust, it was Yudhishthira, for the champion of dharma never lied. With great reluctance, Yudhishthira confirmed that Ashwatthama was indeed dead. Drona went numb on hearing the words come out of Yudhishthira's lips.

Devastated, he stopped his chariot, stepped out of it, and then put down his weapons. Like a man who had lost everything in life, Drona sat down to meditate right in the middle of the battlefield. Seeing an unarmed Drona, Dhrishtadyumna, who was burning for revenge, could not resist the chance. In one fell swoop of his sword, he decapitated the great preceptor of the Kuru dynasty. With the slaying of Drona, Dhrishtadyumna had avenged his father's death. Yudhishthira was not strictly lying when he said Ashwatthama was dead. What Drona did not know was that Pandavas had named an elephant Ashwatthama and Bhima had killed it. But that was not for Drona to know. With the slaying of Drona, the Pandavas had executed their plan to perfection albeit not in line with the codes of the war. In any case, all knightly ethics had been discarded by the 15th day.

RUMOR LEADS TO DRONA'S UNDOING

A temporary ceasefire was declared to mourn the death of the fallen leader. When Ashwatthama heard about his father's death, he went wild. He released the mighty *Narayana Astra* against the Pandava army despite the ceasefire declaration. The *Narayana Astra* was given to him by his father when he was a boy. Drona had wanted to assuage his son, because Ashwatthama always complained about his father's bias toward his favorite student Arjuna. As Ashwatthama launched the weapon in the battlefield, it split into thousand smaller missiles and sped ominously toward the Pandava army. The Pandavas were terrified. No one knew how to handle the *astra* let alone knew how to defuse it except Krishna. Since the missile could not harm an unarmed person, Krishna asked everyone in the Pandava army to step down from the chariots and lay down their weapons.

Everyone obeyed his order except Bhima, who was furious with Ashwatthama and charged toward him in his chariot, holding his mace aloft. Both Krishna and Arjuna rushed at Bhima and got on his chariot. Before Bhima could protest, they managed to drag him out of the chariot and disarm him.

With everyone laying down their weapons, the missile fizzled out harmlessly. Ashwatthama was not impressed. Because the missile did not live up to its hype, he blamed his father. Meanwhile, Duryodhana urged Ashwatthama to launch the *astra* again. Ashwatthama balked. He pointed out that the weapon turns against the person who launched it if it is used more than once.

Thus, the 15th day ended with the death of Drona. With his death, the Pandavas held the upper hand in the war. The onus now fell on Karna to save the Kauravas from a certain defeat.

It takes a great deal of bravery to stand up to our enemies, but just as much to stand up to our friends.

—J. K. ROWLING, 1965—

33

A Fatal Memory Lapse

This chapter describes the significant events on days 16 and 17 of the Kurukshetra War.

After the death of Drona, the Kauravas needed someone equal to him as the commander-in-chief, and the only one qualified was Karna. Because Karna was a skilled archer, the question was whether he should be left alone as an individual fighter like Arjuna or entrusted with directing the military forces. On the morning of the 16th day, Duryodhana made twin appointments. No one was surprised when Duryodhana instated Karna as the commander-in-chief of the Kauravas. When it came to their hatred for the Pandavas, Duryodhana and Karna were conjoined twins, connected by their desire for vengeance. However, the appointment of Shalya as Karna's charioteer raised a few eyebrows. Duryodhana realized that Karna could benefit from having someone like Krishna who could shepherd him in the battlefield. Whether Shalya was the right choice was the question in everyone's mind. As for Shalya, he was a king and he considered it beneath his dignity to become a charioteer to Karna, who was himself a charioteer's son.

When the battle began for the day under the new commander-in-chief, Krishna steered Arjuna's chariot away from Karna to avoid an early engagement. Karna encountered Nakula and Sahadeva and defeated them both. But Karna spared their lives because of his promise to Kunti not to kill any of the Pandavas except Arjuna. Meanwhile Yudhishthira challenged Karna for a fight and wounded him initially. But Karna fought back and broke Yudhishthira's bow into pieces. He smashed Yudhishthira's chariot and with another arrow broke his armor. Utterly stranded, Yudhishthira ran for his life. Bhima became indignant at seeing his brothers' plight and attacked Karna menacingly. In the tussle Karna was hurt badly and fainted. But Bhima spared Karna's life because he wanted Arjuna to finish him off.[53] When Karna recovered, Yudhishthira challenged him to another duel. In the ensuing combat, Yudhishthira was wounded and ignominiously fled for the second time. Since Arjuna was fighting in another sector, he did not meet Karna on his first day as commander-in-chief.[54]

By now Bhima had single-handedly demolished 98 of the Kaurava brothers. Only two remained—Duryodhana and Dushasana—the two Bhima held in greatest contempt for Draupadi's humiliation. On the 17th day, Bhima confronted Dushasana and the two exchanged arrows in a fierce battle. One arrow from Bhima hit Dushasana with such force that he was thrown off afar. Bhima ran toward Dushasana and saw him lying prone on the ground. Momentarily, the scene of Dushasana disrobing Draupadi flashed across his mind. Bhima grabbed Dushasana by his hair and with a twist, broke his right arm. He then lifted Dushasana and threw him down with tremendous force. As if that was not enough, he ripped apart the body with his hands and drank his blood thereby fulfilling his vow. The warriors from both sides were horrified to watch this macabre scene.

---

[53] Another version of this event has Bhima being defeated by Karna in the duel.
[54] B.R. Chopra's version (TV serial) depicts Arjuna and Karna facing each other on this day. In this version, Karna spares Arjuna's life after rendering him weaponless because the sun had set for the day.

A FATAL MEMORY LAPSE

Meanwhile, the Pandavas realized that Karna was the last man standing between them and victory. The time had arrived for Arjuna and Karna to face each other. Both harbored an intense hatred toward the other. For the Pandavas, victory over Karna was crucial, for they knew how strong a warrior he was and only Arjuna was capable of defeating him. Soldiers from both sides stopped fighting to watch the duel between the greats. Arjuna initiated the engagement by sending a steady stream of arrows at Karna pushing his chariot a hundred yards away. Karna retaliated with a blistering attack of arrows. As the fight went on, more and more potent weapons were displayed. Karna decided to release the potent weapon, *Naga Astra*. This fiery weapon, in the shape of a hissing cobra with its mouth and fangs open, darted toward Arjuna at lightning speed. Seeing the speeding missile, Krishna pressed his feet on the floor causing the chariot to sink into the mud. The missile missed Arjuna but split his crown into two. Although Arjuna was not hurt, he was badly shaken by his narrow escape.

The battle between Arjuna and Karna raged on into the evening. Until then Shalya had steered Karna's chariot admirably despite having no prior experience. Just as the sun began to set, however, Shalya inadvertently steered the chariot into a tract of swamp and one of the wheels sunk into the mud. Arjuna was presented with a stationary target, and he began closing in on Karna. The arrows from his bow whizzed past Karna. Realizing that Arjuna was gaining over him, Karna decided to resort to his most powerful missile, the *Brahma Astra*. To launch the missile, he had to chant a mantra, which he had learned from his preceptor Parashurama. To his dismay, Karna found that he could not remember the mantra. The curse had struck. When he was a boy, Karna had lied to Parashurama that he was a Brahmin to become his student, since Parashurama taught warfare only to Brahmins. Later, when the hot-tempered Parashurama found out that Karna had lied, he became enraged and pronounced a curse on Karna that he would forget everything when he needed it the most.[55]

---

[55] This incident will be revisited in a later chapter.

Unable to launch his most potent weapon, Karna became alarmed. He wanted to free the chariot wheel to avoid Arjuna's blistering attacks. Karna asked his charioteer to step out and release the chariot wheel from the mud. At the moment, Shalya chose to throw a temper tantrum and refused. He was offended by the request and considered it below his dignity to do menial chores like fixing wheels. Since Shalya refused to budge, Karna had no choice other than alight the chariot and free the wheel himself. So he invoked the laws of chivalry and stepped out. As soon as he turned, his back was exposed to the warriors. Krishna exhorted Arjuna to shoot him. But Arjuna was hesitant because it was against the rules of the war to attack someone from behind. Krishna reminded Arjuna that Karna expressed no such qualms during the public disrobing of Draupadi or slaying of Abhimanyu. Arjuna needed no further persuasion. Spurred by those memories, he shot straight at Karna's back. The arrow went through his back and came through the front ripping his heart. Karna fell dead, instantly.

When Duryodhana came to know about Karna's death, he sobbed uncontrollably. If there was anyone in the world that Duryodhana was genuinely fond of, it was Karna. He never cried at the death of his own brothers, yet he became inconsolable over Karna's death.

A FATAL MEMORY LAPSE

Karna's chariot wheel gets stuck in mud, artist unknown

34

Duryodhana Hides in a Lake

This chapter describes the significant events on the 18th day—the last day—of the Kurukshetra War.

Either the Kauravas would utterly collapse or surrender meekly after the death of Karna—that's what everyone thought. But that did not happen. In fact, one of the most ghastly incidents of the entire war happened right after his death. However, with only a few heroes remaining among the Kauravas, the tide had definitely turned in favor of the Pandavas. With a handful of choices remaining, Duryodhana appointed Shalya as the commander-in-chief of the Kauravas.

On the 18th morning, Krishna pitted Yudhishthira against Shalya. That's because Krishna realized that Shalya was the type who returns fire with fire but with double the intensity. That is, if you fight hard with Shalya, he will go harder on you; but if you are nice to him, he will be doubly nice in return. Yudhishthira was picked because he was not naturally aggressive and therefore unlikely to stir up the worst instincts of his enemy. As Yudhishthira faced off his uncle in the battlefield, his gentle demeanor zapped the aggressive instinct of Shalya. They fought gently for some time. Eventually, Yudhishthira threw a spear at Shalya, who offered not even a semblance of resistance. The weapon pierced though his heart, killing him instantly.

With the Kaurava army in shambles, Shakuni came up with one last attempt. He organized his Gandhara army to ambush the Pandavas from the rear. Anticipating such a move, the Pandavas sent Nakula and Sahadeva to confront Shakuni. A fierce fight unfolded between the two Pandavas and the forces of Shakuni. After a prolonged battle, Sahadeva defeated Shakuni and cut off his arm. The mastermind of Mahabharata thus met his end after being left to die bleeding.

With the death of Shakuni, only four Kauravas remained—Duryodhana, Ashwatthama, Kripa, and Kritavarma—and the attention shifted to Duryodhana. Sensing defeat and fearing for his life, Duryodhana beat a hasty retreat and hid himself in a nearby lake. The leader of the Kauravas who patronized his commanders and attacked them for apathy could only whimper when it was time to take charge. With Duryodhana absconding, the Pandavas spent the rest of the 18th day searching for him. Some hunters, who happened to witness Duryodhana hiding in the lake, reported the matter to the Pandavas. They hurried to the lake where Duryodhana had hidden by immersing himself in the water and breathing through a reed.

"Come out coward and fight for your life," bellowed Bhima. At this, Duryodhana emerged from the water. Eager to take on Duryodhana, Bhima removed his armor since Duryodhana had none. This was his opportunity to finish off the 100th Kaurava brother. The fatal day on which Draupadi was humiliated flashed through his mind again. On that day Duryodhana had bared his thighs and beckoned her with vulgar gestures.

The sound of maces boomed and reverberated in the air, as the bitter enemies clashed. Despite the Kaurava army in tatters, Duryodhana put up a brave show. Bhima knew that Duryodhana was trained by Balarama and was skilled in mace fighting. But he was astounded to see him not only parry his powerful blows but occasionally mount a riposte. Duryodhana was supposed to go out with a whimper; instead, he was fighting like hell. It seemed some higher force was assisting Duryodhana.

What Bhima did not know was that Duryodhana was shielded by Gandhari's blessing. After the death of his brother Dushasana, Duryodhana went to his mother and begged her to save his life. Gandhari was sympathetic to her son's plight. Devastated at the loss of her 99 sons, she desperately wanted to save the life of her last remaining son. She told him to come to her abode at dawn without any attire. She would then remove her blindfold and then impart the strength of a hundred elephants to his entire body by the power of her gaze. As instructed, Duryodhana met his mother early next morning and was subjected to her gaze. However, because he was wearing a loincloth, the area below his waist did not receive the benefit of her powerful rays.

Meanwhile, Bhima was becoming exasperated at his own inability to finish off Duryodhana. Try as he might, he could not penetrate his defenses and turned to Krishna in despair. Krishna has been the savior of the Pandavas on multiple occasions during the war. He gave a clue by slapping high on his thighs. Bhima then swung his mace with all his might at Duryodhana's body where he least expected—below his waist. Duryodhana convulsed, then wobbled, and fell to the ground in deep agony. The last of the Kauravas had fallen, mortally wounded.

Not everyone was pleased by Bhima's tactics. By hitting Duryodhana below the belt, Bhima had flouted the rules of the war. Among the crowd that had gathered to watch the fight was Balarama, Duryodhana's mace instructor. He became furious at the blatant violation of war rules and raised his plow threatening Bhima. But Krishna intervened and stopped Balarama reminding him that those who perform ignoble deeds in life cannot expect to meet a noble death.

As the sun set on the 18th day of the epic battle, the victorious Pandavas returned to the battle camp. But they did not celebrate. Scattered on the bloody plains of Kurukshetra lay thousands of bodies. The Pandavas had won an empire at a stiff price.

KRISHNA AND THE LATER AVATARS OF VISHNU

Real men despise battle, but will never run from it.

—GEORGE WASHINGTON, 1732–1799

35

Midnight Massacre by Ashwatthama

It's always darkest before the dawn.

—PROVERB

The war had virtually come to an end at dusk on the 18th day with only three survivors from the Kaurava army—Ashwatthama, Kripa, and Kritavarma. The leader of the Kauravas, Duryodhana, lay mortally wounded near a lake. The surviving Kauravas, however, were not finished yet and fumed at the unfair tactics deployed by the victors. Bhishma was wounded by foul play. Likewise Drona, Karna, and Duryodhana were all brought down by underhand tactics. All these fumed in young Ashwatthama's mind, as he gave into his rage and vowed to avenge the Kaurava defeat, even if the war was already lost. The three of them visited Duryodhana and sought his blessings for a last-minute strike at the enemy. Despite being on the throes of death, nothing much changed in

Duryodhana. He endorsed the plan and appointed Ashwatthama as the leader of this special purpose squad.

As night fell on the 18th day, the three rested under a large banyan tree. A hundred crows were sleeping on the tree's many branches. Suddenly a fierce owl swooped in surreptitiously toward the tree and killed the sleeping crows. Watching this scene from below, Ashwatthama was taken aback by this incident. But soon a sinister plan for revenge began to take shape in his mind. Hastily, he woke up the other two and detailed the plan to them—a cold blooded massacre of the sleeping Pandavas in the stealth of night. The other two protested that it was immoral to attack a sleeping warrior. But Ashwatthama reminded them that he was merely taking a page out of the Pandava playbook. The Pandavas had resorted to unfair tactics and violated every canon of the law throughout the war.

In the small hours of the night, the trio stealthily arrived at the Pandava camp. Leaving Kripa and Kritavarma to guard the exits, Ashwatthama slipped into each tent. At the first tent he found Dhrishtadyumna snoring and promptly woke him up. Before the half-awake Dhrishtadyumna realized what was happening, Ashwatthama grabbed him by his neck and strangled him to death. Moving to the second tent he encountered Shikhandi and readied his sword. Taken by complete surprise, Shikhandi had no chance when the sword sliced his head. In the next tent, Ashwatthama saw what appeared to be the five Pandava brothers sleeping soundly. He flew into a terrifying rage on seeing them and chopped off their heads. Having fulfilled his vow, Ashwatthama collected the heads and put them in a sack. He set fire to the tents before leaving the camp.

Ashwatthama went back to meet the dying Duryodhana and proudly presented him the severed heads. Duryodhana was thrilled to hear about the squad's success. He wanted to have the pleasure of seeing his arch nemesis dead, so he asked Ashwatthama for Bhima's head. When Ashwatthama showed him the head, Duryodhana took it in his hands and crushed it like coconut. But the head crushed easily, and Duryodhana was uncertain. He reckoned it was not Bhima's head. Ashwatthama did a closer inspection of the heads and realized his blunder. He had killed the five sons of Draupadi instead of the Pandavas. Duryodhana was disappointed to learn the mission was a failure. He realized that he may not have another opportunity to strike at the Pandavas, for his health was deteriorating by the minute. Nevertheless, he was gratified that killing any Pandava was better than nothing at all. Meanwhile, the wounds were taking their toll. "I may have lost the war, but the Pandavas lost everything too," muttered Duryodhana. Shortly thereafter he breathed his last. The leader of Kauravas died unattended and lonely.

The next morning, the Pandavas came to know about the attack in the night. Draupadi was indignant to learn about the death of her brothers and sons. She urged the Pandavas to wreak vengeance on Ashwatthama and vowed to fast unto death until the Pandavas brought to her the jewel on his forehead as proof of his destruction. The jewel was not only Ashwatthama's signature facial feature but also the source of his strength. Legend has it that Drona did not have a child for a long time. He undertook penance to obtain a child of Shiva's valor, and was blessed with a child. A shining jewel was embedded on the child's forehead that became his permanent identification.

The Pandavas, accompanied by Krishna, immediately set forth to hunt down Ashwatthama and found him hiding in sage Vyasa's abode. On seeing the approaching Pandavas, Ashwatthama raised his bow and released the deadly missile *Brahmashira Astra* at them. The *Brahmashira* was the most potent weapon of that age. On sighting the speeding missile, Krishna instructed Arjuna to counter it. A *Brahmashira* can be neutralized only with a matching *Brahmashira*, and only Arjuna possessed one. The collision of these supreme missiles, however, would have destroyed the world if not for the intervention of Narada and Vyasa. The sages arrived at the scene to reprimand both warriors for unleashing these powerful weapons and urged them to recall their missiles. While Arjuna complied with their request, Ashwatthama, still burning for vengeance, deflected the missile to the wombs of the Pandava women in order to destroy the entire Pandava lineage. As the missile came hurtling toward the pregnant wife of Abhimanyu, Krishna intervened with his divine powers and prevented it from harming the unborn baby.[56]

The Kauravas were well and truly defeated by now. The sages insisted that Ashwatthama surrender his gem to the Pandavas for his wicked act. The depravity of Ashwatthama's exploits did not escape Krishna. Not only did he kill innocent children, he attempted to destroy the entire lineage of the Pandavas. He was the only warrior who crossed all limits of conduct and even misused divine *astra*s. A death sentence would not have done justice to his wickedness. For that reason Krishna pronounced a curse on Ashwatthama. He condemned him to wander over the world forever like a leper, afflicted by disease, and shunned by all. For Krishna, this was a more appropriate sentence than death because leading a wretched life will make you wish for death, yet death will always evade you. Incidentally, this was the first time Krishna cursed anyone.

Ashwatthama joined the ranks of immortals or *chiranjeevi*s, as they are known in Hinduism. They include Bali, Vyasa, Hanuman, Parashurama and others. While members of this elite group attained the fountain of longevity for heroic deeds, Ashwatthama became the only cursed *chiranjeevi*, punished to suffer for his despicable acts.

---

[56] The son was named Parikshit and he succeeded Yudhishthira as the king of Hastinapura.

36

Aftermath of the War

Only the dead have seen the end of war.

— GEORGE SANTAYANA, 1863–1952

After the end of the Kurukshetra War, the women went to the battlefield to look for their men. Among them were the wives of the fallen Kaurava brothers. Each of them prayed that her husband would be found alive, but all they found were headless torsos and maimed bodies. The atmosphere was filled with women squealing after discovering the bodies they recognized. Yet every now and then, a cry of joy would pierce through the somberness when a woman found her husband or brother still alive.

A somber Yudhishthira took his brothers on a tour of the battlefield. He wanted to show them the cost of their victory. Grimly, the brothers walked between piles of corpses that they themselves had unleashed. They noticed Kunti at a distance weeping uncontrollably over the body of a fallen warrior. The Pandavas went up to Kunti and surrounded her.

Arjuna was the first to speak, "Mother, why are you weeping over the death of Karna, our arch enemy?" Kunti turned around. Her face soaked in tears, she addressed Yudhishthira. "Karna was your brother, my first-born son." The Pandavas were dumbfounded. Kunti then told them how Karna was born and how she had left him at the riverbank. On hearing the story, the Pandavas went weak at their knees. Already struggling with the guilt of killing Bhishma, Arjuna became more remorseful with the realization that he had killed his own brother.

"Did Karna know?" asked Yudhishthira. Kunti nodded. "I told him before the war because I wanted him to join your side. He chose to remain loyal to Duryodhana but promised me never to harm any of my sons except Arjuna. He spared the lives of Bhima, Nakula, Sahadeva, and yours in the battlefield because of that promise." Arjuna turned away unable to come to terms with what he had done. He had killed his own brother and gloated over it. Yudhishthira caressed Arjuna's shoulders trying to comfort him from his agony. He told his brothers that they should perform Karna's funeral rites along with those of their other family members.

Both Dhritarashtra and Gandhari were inconsolable on learning that all their sons had been killed. Dhritarashtra found it harder to forgive the loss of his sons and mourned especially for Duryodhana, who was killed by Bhima. Krishna asked the Pandavas to set aside their sorrow and pay their respects to Dhritarashtra and Gandhari. When the Pandavas came to meet them, Dhritarashtra embraced Yudhishthira as a token of peace. His wrath for Bhima, however, was obvious. When Dhritarashtra got the opportunity to embrace Bhima, he crushed him into fine powder with his strength. Luckily Krishna had anticipated such behavior, and had substituted Bhima for a metal statue of him.

Like Dhritarashtra, Gandhari was heartbroken at the loss of her sons. She refused to return to the palace from the battlefield even after the sun had set. No words of consolation or power of persuasion could relieve her pain. She blamed Krishna for using his divine powers to help the Pandavas. She pronounced a curse on Krishna that he too would one day experience the pain of losing his beloved ones. Gandhari's dreadful curse struck 36 years after the Battle of Kurukshetra. (We describe that in another chapter of this book.)

The bodies of the slain warriors were collected, wrapped in perfumed linen, laid upon a funeral pyre, and burned in accordance with the Hindu traditions. After a long period of mourning, Yudhishthira was crowned the king of Hastinapura. People rejoiced and bowed to the new king. The city of Indraprastha was unified with Hastinapura. Yudhishthira, however, could not bring himself to celebrate the occasion. He was overcome with guilt for the loss of many lives. Meanwhile, Krishna returned to his city, Dvaraka. Despite the war and deaths, all was not lost for the Kuru clan. There was great joy in the palace on the birth of Arjuna's grandson, Parikshit. The birth also ensured the continuity of the Kuru empire. Both Dhritarashtra and Gandhari stayed at Hastinapura and Yudhishthira treated them with respect. After Bhishma's death, Dhritarashtra and his wife, together with Kunti, retired to the forest where they perished in a forest fire two years later.

37

The Cruel Destiny of Karna

In this seemingly never-ending saga of intricately woven tales called the Mahabharata, there are no superheroes, only many heroes. Among the myriad of characters, Karna stands head and shoulders above the rest for his unflinching loyalty and boundless generosity. With an unforgettable role, Karna is also a hero in the epic, alas a tragic one, for Karna was the brother the Pandavas never had. As the eldest son of Kunti, he became the enemy of his own brothers and had the ignominy of fighting against them. Yet, it is to the character of Karna that you can relate to in the ebb and flow of everyday life. Throughout his life, he had to fight against setbacks and overcome the disgrace of belonging to a lower caste. Above all, the story of Karna illustrates how situations and circumstances in life can influence you and play a crucial part in destiny.

Although Karna was the oldest brother of the Pandavas, he was, strictly speaking, not a Pandava, for the sons of Pandu are referred to by that term. At the time of Karna's birth, Kunti was not married to Pandu. The sage Durvasa was once a guest at her father's palace. Kunti was in charge of the religious rituals during his visit. Kunti served the sage so well during his stay that the sage taught her a mantra by which she could invoke any *deva* (demi-god) and beget a child through him. Eager to test the power of the mantra, she saw the beautiful sun rising and prayed to

Surya, the sun god, without realizing the consequences of her actions. The mantra worked. Surya appeared before her and bestowed upon her a beautiful son wearing a pair of earrings and a golden armor protecting his chest. Ashamed of being an unwed mother, Kunti abandoned the baby by setting it afloat in a basket on a river. Kunti then returned to the palace burying the secret in her heart. The baby was found by a charioteer, who did not have any children of his own. The child later became known by the name of Karna.[57]

Karna grew up to be a valiant boy and became interested in warfare at an early age. He approached Drona, the established authority, who was also the royal preceptor of both the Pandavas and the Kauravas. But Drona refused to accept Karna as his student, since he was the son of a lowly charioteer. He further snubbed Karna by telling him to stick to his father's trade. A determined Karna went to Parashurama, Drona's teacher, to fulfill his childhood ambition. At the time Parashurama was waging a crusade against the Kshatriyas. He had a policy of accepting only Brahmin students, because he wanted Brahmins to learn how they could defend themselves against the Kshatriyas. To become his student, Karna disguised himself as a Brahmin. Karna soon proved himself to be Parashurama's top student.

One afternoon, exhausted from training, Parashurama took a nap resting his head on his student's lap. While Parashurama was dozing, a bee stung Karna's leg. Not to disturb his guru, Karna endured the pain even though he was in agony. Later when Parashurama came to know about the incident, he became suspicious. "You cannot possibly be a Brahmin because only a Kshatriya is strong enough to suffer such pain silently. Who are you really, son?" At once Karna fell at his feet and confessed, "I am no Brahmin, but a charioteer's son. I put on this charade to become your student." Karna did not cover himself in glory with his confession because Parashurama became enraged for being duped. "I taught you the

---

[57] Karna joins the list of famous adopted children alongside Krishna and Lakshmi in Hindu mythology. In modern times, this list includes Bill Clinton (ex-US President), Steve Jobs (Apple), John Lennon (Beatles), and Nelson Mandela.

use of divine weapons in good heart, but you fooled me." Saying this he pronounced a curse on Karna. "You will not remember how to use the divine weapons when you need them the most."

The turning point in Karna's life would soon arrive. At Hastinapura, Drona held a big event to mark the graduation of his royal students—the Pandavas and the Kauravas. Each of the boys came forward and showcased their skills in front of an audience. While Bhima and Duryodhana demonstrated their strength in mace, Sahadeva displayed his skills in swordsmanship. Arjuna impressed the local crowd with his extraordinary skills in archery. Karna stepped forward from the spectator's stand and performed all the feats demonstrated by Arjuna with ease. Recognizing the boy in golden armor and earrings as her first-born child, Kunti fainted in the stands. Karna challenged Arjuna to a duel, but Drona intervened and refused the challenge. Under the rules only royals could challenge royals. Upon seeing Karna's charioteer father, Bhima taunted Karna by comparing him to a stray dog for his mixed caste and lineage. Meanwhile, Duryodhana realized Karna could be a worthy opponent to the Pandavas. He conferred the kingdom of Anga on Karna at that moment so that he could challenge Arjuna. But because the sun was about to set for the day, the much-anticipated one-on-one duel between Karna and Arjuna did not go ahead. This event marked the beginning of a lasting friendship between Duryodhana and Karna. From a commoner, Karna became a prince overnight for which he was forever grateful to Duryodhana. This event also intensified his rivalry with the Pandavas, particularly with Arjuna.

At Draupadi's *swayamvara*, kings and princes came from afar. Among the guests were Karna, now the prince of Anga. At the center of the marriage hall was an artificial revolving fish suspended from a pole placed in a bowl of water. The challenge was to shoot the eye of the fish looking at its reflection using a heavy bow. Many suitors came forward. Some could not even lift the bow let alone string it. Unlike other contenders, Karna lifted the bow and strung it with ease. When he was about to shoot at the target, Draupadi remonstrated saying that only higher castes are allowed to participate in the *swayamvara*.

Karna got his chance to exact revenge thereafter. After Yudhishthira lost his kingdom in a game of dice, Draupadi, who was now queen to all five Pandavas, was taken captive by the Kauravas and dragged into the court. Karna insulted the helpless Draupadi by saying that a woman with five husbands was nothing but a glorified whore. Incensed, Arjuna swore he would kill Karna for this insult.

After the Pandavas were exiled to the forest, Duryodhana embarked on a military adventure with Karna as his commander, subjugating kings and conquering kingdoms. From the heavens, Indra became concerned about Duryodhana's might and power. With Karna by his side, Duryodhana appeared formidable in battle. But Indra knew that Duryodhana was nothing without Karna, and the secret to Karna's invincibility was his protective armor and earrings. So, disguising as a poor Brahmin, Indra approached Karna when he was praying and asked for his armor and earrings as alms. Karna cheerfully handed over the items to Indra even though his father, Surya, had warned him of Indra's deceitful nature. Karna was generous by nature, and could not turn away anyone empty handed.

After peace negotiations broke down between the Pandavas and Kauravas, war became imminent. While Arjuna was having pangs of conscience about the war, both Kunti and Krishna were faced with the dilemma of revealing Karna's true identity to Karna himself. In an attempt to placate Karna, Krishna told him that he was the eldest of the five Pandava brothers. He then pleaded with Karna to join the side of the Pandavas, assuring him that Yudhishthira would certainly give up the crown of Indraprastha for this older brother. But Karana declined the offer, for he had already promised his loyalty to Duryodhana. Krishna was saddened, but accepted the decision. He acknowledged Karna's sense of loyalty and promised that his true lineage would remain a secret.

As the war approached, Kunti became restless and went to meet Karna to reveal his true identity. Both mother and son shared a touching moment, but when Kunti asked Karna to call her mother, Karna gently refused. Like Krishna, Kunti asked Karna to join the Pandavas. Once again, Karna refused saying it was too late, and that he could not sever his ties with Duryodhana, however evil he might be. Karna promised that he would not kill any of the Pandavas except Arjuna.

In the Battle of Kurukshetra, Bhishma became the commander-in-chief of the Kaurava army. Karna refused to serve under Bhishma since he refused to recognize his skill. After Bhishma was mortally wounded, Drona became the commander-in-chief of the Kauravas. It was then that Karna entered the war on behalf of the Kauravas. After Drona died in battle, Karna was appointed the commander-in-chief. On that day, Karna fought with each one of the Pandava brother except Arjuna. A man of his word, Karna did not kill them even though he had the opportunity.

The following day he asked his charioteer to take him to Arjuna, and a major battle ensued between the brothers. It was the battle of the greatest heroes India had ever produced. When Arjuna surged forward with Krishna as his charioteer, Karna sent him backwards with a blistering array of arrows. As the battle raged, a wheel of Karna's chariot got trapped in the mud, and Karna was forced to descend from the chariot. Utterly helpless, Karna tried to invoke the divine weapons taught to him in his childhood. But he could not remember the incantation because of Parashurama's curse. Karna then signaled to Arjuna that he was in a non-combat role to fix the wheel of his chariot. The rules of engagement forbid attacking a warrior from behind. But rules were consistently being broken by both warring parties in desperation. Earlier, Drona had not only used divine weapons against ordinary soldiers but violated the rules of war by killing a defenseless Abhimanyu. In the last throes of war, all sense of honor and ethics were being discarded. Upon Krishna's exhortation, Arjuna shot an arrow at Karna when he was pulling the wheel. And thus Karna fell dead, his death, like his entire life, was unfair. The Kauravas did not last long after Karna's death. Duryodhana was utterly devastated. It is said that Duryodhana never shed a drop of tear when any of his brothers were killed, but became inconsolable at the death of his dear friend.

At the cremation of Karma, Kunti asked her sons to perform the funeral rites. When they refused, she revealed the truth about Karna's birth. The Pandavas were shocked to realize that they had killed their own brother. Yudhishthira, in particular, was furious with his mother for not revealing the truth earlier.[58]

The Mahabharata had many powerful characters, but if there was an individual endowed with the attributes of a good human being, it was Karna. Even today, the debate rages on whether Karna was a better archer than Arjuna, and whether Krishna feared Arjuna was losing and therefore prodded him to employ illegitimate tactics in war. Regardless of whether you agree or not, there is no doubt Karna was the ultimate epitome of a self-made hero. There are few donors more gracious than him. At every stage in his life, he had to endure hardship. Yet, he kept his mental anguish within himself and never made a public show of his tragedy. Karna was extremely loyal. But loyalty is a double edge sword, and he paid the price for it. His loyalty toward Duryodhana was as a friend, but it made him fight on the side of evil. In the end, however great Karna turned out to be, his image was tarnished by his association with bad company—which even an exemplary personality like Bhishma could not escape.

> *I can control my destiny, but not my fate. Destiny means there are opportunities to turn right or left, but fate is a one-way street. I believe we all have the choice as to whether we fulfill our destiny, but our fate is sealed.*
>
> —PAULO COELHO, 1947—

---

[58] This is another version of how the Pandavas came to know about Karna's true identity.

38

Why Drona Is a Controversial Guru

A feature of ancient Indian tradition is the *guru-shishya parampara* or the "teacher-student tradition," in which a learned teacher imparts his knowledge—spiritual, martial, arts, etc.—by developing an altruistic relationship with the student. In this tradition, the guru is held in utmost respect, next only to parents in the social hierarchy. It is a common practice for the guru to ask for *guru dakshina* or "token payment" at the end of studies. Drona is considered the role model of the *guru-shishya parampara*, and the Government of India confers the Dronacharya Award yearly in his honor for outstanding coaches in sports and games. As a guru, however, Drona used the sacred relationship to settle old scores. He also made the most outrageous demand for *guru dakshina* by asking a student to chop off his right thumb. Why is a controversial guru being revered at the highest level?

Most of our knowledge about Drona comes from the Mahabharata, where he is not portrayed as an evil character even though at times, he had no qualms about using divine weapons on ordinary soldiers or unethical tactics in war. Drona was a strict conformist of the caste system of those times. He had a personal bias toward three things—his son Ashwatthama, his star pupil Arjuna, and his motherland Hastinapura—all of which conjured to cloud his dharma. Although he fought on the side of the evil Kauravas in the war, he was often at odds with Duryodhana and could not stand his immoral ways. Drona is famously remembered for rebutting the contention that "friendship can exist only between equals."

Like many characters in Hindu mythology, Drona did not have an ordinary birth. It is said that his father, sage Bharadvaja, once went to perform ablutions on the banks of river Ganga where he saw the beautiful apsara, Ghritachi, bathing. The sage celebrated the occasion by depositing his seeds into a vessel. Over time a boy sprouted from it and was aptly named Drona since "Drona" means "vessel" in Sanskrit. The child grew up at his father's hermitage. Around this time Drupada, the prince of Panchala, used to frequent the ashram for study and play. The boys got close and developed a strong bond. Such was their friendship that Drupada once boasted that he would give away half his kingdom to Drona when he became king.

After their studies, Drona and Drupada parted ways. Drona married Kripa's sister and had a son called Ashwatthama. At that time the Brahmin was impoverished and struggled to make ends meet. The birth of the child led to further financial woes. His wife could not bear the financial strain anymore and asked her husband to find a way to escape poverty. Drona learned that Parashurama was distributing the wealth he had acquired by defeating a number of Kshatriya kings. So he went to Parashurama, but it was a tad late—Parashurama had already donated his wealth, and only weapons remained. Moved by the Brahmin's plight, Parashurama offered him weapons and free training—which Drona accepted. Soon Drona became a highly skilled archer and an unrivaled master of the military art—which earned him the title "Acharya."

Although Drona became an outstanding archer, his family continued to struggle financially. He then remembered his childhood friend Drupada, who was now the king of Panchala, and decided to seek his assistance. But Drupada refused to acknowledge their friendship. "O Brahmin, what friendship can exist between a crowned king and a wandering mendicant? Friendship can exist only between equals! How can a pauper be a friend of the rich, an ignoramus, a friend of a scholar, or a coward, a friend of a hero?" According to Drupada, he was a friend of Drona during childhood because then they were equals. Now he was a king, and Drona, a pauper. It would be more appropriate for Drona to ask for alms befitting a Brahmin rather than claim his right as a friend.

Utterly humiliated, Drona left the palace without saying a word, longing for retribution. But he had more pressing issues to deal with. He needed a steady job to keep the wolf from the door. So Drona headed to Hastinapura to meet his brother-in-law Kripa, the royal preceptor of Kuru princes, with the prospect of securing employment. When Drona reached the city precincts, as luck would have it, he strolled past a group of boys playing a ball game. All of a sudden, the game was stopped because their ball fell into a well. The boys gathered around the well seeking a way to retrieve the ball.

Seeing the anxious boys hunched over the well, Drona went up to them and asked about the matter. He then picked a stalk of grass from the ground. Chanting a mantra, he took careful aim and threw the stalk at the ball. The stalk pierced the ball, as the boys looked at the stranger in amazement. Drona threw another stalk that pierced the end of the first and soon a chain of stalks was formed. When the chain was long enough, he pulled out the ball from the well effortlessly. The boys couldn't believe what they had just witnessed. Impressed by his visitor's skills, Yudhishthira introduced himself to Drona and invited him to the palace. At the palace, Bhishma welcomed Drona after learning that he was a student of Parashurama. He appointed him as a guru to train the princes in the use of arms.

The princes learned archery from Drona. Among them, the one who showed the most interest was Arjuna. Soon Arjuna became Drona's favorite pupil but only after his son Ashwatthama, who also studied with the princes. Although gurus are supposed to be fair and impartial in disseminating knowledge, Drona revealed the secrets of divine *astra*s to his son when others were not around. He used to create elaborate schemes to hold special one-on-one training sessions with his son. For instance, he would challenge his students to fetch water from a nearby river with the condition that whoever returns fastest would receive special knowledge in the use of weapons. He would then ensure his son came first by giving him a wide-necked pot and others a narrow-necked pot. Soon, Arjuna figured out the guru's trick and began returning alongside Ashwatthama thereby receiving some of the special training for himself.

Drona once subjected his students to a test. He placed a wooden bird high up on a tree and asked each student to come forward with his bow and arrow. When Yudhishthira came first, Drona asked him to take aim at the bird. "What do you see?" asked Drona to which Yudhishthira replied, "I can see the bird!" When Drona pressed him on what else he could see, Yudhishthira replied, "I can see the bird, the tree, you, and my brothers and cousins standing behind!" Drona was unimpressed by his answer and asked Yudhishthira to stand aside. He then posed the same question to each of the princes in turn. Each of them said the same and was made to stand aside. Arjuna was last. When Drona asked the same question, he replied, "I can see the bird and nothing else!" Drona was impressed by this answer, and asked him to proceed. With a single shot, Arjuna brought down the bird much to the delight of Drona.

Drona was greatly impressed with Arjuna's commitment and concentration. He wanted to make Arjuna the greatest archer on earth—at any cost. About this time, Ekalavya, the son of a tribal chief, came to Drona to learn archery. Drona refused to accept him as his student because he was not a Kshatriya prince. Furthermore, he felt an obligation to defend Hastinapura, the land that gave him shelter and recognition. He was concerned that Ekalavya would become an unconquerable warrior for the rival army since his father was a commander of Jarasandha, the king of Magadha. But Ekalavya did not abandon his ambitions. Creating a clay image of Drona, he learned the intricacies of archery by himself and became a warrior of exceptional prowess. Soon Drona came to know about his skills, and came to meet the young warrior. On seeing Drona, Ekalavya prostrated at his feet and called him his guru. Seizing the moment, Drona reminded Ekalavya that it was his duty to pay *guru-dakshina* to his guru. When Ekalavya obliged, Drona demanded that he chop off his right thumb. Ekalavya was horrified with this request, but nevertheless complied. Another person who wanted to learn archery from Drona was Karna, who was also rejected because he was the son of a lowly charioteer and not a Kshatriya. Like Ekalavya, Karna did not forsake his ambition, and became a student of Parashurama, who later declared Karna equal to himself in warfare.

After the Pandava and Kaurava princes completed their training in the use of arms, the thought of settling scores with his nemesis Drupada dawned upon Drona. Once again, he used *guru dakshina* as the means to achieve his end. He asked the Kaurava princes to defeat Drupada as payment for their training and bring the king before him. Duryodhana led the battle but conceded defeat at the hands of the formidable Drupada. Next the Pandava princes were asked to attack and seize the capital of Panchala. Arjuna led the army for the Pandavas and a fierce battle ensued upon which Drupada was defeated. Drupada was tied up and brought to Hastinapura. But Drona was humble in victory and appropriated only half of Drupada's kingdom, thus becoming his equal. To the captured king of Panchala, Drona queried, "Did you not say friendship was between equals? We were friends once, can we not be friends again since we have become equal?" This time it was Drupada's turn to become silent. Although Drona forgave the king's misdeeds, Drupada vowed to take revenge on Drona. After Drupada returned to Panchala, he performed a great fire sacrifice to beget a son as powerful as Arjuna who could destroy Drona. Out of the fire came two luminous children, one a son called Dhrishtadyumna, and the other his sister, Draupadi.

As a faithful servant of Hastinapura, Drona was duty-bound to fight for the Kauravas and against his favorite Pandavas in the Kurukshetra War. After Bhishma was mortally wounded on the tenth day of the war, Drona became the commander-in-chief of the Kauravas. At this time, Duryodhana came up with the strategy of trying to end the war by capturing Yudhishthira alive. Drona accepted the plan because he didn't want to see Yudhishthira killed. On the battlefield, however, he met with little success in capturing Yudhishthira since Arjuna was always present to foil his advances. In desperation Drona used divine weapons against ordinary foot-soldiers and killed a number of them. A voice from heaven admonished him for using divine weapons recklessly.

The Kauravas realized they could not capture Yudhishthira when Arjuna was protecting him. So they made a plan to distract Arjuna to another part of the battlefield. A multi-tier defense formation in the shape of a blooming lotus, known as *chakra vyuha*,[59] was organized to capture Yudhishthira. The Kauravas knew only Arjuna and Krishna had the knowledge to penetrate and overcome this war formation. On that day, at the behest of Yudhishthira, Abhimanyu led the Pandava army and, he was able to penetrate the elaborate defensive formation. Although Abhimanyu knew how to move into the formation, he did not know how to escape from it. After cornering Abhimanyu and surrounding him with enemy soldiers, Drona asked them to slay his horses, kill his charioteer, and then destroy his chariot. Trapped, Abhimanyu faced an army of Kauravas attacking him from all sides. Abhimanyu fended off the entire Kaurava army with the chariot wheel as his only weapon. Eventually, he succumbed to the Kaurava army and was killed. This was a gross violation of the rules of war whereby a lone weaponless warrior was attacked by many soldiers.

The gruesome killing of Abhimanyu infuriated the Pandavas and they retaliated in kind. The Pandavas realized that it was next to impossible to defeat an armed Drona. Therefore Krishna and the Pandavas devised a ruse to trap Drona. During a lull in the fighting, the Pandavas spread the rumor that Ashwatthama was dead. As an only child, Ashwatthama was Drona's weakness. It was prophesied that no harm would come to Ashwatthama as long as Drona lived. At first Drona would not buy into the rumor, but after some time he decided to verify it from the lips of Yudhishthira, for he knew Yudhishthira would never lie. When Drona asked for the truth, Yudhishthira confirmed that Ashwatthama indeed was dead. On hearing this, Drona became inconsolable. He descended from

---

[59] *Chakra vyuha* is also known as *padma vyuha*.

his chariot, laid down his arms, and sat in meditation to pray for his son's soul. Dhrishtadyumna seized this opportunity to behead the unarmed Drona in another gross violation of the rules of the war. Drona did not know that his son was alive at the time of his death. Yudhishthira was referring to an elephant by that name which Bhima had killed that morning.

Although Dronacharya died thousands of years ago in the battlefield, he remains a revered figure among the Hindus. Not all Hindus, however, see Drona in the same light. His detractors point out that he misused the sacred relationship for personal gain. Besides being reckless with divine weapons, Drona used questionable tactics in war. Furthermore he showed his caste prejudice in the treatment of Ekalavya and Karna, but conveniently ignored it to advance his own purpose. Born as a Brahmin, Drona should have been in the traditional occupation as a priest, yet he chose to become a warrior and transgress the caste barrier.

Drona's supporters, however, contend that it is unfair to single out Drona for using unethical tactics in war. They agree Drona is far from perfect, but the battlefield is not the place to judge exemplary behavior. They point out that Krishna did not hesitate to recommend such tactics to Arjuna.

Yet there is no doubt Arjuna became the greatest archer of his time because of Drona's tutelage. For that reason Drona is considered the role model of *guru-shishya parampara* and an award bearing his name is meted out for exceptional coaches every year. The city of Gurgaon—now a leading financial and industrial hub—located near Delhi is believed to be Drona's home.[60] The land was awarded to him by Dhritarashtra in recognition for his services as the royal preceptor to the princes—according to legend.

Tell me and I forget. Teach me and I remember.
Involve me and I learn.

—BENJAMIN FRANKLIN, 1706-1790

---

[60] Gurgaon recently underwent a name change to become Gurugram.

39

Amba Is Reborn as Shikhandi

Background: Amba, the princess of Kashi, was abducted along with her sisters from their swayamvara by Bhishma and taken to Hastinapura, where arrangements were made for their marriage with his king-cum-step-brother, Vichitravirya. Prior to her nuptials, Amba confides in Bhishma that she is already in love with King Salva. Bhishma grants her permission to leave Hastinapura. On meeting Amba, Salva has a change of heart and refuses to accept her since Bhishma, by his abduction, had earned the right to marry her. Distraught, Amba returns to Hastinapura only to be rejected by Vichitravirya because she was already in love with another man. Nowhere to turn to, Amba pleads with Bhishma to marry her, but he reminds her of his vow of celibacy taken earlier in life. Blaming Bhishma for ruining her life, Amba seeks the help of sage Parashurama to kill Bhishma. Although Bhishma was his former student, Parashurama feels sorry for Amba and challenges Bhishma for a duel. The battle lasts several weeks, and in the end both combatants, completely fatigued, call off the fight. But Amba is firm in her resolve to destroy Bhishma and enters a forest to practice austerities.

After 12 years of extreme austerities in which Amba survived for days without water, Shiva was pleased and granted her a boon. "You will be the cause of Bhishma's death in your next life," said Shiva and disappeared. Amba was so pleased by the boon that she could not wait anymore. She jumped into a raging funeral pyre and killed herself.

Far away at the kingdom of Panchala, King Drupada was delighted when Shiva appeared before him. Having been childless with his eldest queen for many years, he was practicing harsh austerities. When Shiva blessed him by saying, "You will have a son who will be born as a girl," Drupada was startled. He was not sure whether it was a blessing or a curse. Shiva's words came true, for in due course the queen became pregnant and gave birth to a girl. The parents announced they had a son since they did not want to overcomplicate matters in society. They named the baby Shikhandi. Although born with female genital organs, the child was raised as a son and taught warfare and statecraft. The gender of the child was kept a secret from everyone.

As a child, Shikhandi could remember events from her past life, including her hatred for Bhishma. When she attained youth, her parents chose a princess as a bride for her. Soon Shikhandi was married, but on the wedding night, the princess was intrigued to discover both of them had identical genital organs. She promptly reported the matter to her father, who became furious and at once mobilized a large army to fight Drupada for his deception. Shikhandi was saddened that her parents had to go through this ordeal because of her. So she went to a forest to end her life. Luckily a *yaksha* (forest spirit) called Stuna took pity on Shikhandi for being so unfortunate in life. To save Shikhandi from her predicament, Stuna agreed to swap his genital organ with hers for one day. Meanwhile Shikhandi's father-in-law dispatched a woman to ascertain whether Shikhandi was male or female. The woman performed a physical examination on Shikhandi and reported back to the king that Shikhandi was indeed a man—and a rather powerful one at it. Relieved, the king reprimanded his daughter for lying about Shikhandi's gender. Soon the king of yakshas learned about Stuna's genital swap and became angry at Stuna for showing disrespect to the yaksha clan. He cursed Stuna that

AMBA IS REBORN AS SHIKHANDI

he would be a woman until the death of Shikhandi. Since Stuna could not reverse his action because of the curse, the temporary genital swap performed on Shikhandi became permanent.

Meanwhile at Hastinapura, war broke out between the Pandavas and Kauravas. Although Bhishma was the father figure for the cousins, he chose the side of Kauravas in the battle. On the ninth day, the Kauravas led by Bhishma proved to be insurmountable for the Pandava brothers. After sunset the Pandavas deliberated on how to achieve a breakthrough, but came to the conclusion that Bhishma could not be beaten as long as he held a weapon. Sensing a chink in his armor, the Pandavas devised a wicked plan to take on Bhishma. They invited Shikhandi on the tenth day to the battlefield along with Arjuna and Krishna. As the chariot rolled on the next day, Bhishma noticed Shikhandi at the forefront and hesitated. It was against his dharma to raise weapons against a woman. "Women are not allowed in the battlefield," protested Bhishma. But Krishna retorted, "Shikhandi is no woman and was raised as a man. You see her as a woman because in your heart she is Amba, the one you humiliated in her previous life." Memories of Amba suddenly flashed through Bhishma's mind. Taken aback, he lowered his bow and muttered, "No, I cannot fight this woman. I have tormented her enough." At this moment Krishna gave the cue to Arjuna to strike. A barrage of arrows soon found their way toward Bhishma and punctured every limb of his body until the grandsire fell like a huge tree in the middle of a forest. While Bhishma was bound by his guilt and ethics, for Krishna, everything was fair in war.

The fall of Bhishma became the turning point of the war. With his descent, the war inexorably tilted in favor of the Pandavas. Eight days later, the Kauravas were annihilated and dharma was re-established. There is no doubt Bhishma was a formidable warrior with extraordinary ethics. There is no doubt Bhishma was a die-hard defender of dharma. In the real world, every action is linked to multiple ethical issues and the question of what is right or wrong is never clear. Just as a morally right action can lead to a negative outcome, a morally wrong action can also have a positive outcome. Krishna is seen exhorting Arjuna, for instance, to perform acts that are against the code of conduct in the war, yet they result in a positive outcome. In Bhishma's case, he got trapped in this conflict between dharma (duty) and karma (right action) although he is occasionally seen trying to advance his self-serving interest. Bhishma was arrogant enough to disrupt a *swayamvara* and kidnap the princesses, yet he was also chivalrous enough to release Amba as soon as he realized she was already in love. Against his own guru, Bhishma had no hesitation in using the *Praswap Astra*.[61] And in the Kurukshetra War, he sided with the evil-minded Kauravas fulfilling his dharma—which led to a negative outcome. In the end, Bhishma suffered tremendously from the consequences of his actions.

There is also poetic justice in the story of Amba. The queen Satyavati prevented her step-son Bhishma from fathering children to ensure her own children could inherit the throne. What she did not anticipate was that her descendants ended up fighting over the crown. The Mahabharata captures the grand Hindu discourse on destiny and conveys in no uncertain terms that no matter how hard humans try to control their destiny, they will fail. No human can manipulate the mysterious working of karma.

The story of Amba is also a curious tale of gender fluidity in ancient India. Many stories of sex change, both temporary and permanent, exist in Hindu scriptures suggesting that ancient India considered gender to be flexible. More importantly, the variations in gender were acknowledged and accepted wholeheartedly. While "Amba" symbolizes fearlessness and resolve in modern times, the word *shikhandi*, however, has taken on a negative connotation. Although the word *shikhandin* literally means a crested peacock, today it is used to refer to queers—from gays to *hijra*s (eunuchs) to bisexuals, or LGBT in today's terms. In fact, the character of Shikhandi in the epic has become such an embarrassment that many modern authors either downplay the significance of his role in the war or exclude it in its entirety.

---

[61] This story is described in book 3 of this series (see Chapter 9).

40

Samba - The Black Sheep of the Family

When the gods wish to punish us they answer our prayers.

—OSCAR WILDE, 1854–1900

It is a universal truth that every family has its own share of bad apples who shame and embarrass them. For the Gandhi family, the black sheep was their eldest son, Harilal Gandhi, who wanted to study in England when Mahatma Gandhi was leading India's freedom struggle against the British. When his father opposed the idea, Harilal protested by renouncing all family ties. He even converted to Islam temporarily to humiliate his father. The Krishna clan was no different. Krishna may have managed to keep his 16,108 wives happy, but his relationship with his sons was fraught with tension and conflict. Although Krishna did have an outstanding son in Pradyumna,[62] the black sheep of the family turned out to be Samba, who ultimately caused the ruin of the entire Yadava clan.

Samba was the child of the bear princess Jambavati, one of the eight principal queens of Krishna. While the other wives of Krishna were having babies, Jambavati did not have a child for a long time and was despondent. Because Jambavati was distraught, Krishna went to the Himalayas and worshipped Shiva, who appeared before him as "Sambashiva," the "half-woman half-man" form.[63] Thereafter Jambavati gave birth to a son, who was named Samba in honor of Shiva. After giving birth to Samba, Jambavati went merry and had many children. Little did she know that Samba was the seed that would sow the destruction of the entire clan, including his father.

No early warning signs of an impending disaster were apparent. Samba grew up into a handsome prince; in fact, he was so handsome that he looked like a replica of his father. About this time, Lakshmana, the beautiful daughter of Duryodhana, came of age. As was the custom those days, Duryodhana arranged a *swayamvara* and invited princes from afar for her wedding. Not only did Samba attend the *swayamvara* without invitation, he abducted Lakshmana at the ceremony—just like Krishna had abducted Rukmini at her wedding. But there was a key distinction. Unlike Rukmini, Lakshmana never had any romantic feelings for Samba, who was promptly apprehended by her father.

Duryodhana realized that Samba should not be living in a mansion; rather he must be confined to a cell. Samba was promptly dispatched to jail. Balarama negotiated for his nephew's release thinking Duryodhana might soften his stance because he was Duryodhana's guru and had taught him mace fighting. But Duryodhana remained unmoved to his pleas and refused to free Samba. Since diplomacy ended in failure, Balarama changed tactics and threatened to uproot the entire kingdom into the sea with his plowshare. That was enough to break Duryodhana's resistance and

---
[62] Pradyumna is described in book 1 of this series (see Chapter 27).
[63] Shiva is the god of fertility even though he is more famous for his destructive tendencies.

Samba was released. Meanwhile, a strange thing happened. Lakshmana became afflicted with the Stockholm syndrome and felt sympathy for her captor.[64] Samba and Lakshmana were married shortly thereafter.

Samba not only inherited his father's looks but also shared his pastimes. Just as Krishna was a prankster in his youth, so was Samba. Capitalizing on his good looks, Samba would often impersonate his father and play pranks in the palace. Some of Krishna's junior wives were drawn toward him, and one wife even tricked him into embracing her. Enraged at his son's behavior, Krishna cursed Samba that his face would be covered with skin lesion. Samba was advised to worship the sun god, Surya, to free himself from the lesions. For that reason, Samba built a number of temples honoring Surya, and his disease was cured. That's why all sun temples in India, such as Konark (Odisha), Modhera (Gujarat), and Markand (Kashmir) are attributed to Samba.

Samba paid the ultimate price for his mischief when he along with his friends played a prank on a group of sages visiting Dvaraka. With an iron mace tied to his stomach, he dressed as a pregnant woman and asked the sages whether the unborn child would be a boy or girl. But the sages came to know about the hoax and were not amused. "Neither male nor female, but an iron mace resides inside your body that will destroy the Yadavas. Beware!" Samba and his chums burst into laughter at the verdict, but their glee was short lived. Just as the sages foretold, an iron mace ripped out of Samba's thighs. Terrified, Samba and his friends sought the advice of the Yadava elders, who told them to grind the mace into a fine powder and throw it into the sea. The young men pounded the mace and scattered the remains into the sea, as they were told. These iron filings were washed by the sea to the shores of Prabhasa,[65] where they grew into a grass with sharp, serrated edges. Meanwhile, a fish happened

---

[64] Stockholm syndrome refers to the bonding that occurs when a captive begins to identify closely with the captor. The name comes from a botched bank robbery in 1973 in Stockholm, Sweden.

[65] Prabhasa is an ancient pilgrimage site for the Hindus situated in the state of Gujarat. It is home to the renowned Somnath Temple.

to swallow a scrap of iron, but was caught by a hunter called Jara, who used the iron piece as the arrowhead for his weapon.

As events would unfold, the Yadavas fought among themselves over an argument. The grass blades became swords in their hands and eventually led to the destruction of the entire clan. Worse still, an arrow from Jara's bow found its mark on an unsuspecting Krishna, wounding him fatally and putting an end to his reign on earth—which we describe in the next chapter.

41

The Tragic Death of Krishna

A mother's love for her child is like nothing else in the world. It knows no law, no pity, it dares all things and crushes down remorselessly all that stands in its path.

—AGATHA CHRISTIE, 1890–1976

No sorrow is greater than the loss of a child for a mother—except the loss of hundred sons. Such was the plight of Gandhari, the hapless mother of the Kauravas, who lost all her sons in the Battle of Kurukshetra. Inconsolable in grief, she blamed Krishna for her woes. "So many lives were lost because of you. You will never understand the depth of my despair." Krishna demurred, "Mother, please do not hold me responsible for the death of your children. I begged them not to fight, but they would not listen." But Gandhari was not listening. "You are the lord and could have averted the war if you wanted to. You could have saved all my children. Because you had a soft spot for the Pandavas, you did not do anything." Casting her grief away for a moment, Gandhari swore at

Krishna, "One day your dear ones will squabble among themselves and end their lives. Then, you will understand the true grief of a mother who lost all her children."

Neither Krishna nor his family was able to escape the laws of karma. Gandhari's dreadful curse struck 36 years after the Battle of Kurukshetra. By that time, the Yadavas had become utterly corrupt. The relatives and sons of Krishna—particularly Samba—had become arrogant and disrespectful. Signs of an impending doom had started to appear. Natural calamities occurred almost daily. Mysterious events seemed to happen on a regular basis. The once peaceful and prosperous city of Dvaraka seemed to have sunk into misery. Worried, the Yadavas went to their elders and asked him how they might avert the catastrophe. On their advice, the men set off on a pilgrimage to Prabhasa, the Jyotirlinga site of Somnath in present day Gujarat.

At Prabhasa, the Yadavas made offerings to those who had died at the Kurukshetra War. But in due course the reason for the pilgrimage was forgotten. Praying and fasting were replaced by feasting and revelry. Liquor made its appearance among the pilgrims. An argument erupted as to who was right and who was wrong at the time of war. The Yadavas had participated in the war, and many of them fought on the Kaurava side. At that time Krishna did not want to take sides and offered to be Arjuna's charioteer, while commanding his army to fight for the Kauravas. One such army chieftain of Krishna's was Kritavarma, who fought for the Kauravas. Another warrior called Satyaki did not heed Krishna's advice and fought for the Pandavas.

Split into two camps, the Yadavas who supported the Pandavas thought they were righteous, while the other camp believed the Kauravas were wronged. Satyaki taunted Kritavarma for his actions during the war and enraged him. He responded in kind and reminded Satyaki how he killed an unarmed Bhurishravas on the 14th day of the war. The squabble spread like cancer through the whole camp, and soon a fight ensued without regard for their kinship. As more people joined the fray, the fight turned into a full-blown civil war. Mayhem and terror reigned as sons fought against fathers, uncles against nephews and brother against brothers, all determined on self-destruction. When the weapons and arrows were exhausted, they fought with reeds found on the shores.

But these were no ordinary reeds. They were sharp and serrated and made of the same iron dust Samba had thrown into the seas. The deadly blades of grass became swords in the hands of the fighters. In a fit of rage, Satyaki decapitated Kritavarma. The supporters of Kritavarma ganged up and attacked Satyaki. Within a few hours, the shores of Prabhasa were littered with bodies of slain Yadavas. In the end, all of them perished, including Satyaki. It seemed as if another Kurukshetra had played out over a political disagreement.

With the demise of his clan, Balarama retreated to the forest despondently. A serpent crawled out of his mouth and rose up into the skies leaving his lifeless body behind. Ananda Shesha's time on earth as Balarama had formally come to an end. On learning that his elder brother had passed away, Krishna realized it was time for his departure from mortal existence. He made his way into the forest, where he sat under a tree and went into meditation. A passing hunter by the name of Jara[66] mistook the foot of Krishna for the face of a deer and shot an arrow, fatally wounding him. Although Krishna's limbs and other body parts were invincible, the foot was his weak spot. When the hunter came to claim his deer, he saw Krishna lying in a pool of blood. Aghast, he threw himself at the lord's feet and begged for mercy. Before breathing his last, Krishna forgave the hunter. Just as this birth was mysterious, so was his death. Ironically, Krishna, who talks so much about karma in the Bhagavad Gita, became a victim of karma himself.

The news of Krishna's death soon reached his family. Vasudeva, Devaki, and Rohini died of grief. A grand funeral was held for Krishna and Balarama. They were joined by Krishna's eight principal wives, Balarama's wife, and King Ugrasena. During the funeral, the wives threw themselves into the flames and met with their deaths.

---

[66] Jara (hunter) should not be confused with Jarasandha (king) or Jara (ogress). Although Jarasandha made many attempts on Krishna's life, it was Jara, the hunter, who killed him accidentally.

Before we leave this chapter, let us answer this question: Did Krishna have a weak spot? Many stories vouch for its existence. One version is attributed to sage Durvasa, the powerful but bad-tempered teacher, who either censured or cursed anyone who dared to cross him. Durvasa had this habit of always being on the lookout for an invitation to stay at someone's home. Once Krishna and Rukmini met with the sage and invited him to their abode. Instead of showing his appreciation, Durvasa made them pull his chariot like horses, beating them all the way. Krishna and Rukmini did not protest, for they did not want to incur the sage's wrath. Later, Durvasa blessed the couple for their hospitality by giving them the boon of invincibility—provided they smeared their bodies with a pudding. It is said that Krishna smeared the pudding over his entire body except the foot, thereby, only obtaining partial invincibility. That's how that myth goes.

42

Yudhishthira and the Dog

Among the Pandavas—Bhima, Arjuna, Yudhishthira, Nakula, Sahadeva—who would you trust if your life depended on it? If you picked Yudhishthira, you are mostly okay. In fact Drona did the same thing during the battle to confirm rumors about his son's death. When asked the question, Yudhishthira was caught in a dilemma. If he spoke the truth, it would be detrimental to the Pandavas and would sabotage their war strategy. If he lied, he would be going against his own dharma. Caught between the two, Yudhishthira equivocated and mislead Drona. But that was war, and Drona deserved his just comeuppance for discarding ethics and employing extreme tactics. Well, that's not to say Yudhishthira is perfect. His archery skills were average and he had a serious gambling problem. Despite the flaws, there was no doubt that the righteous Yudhishthira was the most trustworthy among the Pandava brothers.

After the Battle of Kurukshetra, Yudhishthira was crowned the king of Hastinapura. Several years later, on the advice of sage Vyasa, the Pandavas decided to retire. Instead of checking into a nursing home or a retirement village, Yudhishthira renounced his kingdom, anointed his nephew Parikshit as the new king, and set out with his brothers, along with Draupadi, on the long journey to Mount Meru, the abode of Indra in the Himalayas. At the start of the journey, a dog[67] befriends them and keeps them company throughout the grueling journey.

During the journey, one by one, the Pandavas succumb to their weakness and fall to their deaths. Draupadi was the first to depart. A sad Bhima asks Yudhishthira why a virtuous, straight-shooter like Draupadi should fall first. "Her fault was too much attachment to Arjuna," explains Yudhishthira. After Draupadi, Sahadeva succumbs to which Yudhishthira explains that excessive pride led to his undoing. Next to pass away was Nakula, and the reason for his failing was narcissism. When the protagonist of the epic, Arjuna, collapses next, Yudhishthira comforts an alarmed Bhima by saying, "He was brilliant but boastful." Lastly, Bhima falls without completing the journey, and as he lay dying, Yudhishthira explains to him that his death was a punishment for the excessive hatred he felt toward his enemies.

Undeterred by the loss of his family, Yudhishthira plows on with the dog in tow. Just before it is time to ascend to heaven, Indra arrives in his chariot. He welcomes Yudhishthira to come onboard. But Yudhishthira balks saying he cannot travel to heaven without Draupadi or his brothers. Indra assures Yudhishthira that though they are dead, their spirits have risen to heaven. The righteous Yudhishthira still hesitates to join Indra unless his dog, who has been faithful throughout the long journey, accompanies him. But Indra is adamant that dogs have no place in heaven. Yudhishthira insists that the dog must be rewarded, and as long as the faithful creature lives, he will never abandon it.

As they argue about the pros and cons of introducing a canine to heaven, the dog undergoes a miraculous transformation and becomes Dharma,[68] the god of moral and religious duty, and the father of Yudhishthira. This was after all a divine experiment to test Yudhishthira's commitment to dharma, and Yudhishthira proves his righteousness by not abandoning those who stayed with him. Yudhishthira has passed

---

[67] Scholars claim this dog to be the Indian Pariah dog, the world's first domesticated dog. The animal is considered an ancestor to the Australian dingo.
[68] Dharma is also identified as Yama, who sends his watchdog to fetch the dead.

the test with flying colors and the gods are hugely pleased. Thereafter, Yudhishthira is led to the Ganges to bathe and cast off his mortal body. He becomes an immortal and is welcomed to heaven, where he is joined by Krishna, his brothers, Draupadi, and others.

43

Bhagavad Gita - The Song of the Lord

The soul is neither born, nor does it ever die.
The soul is birthless, eternal, and ageless.
It is not destroyed when the body is destroyed.

—KRISHNA IN BHAGAVAD GITA 2.20

Which is more important to you in a song—music or lyrics? Some say lyrics, but I have always vouched for music. It was also music that led me to Bhagavad Gita. The Bhagavad Gita literally translates to "The Song of the Lord," but the wisdom of the Bhagavad Gita lies in its words—which I didn't realize for a long time. The Gita was a beautiful song for me in my teenage years. By then, many artists had sung the verses of Gita—from gifted singers to wannabes with buffalo voices—but when the verses were rendered by the legendary Indian singer Jesudas in his inimitable voice, the song was melodious and utterly captivating.[69] It became my constant companion in the mornings, afternoons, evenings, not to mention during times of uncertainty and stress. The melody of the Sanskrit shlokas was mesmerizing even though I did not understand a single word.

I cultivated a sharper appreciation for the meaning of words when I was confronted with—problems, problems, problems—in my late twenties. My Jesuit priests at school taught me to always show the other cheek and practice forgiveness. My Hindu gurus were convinced that the astrological position of the stars was the cause of my troubles. But here in the Gita, Krishna tells Arjuna to fight the Kauravas and not shirk his duty. He urges him to boldly confront his rivals and not to worry about the consequences. This was refreshing and resonated with me. It was a welcome relief from the insincere platitudes or shrinking in fear. No offence to the Hindu priests or Jesuit fathers. I know they meant well. It's just that in my twenties I was not thinking of attaining moksha or salvation from the world let alone becoming a *sthitaprajna*.[70] We'll get to this concept shortly.

Regarded as the bible of Hinduism, the Bhagavad Gita is commonly referred to as the Gita in the land it was born. It is the most loved holy book in Hinduism, and many Hindus have memorized many lines of the book including yours truly. Although the Gita dates back to several thousand years, it was delivered under extraordinary circumstances. The Pandavas and the Kauravas had assembled on the sweeping Kurukshetra plains early in the morning ready for battle. As the war was about to begin, Arjuna asked his charioteer Krishna to drive forward into the open space between the two armies so that he could have one last look at the two sides. On seeing the tragically divided families, Arjuna had a meltdown. Several good men on both sides were about to die in the

---

[69] The Gita sung by Jesudas can be found on YouTube.
[70] The concept of *sthitaprajna* is said to have left a lasting impression on Mahatma Gandhi, who equated this principle to the Buddhist concept of nirvana where the mind is in perpetual equilibrium.

name of war. An emotionally paralyzed Arjuna collapsed to the floor of his chariot. It was then Krishna turned to him and spoke these famous verses. Bhagavad Gita is the conversation between Krishna and Arjuna prior to the war. It forms the sixth *parva* (book) of the Mahabharata, and scholars believe it was inserted into the epic sometime between 4 BCE and 4 CE. While the Mahabharata has 18 chapters and consists of a whopping 100,000 shlokas (two-line stanzas), the Gita also has 18 chapters, but only 700 shlokas. If the Mahabharata is convoluted and intriguing, then the Bhagavad Gita is motivating and uplifting.

In the Gita, Krishna consoles a despondent Arjuna by pointing out the impermanence of the universe. It is the law of the universe that anything created must eventually perish. Krishna comforts Arjuna saying that death happens only to the perishable body. Although death is unstoppable, the living core of each human is untouched. Just as we change clothes, the soul moves into a new body. It is wrong to identify ourselves with our perishable body. The souls of all those gathered on the battlefield are immortal, so there's no need to be sorrowful. The greatest honor in life is to die fighting for your dharma.

Krishna boosts up Arjuna's flagging morale by pointing out that good people, by their very nature, think about the consequences and are unable to act. But control of the world should not be handed over to evil men by those who are too weak-willed to stand up against them. When all peaceful options are exhausted, men of good conscience should get up and fight. But war can be cruel and victory will not be delivered on a silver platter. Krishna urges Arjuna to detach himself from desired outcomes and concentrate on his dharma, for the dharma of a Kshatriya prince is to protect his country regardless of the personal costs. To illustrate the notion of detachment, Krishna expounds the concept of *sthitaprajna* or "the one with steady wisdom." He is one who performs his duties without being concerned about the consequences because he is not attached to the fruits of the action. For a *sthitaprajna*, "a clod, a stone, and a nugget of gold are the same." He has no selfish goals to achieve through his actions, and takes no pride in what he accomplishes. Just as his mind is free from desire in the midst of pleasures, his mind is untroubled in the midst of sorrow.

But why are some people ready to pick up a fight when others are extremely reluctant to do so? The Gita explains the discrepancy through the notion of *guna*s. According to the Gita, the distribution of *guna*s in a person defines their mental makeup, the distribution being determined by the actions of past life. Although the soul is eternal, the *guna*s attach themselves to the soul and influence its behavior. The Gita further explains that the *guna*s come in three varieties: *sattva*, *rajas*, and *tamas*. Everyone has these three *guna*s, but their combinations and concentrations are never the same in two people. And they keep changing. The *guna*s exist even in your food and therefore can influence your behavior. According to the Gita, a preponderance of *sattva guna* leads to virtuous actions that are free from attachment. A dominance of *rajas*, however, leads to selfish acts. The abundance of *tamas* leads to actions that are delusional—which do not consider the impact on others. The Gita states that even though the *guna*s characterize our nature, there is enough freewill in each of us to choose a path and change course.

As the words of wisdom began to sink in, Arjuna realizes that Krishna is no ordinary person. He implores Krishna to reveal his true identity. It is then that Krishna reveals his Vishvarupa or cosmic form. With the radiance of a thousand suns blazing forth, the vision was both beautiful and frightening. With a wide gaping mouth, the sight of Vishnu draped in heavenly garments with countless limbs and eyes overwhelmed Arjuna so much that the greatest archer of the world trembled in fear and begged his cousin to forgive him if he had ever treated him disrespectfully. Krishna then reverts to a more bearable human form much to the relief of Arjuna. In this Vishvarupa form, Krishna was teaching Arjuna the individual soul's identity with the universal soul, or *Brahman*. The goal of human life is the union of individual soul with the *Brahman*—which would allow the soul to escape from the countless cycles of death and rebirth. In the Gita, Krishna presents a shortcut to Arjuna when he declares, "Abandon all sorts of dharma and take refuge in me alone, and I shall release you from all evils."

In the preceding paragraphs, we have discussed some of the teachings of the Gita, albeit in brief. The Gita presents even more options to Arjuna, for it is believed the text has an answer to every problem faced by humankind. Yet the beauty of Gita is that it never commands you to choose a particular course of action, recognizing the diversity in our beliefs. As one of the world's greatest literary and spiritual works, the Gita can speak to just about anyone whether Christian, Muslim, Buddhist, Shinto, Jain, Zen, or Shaman. When Robert Oppenheimer, the father of the atom bomb, witnessed the massive explosion of a nuclear weapon, the American physicist claimed two verses from the Gita came to his mind:

If a thousand suns were to blaze forth together in the sky, they would not match the splendor of that great form.

—BHAGAVAD GITA 11:12

I am time, the destroyer of all; I have come to consume the world.

—BHAGAVAD GITA 11:32

No other Indian text has commanded more attention from foreigners than the Gita. In the 19th century, Ralph Waldo Emerson, a Unitarian minister who lectured at Harvard University on theology, was drawn toward the wisdom of the Gita. As he perused translations of the text, Emerson was astonished that he could not find a single line starting with *Thou shall not*. Fascinated, Emerson introduced other Americans to Hinduism including his protégé Henry David Thoreau, who famously wrote: "In the morning I bathe my intellect in the stupendous and cosmogonic philosophy of the Bhagavad Gita, in comparison with which our modern world and its literature seems puny and trivial."

KRISHNA AND THE LATER AVATARS OF VISHNU

The Gita is an honest book. It does not shrink from the realities of life like many other holy texts. The astrological position of the stars offers little comfort when your house is on fire. There is no ethical sentimentalism in the Gita such as pretending to look upon nature as always beautiful and refusing to accept its grim reality. Its philosophy is not for the weak who is afraid to face life; rather, it is for the heroic one, who is ready to face the challenges in life. The essence of Gita, according to the 19th century mystic Ramakrishna Paramahamsa, can be described by reversing the syllables of Gita—*tyagi*—which in many Indian languages, means "renunciate."[71] Indeed, for Mahatma Gandhi, a well-known exponent of the Gita, renunciation was the key message of the Gita. But, for Gandhi, renunciation did not equate with abandoning the world and retiring to the forest. Rather, it meant detachment from the fruits of the action. According to Gandhi, the spirit of renunciation should rule all activities of life.

You will be surprised to learn that the Bhagavad Gita, as we know it, is not the exact word-by-word conversation between Krishna and Arjuna. The version rendered to us is a filtered and varnished first-hand description of events by Sanjaya, the royal charioteer of Dhritarashtra. At the start of the Kurukshetra War, the blind king asked his charioteer to tell him what's happening in the battlefield. Upon the king's request, Sanjaya narrated the events in court—without being present on the battlefield—using his divine vision that allowed him to see the events unfold from afar. Over the years, numerous commentaries have been written about the Gita with widely varying viewpoints. Because it is rich and varied, the Gita has been interpreted, misinterpreted, and re-interpreted endlessly at many levels. There were some criticisms too including the contention that Gita condones war.

Gandhi was also greatly influenced by the Gita, which he described as his spiritual dictionary. An agnostic in his youth, he became a full-fledged believer after acquainting himself with its teachings. Gandhi did not believe that Gita taught violence. The fight between the Pandavas and

---

[71] Another word for religious ascetic.

Kauravas, according to him, was an allegory and not the description of an actual fight. It refers to a duel that rages in our minds and hearts each day. And Krishna appears in his chariot as the inner voice that counsels and guides us through our turbulent times. However, not everyone subscribes to Gandhi's view of the Gita. Orthodox Hindus contend that although Gita does not rubber stamp violence, sometimes violence, such as one used during self-defense, is a necessary duty and sanctioned by the Gita. Krishna says in the Gita, "What sin is there, O Brother, in killing those who have sworn to kill us." These critics accuse Gandhi of distorting the meaning of Gita by stating that non-violence was the basic principle of Gita.

Whether Gita condones violence or not is debatable, but one thing is clear. It is tough on dharma. You can try to find as many apologies for shirking your responsibility, but none will stick, for the Gita sees through them crystal clear. It is said that Gita guards its wisdom jealously. One reading of the book—however detailed—will only impart a little of its vast wisdom. You will need to keep revisiting the teachings on a regular basis to appreciate the profound wisdom of the Gita.

> *When doubts haunt me, when disappointments stare me in the face, and when I see not one ray of light on the horizon, I turn to the Bhagavad Gita, and find a verse to comfort me; and I immediately begin to smile in the midst of overwhelming sorrow. My life has been full of tragedies and if they have not left any visible and indelible effect on me, I owe it to the teachings of the Bhagavad Gita.*
>
> —MAHATMA GANDHI, 1869–1948

44

Why India Is Known as Bharat

Have you ever wondered why India is called Bharat? Postage stamps of India include the word "Bharat" in Hindi next to "India." Ancient texts like the Puranas and Mahabharata refer to the subcontinent as Bharatavarsha—not India. The Vishnu Purana says the country that lies north of the ocean and south of the snowy mountains is called Bharata and in there dwells the descendants of Bharata. The Constitution of India says "India, that is Bharat, shall be a union of states . . . ." And the word Bharata is embedded in the name of the epic Mahabharata. Let's investigate the origins of Bharata to find out why Indians are going above and beyond to be associated with him?

In Hindu mythology, there are five illustrious Bharatas. The first Bharata is the step brother of Rama from the epic Ramayana. The land he ruled was also called Bharata—but he's not the king in question. The second Bharata is the son of Rishabha, the founder of Jainism. According to the Bhagavata Purana, Rishabha had a hundred sons that looked like him but only Bharata among them had superior qualities and therefore the land was named after him. The third one is described in the Mahabharata, where he is the son of King Dushyanta and Shakuntala and an early ancestor to both the Pandavas and Kauravas. The fourth one is sage Bharata, the author of Natyashastra, a comprehensive treatise on performing arts.[72] The fifth Bharata is another name for the Vedic god Agni or sometimes a name for his sons collectively. Despite the multiple origins of the name, most Hindus associate Bharata of the Mahabharata as the source of India's alternative name though occasionally Rishabha's son Bharata gets mentioned. Dushyanta's son also has the most mythological significance compared to the other Bharatas. We now describe the birth of Bharata, which is one of the celebrated stories in Hindu mythology and centered on Bharata's mother Shakuntala.[73] And by the way, Bharat is the modern, shortened version of Bharata.

Our story goes back to a time when the ascetics were undertaking penance, and the power gained through asceticism was threatening the dominion of gods. This became a concern for Indra, the lord of the heaven.

---

[72] Natyashastra is described in book 5 of this series.
[73] The story of Shakuntala was immortalized by the great Indian poet Kalidasa in his work *Abhijyanashakuntalam*. The poet introduced additional characters and events outside the theme of the original story in the Mahabharata.

One such ascetic was the sage Vishwamitra, the author of Gayatri Mantra. He was performing such extreme austerities that Indra dispatched a voluptuous apsara called Menaka to seduce the sage and disrupt his meditation. Menaka sang and danced but the sage kept temptation at bay. Meanwhile, the wind god Vayu gently disrobed the apsara and the nudity disrupted the sage's concentration. Vishwamitra steadily succumbed to the seductress and became intertwined in *maithuna* with her.

The passionate encounter resulted in the birth of a daughter. With her mission accomplished, Menaka put on her clothes and went back to heaven, but Vishwamitra suffered from guilt. He was dismayed that he had lost the virtue gained through many years of penance. The sage went back to asceticism, leaving the child abandoned on the banks of a river. Fortunately, the infant was found by another sage, Kanva. The sage took her to his hermitage and raised her as his own child. Since the child was nestled under the wings of Shakun birds, Kanva named her "Shakuntala" or the "one protected by birds."

Shakuntala grew up into a strikingly beautiful woman in a carefree and cheerful environment. One day, King Dushyanta came on a hunting expedition to the forest. Chasing a fawn, he became separated from the main party and stumbled on a picturesque hermitage where he saw Shakuntala nursing the deer. The king was stunned by her beauty and fell in love at first sight. He apologized for harming the deer and sought her hand in marriage. Although Shakuntala was impressed with the suitor, she hesitated because Kanva was away on a pilgrimage. Realizing this, Dushyanta suggested they perform a Gandharva wedding, one which involves only mutual consent with nature as witness. Not able to refuse the handsome king, Shakuntala consented. Dushyanta stayed overnight at the hermitage and left for his capital the next day. Before leaving, the king gave her a signet ring as a token of the marriage, and promised that he would return shortly to take her back to his kingdom.

After Dushyanta's departure, Shakuntala could neither sleep nor eat. She spent the rest of the days dreaming about her husband. About this time, sage Durvasa paid a visit to the hermitage. Shakuntala was lost in her thoughts and paid scant attention to the sage. The temperamental sage was offended and cursed Shakuntala that the person she was dreaming of would forget her. But Shakuntala's friends came to her defense and explained to him the reason for her distraction. On hearing this, the sage tempered the curse by saying that the person would be able to regain his memory when she produces a personal token.

Months passed and Shakuntala began to show noticeable signs of pregnancy. She wondered why Dushyanta did not return and confided in her foster father what had transpired during his absence. The sage immediately decided to send her to her husband. On her way, Shakuntala and her entourage had to cross a river in a canoe. During the journey, she playfully ran her fingers through the clear waters. She did not realize that the ring slipped off from her finger, and a fish in the river swallowed the ring.

At the palace, Shakuntala was deeply hurt when her husband could not recognize her. She tried to remind him of their meeting, their marriage, and their stay together at the hermitage. But Dushyanta, under the spell of the curse, remembered nothing. Finally, Shakuntala raised her hand to show him the signet ring. Only then did she realize that the ring had been lost.

A dejected Shakuntala returned to the forest, where, in due course, she gave birth to a baby boy. She named him Bharata. Raised in the forest, the boy had wild animals as friends and grew up to be strong and fearless. Meanwhile, at the capital, a fisherman was surprised to find a ring in the belly of a fish. Recognizing the royal seal, the fisherman took the ring to the palace and gave it to the king. Upon seeing the ring, Dushyanta remembered Shakuntala and fond memories of his lovely bride came rushing back. The king immediately set out to Kanva's hermitage to meet Shakuntala.

But Shakuntala was no longer living in the hermitage. The king learned that she had moved to a remote area in the forest. He continued his search deeper in the forest and came across a brave boy confronting a lion. The boy had pried open the mouth of a lion and was counting its teeth. Amazed by his boldness, the king greeted the boy and enquired about his whereabouts. The boy replied that he was Bharata, the son of King Dushyanta. Tears of joy rolled over his father's face as the son took him to Shakuntala. Dushyanta explained to her how he was able to regain his memory after seeing the ring. Shakuntala forgave him and the family was reunited.

Bharata inherited the throne after Dushyanta and went on to become a legendary Indo–Aryan emperor and a key figure in both Hindu and Jain mythology. He conquered all of Greater India and unified them into a single entity, which was named after him—Bharatavarsha. According to the Mahabharata, Bharatavarsha spanned over the entire Indian subcontinent and included countries like Afghanistan, Tajikistan, Uzbekistan, Turkmenistan, Kyrgyzstan, Bactria, and Persia. Today, Bharatavarsha officially means the Republic of India. Such is Bharata's popularity that there is a movement to change the name of India to Bharatavarsha or simply BHARAT.

BUDDHA & THE LATER AVATARS

45

The Curious Avatar of Buddha

Hatred does not cease by hatred, but only by love; this is the eternal rule.

—BUDDHA

In many ways, the ninth avatar of Vishnu is controversial. First, there are two nominees. While Buddha is the ninth avatar in the northern tradition of Dashavataras, the South Indians have replaced him with Balarama, Krishna's older brother. Second, the candidates themselves are controversial. Although Buddha was borrowed from Buddhism and honored as an avatar of Vishnu, not all Hindu texts refer to him in a favoring light. Likewise, Balarama is described in texts as an avatar of Ananda Shesha, the giant cobra of Vishnu—and not as Vishnu himself. In this chapter, we'll look into the controversy with the choice of Buddha. Balarama will be the subject of another chapter. The life of Siddhartha Gautama, the historical Buddha as we call him these days, and the topic

KRISHNA AND THE LATER AVATARS OF VISHNU

of Buddhism were covered in an earlier book,[74] so no attempt will be made to revisit the same.

You will be surprised to learn that the Buddha avatar was not an attempt to espouse the teachings of Buddha into Hinduism. The principles of Buddhism were, however, incorporated into the religion at a later stage. In early Puranic texts, Buddha is not portrayed as the heroic upholder of dharma like other Vishnu avatars. Rather, he appears as the devil's advocate to misguide demons from the path of dharma and to weaken their spiritual powers. The Vishnu Purana describes the demons once became so powerful because of their steadfast commitment to Vedic worship and asceticism that they defeated the gods and took control of the heavens. In despair, the gods approached Vishnu, who asked them to have patience and promised them that the situation would not last long. "A magic deluder will arrive amongst you, and deceive the demons from the path of the Vedas."

And indeed a bald magic deluder arrived carrying a peacock-feather fan. He approached the demons, who were practicing asceticism on the banks of river Narmada. He discouraged them from the path of asceticism, and taught them contradictory tenets about dharma. About this time, animal sacrifice was a hallowed Vedic ritual. But the magic deluder told the demons that sacrifice of animals was evil. "If the animal slaughtered in the sacrifice is assured of reaching heaven, why does the sacrificer not kill his own father?" The demons imbibed his doctrines and abandoned the Vedas. But their spiritual strength became diminished by their actions. In the next battle, the gods slaughtered the demons, regaining control of the heaven.

Although no one knows the exact dates, the Vishnu Purana, from where we get the above story, is believed to have been written anywhere between 100 BCE and 100 CE. At this time, Buddhism was popular in India, particularly due to encouragement of King Ashoka. While

---

[74] See the book *Many Many Many Gods of Hinduism* by the same author (Chapters 9, 46, and 47).

Hinduism was a religion of complex rituals that appealed to the elite, Buddhism spoke directly to the people. The introduction of the Buddha as a deceptive avatar perhaps reflects the tension between Hinduism and Buddhism during that time, and may have been intended to keep Hindus away from Buddhism. The various Puranic accounts of the Buddha avatar, such as the Bhagavata Purana and the Agni Purana, all identify Buddhists with demons.

Not all Hindu texts, however, present Buddha in a negative light. Sacred works that appear at a later period actually praise the Buddha avatar, a fact first observed by the English philologist William Jones in 1790 CE. While Buddha is described as a magic deluder in the Bhagavata Purana, Jayadeva, in his famous work Gita Govinda of the 12th century CE, says that Vishnu took the avatar of Buddha out of compassion for animals and to put an end to animal sacrifice. The positive theme of Buddha avatar is also present in later texts like the Varaha Purana and the Matsya Purana. The about-face of Hinduism was remarkable for it once described Buddhism as *nastika*, meaning the one that rejects the authority of Vedas and hence non-theistic.

It appears that from fifth century to the 12th century CE, the Buddha avatar transformed from a negative to a positive figure. It is a coincidence that, during this period, Buddhism steadily declined in India, the land where it was originally founded. Many factors have been attributed to the decline of Buddhism—the lack of appeal of the original Theravada sect, the modification of Hindu beliefs to appeal to the common man, the revival of Hinduism under Adi Shankara, and, of course, the absorption of the founder of Buddhism into the Hindu pantheon of gods. It is likely that when Hindus realized Buddhism was not a threat to their own beliefs, they warmed up to Buddhism with open arms. But the revival was short-lived with the arrival of Islam by the late 12th century. With the destruction of monasteries and stupas by the Muslim invaders, Buddhism almost disappeared from India by the end of the 12th century.

But Buddhists were not wildly cheering the acceptance of their spiritual leader into the Hindu pantheon, whether in a positive or negative light. They considered this as an attempt by shrewd Hindu poets to make Buddhism a branch of Hinduism, although they grudgingly accept that the strategy worked well in India. B.R. Ambedkar, a profound scholar and the architect of the Indian Constitution, vehemently denied that Buddha was an incarnation of Vishnu. One of the many vows he prescribed to the Dalit Buddhist movement included, "I do not and shall not believe that Lord Buddha was the incarnation of Vishnu. I believe this to be sheer madness and false propaganda."

Among Hindus, Buddha as an avatar promoting ahimsa remains a popular belief among a number of Vaishnava sects, including the Hare Krishnas. A number of famous figures in modern Hinduism, including Mahatma Gandhi, have been inspired by the teachings of Buddha. Before we leave this topic, it must be mentioned that the Buddha avatar of Hinduism bears little resemblance to the Buddha, revered as the Enlightened One in the Buddhist religion. In fact, Puranic texts attribute different parentage to Buddha and seem to talk about different Buddhas. This has led to the notion of two Buddhas: Adi Buddha and historical Buddha. Some scholars believe Adi Buddha, born around 1800s BCE, was an avatar of Vishnu, who established the philosophy of ahimsa and preached against animal sacrifice. The historical Buddha, or Siddhartha Gautama as we know him, was born in 563 BCE and preached that desire is the root of all suffering, and nirvana is the end goal. According to them, the Buddha of the Puranas has no bearing to the founder of Buddhism. The merging of the two Buddhas was partly due to Adi Shankara, who didn't seem to recognize the difference, and partly due to sloppy European scholars who simply were not careful enough to discern the difference.

You will not be punished for your anger, you will be punished by your anger.

—BUDDHA

46

Ajanta Caves - Louvre of Ancient India

All art, from the paintings on the walls of cave dwellers to art created today, is autobiographical because it comes from the secret place in the soul where imagination resides.

—GLORIA VANDERBILT, 1924–2019

1819, Maharashtra, India. Britain was ruling India and tiger hunting was a popular sport. A British hunting party, close on the heels of a tiger, loses track of the animal at a deep ravine in the thick jungles of Aurangabad. Soon thereafter, they rediscover the trail next to a cliff of rocks. As they follow the footprints of the tiger, an abandoned cave with a prominent arch surrounded by thorny creepers catches their leader's attention. Holding a torch of burning grass, he beckons his group of officers from the Madras Presidency to follow him. Inside the grotto they are welcomed by a long hall flanked on either side by 39 octagonal pillars. As the party advances to the far end of the hall and stops at the circular dome of a stupa,[75] they realize that they are surrounded by ancient paintings depicted on the walls and ceilings. In the flickering flame, the leader pulls out his hunting knife, and inscribes the words "John Smith, 28th cavalry, 28 April 1819" over the body of a bodhisattva without realizing he had vandalized one of the oldest murals of the ancient world.

Ajanta Caves located near Aurangabad, Maharashtra, India

But the discovery of a man-made cave at Ajanta is hardly surprising in a country with a rich heritage of rock-cut caves. The geology of the Deccan plateau, which covers central and southern India, lends itself to a large number of cliff faces and domes perfectly suitable for rock-cut architecture. With over 1500 such caves and new ones being discovered on a regular basis, India is the undisputed leader in rock-cut caves. The most spectacular among them is the Kailash temple at Ellora, only 100 km from Ajanta.[76] Like Ajanta, the Ellora caves are home to some of

---

[75] Stupa is a hemispherical mound containing Buddhist relics, such as the ashes of Buddhist monks.

[76] The Ellora caves are described in detail in book 5 of this series.

the most valued ancient murals and, along with Bagh Caves (Madhya Pradesh), Badami Caves (Karnataka), and Sittanavasal (Tamil Nadu), form the oldest examples of Indian painting. Even though these sites are famous for their exotic settings and impressive architectures, the exceptional paintings of Ajanta set it apart. A major spot for tourism, Ajanta is now visited by over 5000 people every day.[77]

Ajanta has 30 caves of which five are chaityas[78] and the rest are viharas.[79] The cave Smith first entered was later named Cave 10 and is located at the center of the cliff. While the façade and the interior are decorated with sculptures, the walls inside contain the frescoes. The caves appear to have been carved out not in a single period, but over many centuries and have been dated between the second century BCE and seventh century CE. The ravages of climate and time have claimed the delicacy of tone and the luster of colors (see picture) of the paintings, yet it is a miracle that these murals have lasted so long. They probably survived because these man-made caves were only occupied briefly. Inscriptions at the site indicate that the paintings had the patronage of Vakataka dynasty, which ruled the area during the late fifth century CE. The Vakatakas probably lost control of the area since there are a number of unfinished caves. Thereafter the caves were abandoned and their entrances became obscured by vegetation, which left the interiors virtually sealed off from the outside world until Smith walked into one of the caves.

The ancient murals of India generally depict the religious themes of Buddhism, Jainism, or Hinduism—all of which have their origins in the Indian subcontinent. But at Ajanta, the murals are entirely dedicated to Buddhism, and the artists have turned the stone walls into picture books of Buddha's life and teachings. The Jataka tales, which describe the righteous lives of Buddha in his previous incarnations and serve as models for practicing Buddhists, form the subject matter of most of the frescoes.

---
[77] Pre-COVID-19 figures.
[78] Chaitya, sometimes referred to as chaitya griha, is a shrine or prayer hall with a stupa at one end.
[79] Vihara is a Buddhist monastery.

The high artistic standards of these pictures have been achieved through simple techniques, such as the judicious blending of a small number of colors, precise draftsmanship, and balanced composition by spreading figures and forms evenly. The art at Ajanta is undoubtedly the mastery of line. Emotional expressions are achieved by simple modulating the line in different ways. The modeling, relief, vigor, and other features of pictorial art, which are crucial to providing that distinctive character to the painting, are achieved by simple outline and variations of line.

Chaitya griha in Cave 29, Ajanta Caves

If you are a student of art, you will notice that these ancient paintings have incorporated concepts like perspective[80] and color theory,[81] which were thought to be absent in Indian paintings until contact with the West. The clever use of foreshortening and the vanishing point can be seen in

---

[80] Perspective is the technique of creating an illusion of depth and space (three-dimensional) on a flat (two-dimensional) surface.
[81] Color theory refers to the use of judicious use of colors to create contrast and harmony in pictures.

some of the paintings at Ajanta. Although only a handful of colors were used by the Ajanta artists, the use of warms (reds, yellows, browns) and cools (blues, greens) to establish vibrancy and harmony in the frescoes are conspicuous. The greatest strength of these paintings, however, is their simplicity and informality. They are not rigidly bound by the manuals of art making and can be appreciated by both the art historian and the layperson. According to Jawaharlal Nehru, former prime minister of India, "History becomes human and living and not merely a record of some distant age ... the appeal of Ajanta is not merely to the artist or the expert, but to every sensitive human being."

Since the discovery of Ajanta, many hunting groups, archaeologists, scholars, and throngs of tourists from all over the world have made a beaten path to the caves to explore these wonders of the ancient world. Their unsupervised appreciation of the ancient art led to permanent damage to the murals in caves 9 and 10. In the 1920s, the Nizam of Hyderabad sent two of his Italian conservationists to Ajanta, but their efforts at restoration only resulted in defacing the paintings further. By the late 1990s, the Archaeological Survey of India undertook a painstaking effort at restoration using infra-red and micro-emulsion technology. As a result, the once damaged murals have been restored and are on open display. Meanwhile, the sport of tiger hunting, widely cited as the main reason for the significant reduction in tiger population,[82] has been banned in India thereby decreasing the chances of further accidental discoveries of rock-cut caves by British officers.

The Ajanta caves allow a glimpse of not just the artistic traditions of ancient India, but the great handwork of the stone masons, who with hammer and chisels created the incredible cave chaityas and viharas. However, the brilliance of the Ajanta's sculpture is overshadowed not only by its exceptional paintings but by the grandeur of the sculptural art at nearby Ellora. Because of the proximity of these two UNESCO

---

[82] From 100,000 at the turn of the 20th century, the tiger population has dwindled to 2,226 in 2014. India is home to 70 percent of the world's tigers.

World Heritage Sites, both Ajanta and Ellora are often combined into a single trip, and have become the most popular tourist destinations of Aurangabad, a district named after the Mughal emperor Aurangzeb, who ironically banished all forms of art during his reign. Although the paintings[83] are engulfed in darkness, they glow with a brilliant intensity even after more than a thousand years. The multi-colored murals of Ajanta are recognized not only as the icon of Indian art but as some of the greatest art produced by humankind.

> *Worship is invoking the divinity within. Meditation is awareness of divinity within. Enlightenment is realization of divinity within. Nirvana is being the divinity.*
>
> —RASHMIT KALRA

✦ ✦ ✦

---

[83] Tourists are often advised to bring torches on their visit to Ajanta.

47

Padmapani - The Mona Lisa of India

Among the murals of Ajanta, one of the finest masterpieces is a painting that depicts a man wearing a jeweled crown and holding a lotus—the universal symbol of Buddhism—in one hand with his body slightly bent in the famous *tribhanga*[84] pose. Surrounded by a throng of devotees, including both princesses and commoners, he can be seen with eyes cast downwards in a compassionate tone with the face reflecting gentle sorrow. Radiating divine compassion, this glowing figure is the image of bodhisattva Padmapani, the most revered bodhisattva in the Buddhist pantheon. According to Rene Grousset, a French historian, the picture is "worthy of a place in the art of the world by the side of the sublimest incarnations of the Sistine Chapel, or such drawings as that of Christ for the Last Supper in which Leonardo da Vinci has expressed the most intense emotions of the soul."

---

[84] *Tribhanga* is a tri-bent standing pose involving three bends of the body—at the neck, waist, and knee—and appearing like a gently shaped "S." This position is used in traditional Indian arts including painting, sculpture, and dance and is often considered one of the most graceful and sensual position. Krishna is often depicted in this posture.

Bodhisattva Padmapani, Cave 1, Ajanta Caves (slightly discolored and damaged)

In Buddhism, a bodhisattva is an enlightened person who, out of compassion, forgoes nirvana in order to save other human beings from the endless cycle of birth and rebirth. Having practiced the virtues of Buddhism over many lifetimes, a bodhisattva has come for the final transmigration of his soul. There are hundreds of bodhisattvas—the Buddha himself was a bodhisattva—but three of them namely Manjusri, Vajrapani, and Padmapani are extensively represented in Buddhist iconography as protective deities surrounding Buddha. Each of the bodhisattvas symbolizes one of the Buddha's virtues with Manjusri manifesting his wisdom, Vajrapani his power, and Padmapani his compassion.

In the painting, the highly refined character and graceful charm are discernible in the features of Padmapani, who is the central figure of the mural. He is surrounded by his devotees, who are depicted in somber colors. The juxtaposition of contradictory complexions is suggestive of the idea that color distinctions are just external and do not enrich the inner harmony of the spirit. The meditative expression in the eyes alludes to his indifference toward the material world and compassion for those who are heir to the miseries and sorrows of this imperfect life. In the history of Indian painting, this feeling of spiritual equanimity has never been achieved—the closest in terms of brilliance of expression is the sculpted figure of the Sarnath Buddha. It is this representation of the inner spiritual experience that makes this mural one of the masterpieces of the Indian art.

Padmapani, which means the "bearer of lotus" in Sanskrit, is also known by the popular name of Avalokitesvara, who is famed for his generosity. In fact many Buddhists regard Dalai Lama as the manifestation of Avalokitesvara. At Ajanta, Padmapani is accompanied by an equally impressive mural of Vajrapani, the "bearer of thunderbolt." While Padmapani portrays peace, Vajrapani[85] represents the power of the spirit. These murals, placed on either side of the giant statue of the Buddha in a teaching posture, are central in Cave 1, which was built in the fifth

---

[85] Vajrapani is often associated with *vajra*, or lightning bolt. Since the *vajra* is missing in this picture, some scholars do not consider the figure to be a representation of Vajrapani.

century CE and was one of the last caves to be excavated. As one of the outstanding viharas, this cave is home to quality sculptures and narrative murals known for their fine perspective and elaborate detail. Yet, the most famous and iconic of Ajanta artworks is the rendition of bodhisattva Padmapani. According to the famous Italian painter Lorenzo Cecconi, "This painting [Padmapani] in its grand outlines recalls to memory the figures of Michelangelo in the Sistine Chapel; while the clearness of the color of the flesh, so true to nature, and the transparency of the shadows are like those of Correggio. The design and expression of the face are exceptionally surprising, in the breadth of the technique; the interpretation of the shape of the hand, made to realistic perfection, permits of a comparison with the two great artists of the Italian Renaissance."

> *English decorative art in our day has borrowed largely from Indian forms and patterns. The exquisite scrolls on the rock temples at Karli and Ajanta, the delicate marble traces and flat wood-carving of Western India, the harmonious blending of forms and colors in the fabrics of Kashmir, have contributed to the restoration of tastes in England. Indian art-work, when faithful to native designs, still obtains the highest honors at the international exhibitions of Europe.*
>
> —SIR WILLIAM WILSON HUNTER, 1840–1900

❖ ❖ ❖

48

Avatar #9 - The Balarama Avatar

Question: What's common across the eight Vasus, twelve Adityas, seven sages, and the Dashavataras (ten avatars)? If you think they are part and parcel of Indian mythology, you are on the money. Indeed they are, but there's another thing common amongst them. Inconsistency. That's right. The list of eight Vasus or twelve Adityas or seven sages is not constant and keeps varying in the Hindu texts. The same is true for Dashavataras. While the Hare Krishnas and South Indians include Balarama in the list of Dashavataras, others embrace Buddha. Jayadeva, the famous author of Gita Govinda, included both Buddha and Balarama in his list of the Dashavataras, but excluded Krishna. According to him, the members of the Dashavataras were all incarnations of Krishna, not Vishnu.

In mythology, Balarama was the seventh child born of Devaki and Vasudeva when Mathura was under the tyranny of King Kamsa. The news of Kamsa's atrocities reached heaven, and Vishnu decided to take action and restore the balance between good and evil. Devaki gave birth to six children, but they were killed at birth by the king because of a prophecy that her eighth child would destroy him. It is believed that Vishnu

KRISHNA AND THE LATER AVATARS OF VISHNU

plucked a black hair from his body and a white hair from his serpent Ananda Shesha and placed them on Devaki's womb.[86] The white hair became Devaki's seventh child, Balarama, and the black hair her eight son, Krishna. Just before Balarama's birth, the divine powers of Vishnu transferred the embryo from the womb of Devaki to that of Rohini, another wife of Vasudeva, and Kamsa was led to believe the seventh pregnancy ended in miscarriage.

As a child, Balarama was extraordinarily strong. Originally named Rama, he was renamed "Balarama"[87] meaning "strong Rama" due to his strength. And true to his name, he demonstrated his strength in the use of the plow and mace. For that reason, Balarama is often depicted in pictures holding his two weapons—the plow and the mace. Because of the plow, Balarama is sometimes linked to agriculture, just as Krishna is associated with livestock. Although separated at birth, both Balarama and Krishna were united during childhood and they grew up together. Balarama was fair complexioned

Balarama, the ninth avatar, in the South Indian tradition

---

[86] Some texts say both white and black hairs were plucked from Vishnu and not Ananda Shesha. Others state Balarama to be a partial incarnation of Vishnu.

[87] The word "Bala" is a homograph and pronounced differently according to its many meanings. When "Bala" is pronounced "Bela," it means "strength" as in the name of Balarama (strong Rama). When "Bala," is pronounced "Baala," it means "young" as in the name Balakrishna (young Krishna).

AVATAR #9 - THE BALARAMA AVATAR

while his younger brother Krishna was dark. And like their skin colors, their personalities were polar opposites. Krishna was the shrewd operator, but Balarama, the straight shooter. If Krishna had many wives, Balarama had just one. If Krishna was calm and composed, then Balarama had a short fuse. Some Hindus believe Ananda Shesha accompanies Vishnu during his incarnations on earth. They believe Balarama to be the incarnation of the serpent,[88] not Vishnu himself.

Balarama had a fondness for wine in his youth, and he was often found indulging in the beverage while dallying with the *gopi*s. Once when Balarama and the *gopi*s were frolicking on the banks of river Yamuna, they saw wine oozing out from the hollow of a Kadamba tree. It was a special evening at Vraj, and Varuna had dispatched his wife Varuni, the goddess of wine, to lighten the mood with intoxicants. With wine flowing in abundance, Balarama drank lustily and became inebriated in no time. After feeling the heat of the wine, he thought of having a cool refreshing bath. The rippling waters of Yamuna were flowing far away, but a drunken Balarama was in no state to walk to the river. Instead, he commanded goddess Yamuna to move closer to him, but she shrugged off the drunkard's words and gently flowed at a distance. When his repeated requests were ignored, Balarama became enraged and yanked Yamuna toward him using his plow. Realizing the strength of Balarama, Yamuna at once surrendered and flooded the forest with her cool waters.

Balarama married Revati, the lovely daughter of a king. It is said that Revati was so beautiful that her father could not find anyone worthy of her on earth. So the king made an appointment with Brahma to discuss the prospect of securing a suitable groom for his daughter. When the father and daughter reached Brahma's abode, they found Brahma intently watching a musical concert performed by the Gandharvas. After a lengthy wait, they were welcomed by Brahma, who expounded the glories of Vishnu to them. He directed the father to proceed to Dvaraka, where

---

[88] Likewise, Lakshmana, the brother or Rama in the epic Ramayana, is sometimes considered an incarnation of Shesha.

an avatar of Vishnu was available for matrimony. This was Balarama, the incarnate of Vishnu. The father and daughter returned to earth, but to their disbelief they found the land where they lived before resembled the land of Lilliputians. People seemed to have shrunk in size when they were touring heaven. Little did they realize that while they were waiting for Brahma, several *yuga*s had passed on earth, for a day of Brahma is equivalent to a *kalpa* or 4.32 billion human years. In Hindu beliefs, humans diminish in size in progressive eras.

A byproduct of an earlier era, Revati was much larger than her counterparts on earth. Several inches taller, Revati was to Balarama what Nicole Kidman was to Tom Cruise. But Balarama found a solution to the problem. Using his plow, he whittled persistently at Revati until she was reduced to the size of the women of that era.[89] Soon they were married. Balarama seemed to have found his perfect pair in Revati, for she fulfilled her conjugal obligations by begetting him two sons. Besides cooking sumptuous meals, she also became his booze buddy and together they partnered in several drunken bouts. In later years, Balarama weaned himself off his alcohol problem. He was the one who issued the prohibition of alcohol within the city of Dvaraka when the Yadavas fought against themselves over an argument.

The controversial role of Balarama stems from his association with his pupil, Duryodhana, the leader of the Kauravas. Balarama was the guru of both Duryodhana and Bhima and trained them in mace fighting. However, on multiple occasions, Balarama seemed to be favoring Duryodhana instead of Bhima or Arjuna, although, as an avatar of Ananda Shesha, he was expected to be more supportive of the Pandava brothers than the evil Kauravas.

When Draupadi became the wife of the Pandavas, the brothers had an agreement that she spend a year with each husband, and none of the others would enter her private chambers during that time. Once Arjuna broke the pact, and to atone for his breach of contract, he went on a pilgrimage.

---

[89] A similar act can be found in the Vedic age where Vishwakarma, the architect of gods, placed Surya in a lathe and shaved away his brightness because Surya's wife could not bear his brightness.

AVATAR #9 - THE BALARAMA AVATAR

After visiting many sacred sites, an exhausted Arjuna arrived at Dvaraka where he was greeted by his cousin Krishna, who appointed his half-sister Subhadra to look after him. Subhadra fell in love with an already married Arjuna even though Balarama had arranged her marriage to his favorite pupil Duryodhana. Krishna could not find a way out, so he advised Arjuna to elope with Subhadra. When Balarama heard about the elopement, he became enraged and went to attack Arjuna. But Krishna intervened and dissuaded him from doing so. Abhimanyu was born out of this union between Arjuna and Subhadra. Alternate versions of this story exist in mythology. Another version says Arjuna loved Subhadra, but she did not reciprocate his affection and therefore he abducted her much to the vexation of Balarama.

Despite their close friendship, Duryodhana did not have the blind support of Balarama all the time. The Mahabharata describes an incident at the *swayamvara* of Duryodhana's daughter Lakshmana.[90] Samba, the difficult son of Krishna, not only attended the marriage without invitation but abducted the bride, who resisted his attempts. He was promptly apprehended by Duryodhana and sent to jail. Balarama pleaded for Samba's release, but Duryodhana refused, showing no respect for his guru. When Balarama threatened to drag the kingdom of Hastinapura into the sea with his plow, Duryodhana relented and released his nephew.

Balarama had another significant encounter with Bhima toward the end of the Kurukshetra War. Balarama was conflicted when war broke out between the Pandavas and Kauravas, and went on a pilgrimage on the advice of Krishna. He reappeared toward the end of the war, but by this time, the tide had turned in favor of the Pandavas. All the Kaurava brothers were dead except Duryodhana. The leader of the Kauravas, knowing his end was nearing, showed his true colors by going into hiding at the bottom of a lake. Eventually, Yudhishthira discovered his hiding place. Duryodhana refused to emerge from the lake saying that he wanted to retire and spend the rest of his life in meditation, and that Yudhishthira could have the kingdom to himself.

---

[90] This Lakshmana is unrelated to the Lakshmana of Ramayana.

Yudhishthira was not to be fooled this time. He knew Duryodhana would promise anything for his own survival. Bhima taunted Duryodhana and forced him to emerge from the lake. A tremendous battle with maces began between Bhima and Duryodhana. After a fierce struggle, Bhima hit Duryodhana below the belt smashing his thigh, the same thigh on which he had gestured Draupadi to sit, insulting her and the Pandavas. Bhima then danced around the fallen Duryodhana and kicked his head. Yudhishthira was quick to reprimand Bhima, for it was a blatant violation of the rules of chivalry. Watching from the sidelines, Balarama became infuriated at the foul play. He pointed out that Bhima broke the rules of combat not only by kicking Duryodhana but by striking him below the belt. In fact, Balarama became so disgusted with Bhima's behavior that he attacked him with a plow. But Krishna intervened and reminded Balarama that Duryodhana had cheated at the game of dice and Bhima had vowed to smash his thigh for insulting Draupadi. On hearing this, Balarama stormed out of the arena.

From the above, we can conclude that Balarama was more a stickler for ethics and etiquette than a staunch supporter of a particular member of the Kuru dynasty. No guru can stand when his best student uses unethical tactics in combat. For that reason, he can be seen supporting Duryodhana at times, and threatening him at other times. Thirty-six years after the Mahabharata War ended, the Yadavas became corrupt with alcohol abuse and internal squabbling. They fought among themselves until the entire clan was decimated. A despondent Balarama sat on the shores, lonely in meditation. A great white snake emerged from his mouth and arose up into the skies. Leaving the lifeless body behind, the snake carried the spirit of Balarama over the oceans and out of the physical world.

Although Balarama is recognized as one among the Dashavataras, his popularity never equaled that of Krishna.[91] He is the adoring, supportive, older brother of Krishna and constantly seen as attending to him, just as the serpent Shesha attends to Vishnu. Balarama is, however, held equal

---

[91] It can be said that no god in India is as popular as Krishna other than, perhaps, Ganesha.

to Krishna in the Gaudiya Vaishnava tradition, a lineage originating from Chaitanya Mahaprabhu. They believe Swami Nityananda, an associate of Chaitanya, to be an incarnation of Balarama. The Hare Krishnas, a modern-day offshoot of Gaudiya Vaishnavism, also consider Balarama to be an important deity. He is also the favorite god of the farmers of India because of his plow.

Balarama is worshiped in a number of temples including the Jagannath temple in Puri, Odisha, where his image is installed next to those of Krishna and Subhadra.

Strength does not come from physical capacity.
It comes from an indomitable will.

—MAHATMA GANDHI, 1869–1948

49

Avatar #10 - The Kalki Avatar

Vishnu's tenth incarnation—the Kalki avatar—is yet to manifest and reserved for the future. But are the conditions right for the coming of Vishnu's most powerful incarnation? Let's find out. Which among the following encapsulate the present world situation?

1. Falsehood and fake news have become an everyday expression and the common currency of social existence.
2. Marriage has lost its sacramental nature and sensuality has become the sole bond between man and wife.
3. Nations have become belligerent and strive to profit from their powers.
4. Personal responsibility has died in a culture where you blame everyone except yourself.
5. No belief in god or in an alternate shared set of morals that would hold the social fabric of society together.
6. All of the above.

If your choice was **6**, you are spot on. Although all these scenarios are the characteristics of Kali Yuga (our present *yuga*), we still have to wait hundreds of thousand years for its official arrival.

Kalki avatar, at Rani Ki Vav, Patan, Gujarat, India

It is prophesied that the Kalki avatar will arrive at the end of the Kali Yuga, the dark ages of Hinduism. Hindus believe we are about 5000 years into Kali Yuga, which started in 3102 BCE and extends for 432,000 years.

Riding a white horse with a flaming sword in hand, he will arrive at the very end of the Kali Yuga when virtue has deteriorated completely from earth, and then usher us into the new era of perfect dharma.

The prediction of the future has always been a favorite pursuit of religious faiths. The Hindu beliefs are rooted in the notion that noble values, or dharma, decay slowly with the passage of the *yuga*s, by which time is measured. There are four *yuga*s, each with its own span, as indicated below.

1	Satya/Krita Yuga	1,728,000 years (4 x Kali Yuga)
2	Treta Yuga	1,296,000 years (3 x Kali Yuga)
3	Dvapara Yuga	864,000 years (2 x Kali Yuga)
4	Kali Yuga	432,000 years
	Total	**4,320,000 years**

One complete cycle that encompasses the four *yuga*s spans 4.32 million years. Thus, a complete cycle starts with the longest Satya Yuga, followed by Treta, then Dvapara, and finally Kali. Hindus believe time moves in these cycles, eternally. Each age witnesses a decline in dharma or virtue from the previous age. If dharma is compared to a bull, then the dharma bull is able to stand on all four legs in the first age. By the Treta or second age, the animal wobbles on three. By the time of Dvapara or third age, the bull has lost two of its legs and it struggles to stand. Finally, in the last age, Kali Yuga, the bull can barely stand on one leg.

The farther we are from the inception, the worse off we are in the period, and the more powerful the incarnation. Thus, the Krishna avatar in the third age (the Dvapara Yuga) was more potent than the Rama avatar of the second age. The Hindus believe that morality will reach its nadir toward the end of the Kali Yuga, and would require the most potent incarnation for correction and restoration of order in the world. The Kalki avatar, therefore, would be a heavy-duty Category 5 avatar in our *yuga*, although the manifestation will occur well after our times.

Two major texts dedicated to the Kalki avatar are the Bhavishya Purana and Kalki Purana. Descriptions of the Kalki avatar can also be seen in the Mahabharata where the sage Markandeya describes the avatar to Yudhishthira. Kalki is said to arrive as the son of a Brahmin named Vishnuyaksa in the land of Dravida in the village of Shambala. This Brahmin boy shall be extremely powerful, intelligent, and valiant. He shall receive from Shiva a miraculous sword, a parrot, and a white winged horse called Devdatta. Trained by Parashurama in the art of fighting, he shall assemble a huge army of Brahmin warriors and go about setting order of righteousness in the world. Not only will he re-establish the rule of dharma, he will also herald the advent of Satya Yuga of the next cycle.

It is difficult to say where the legend of the Kalki avatar originated. Parallels have been drawn with the concept of the messiah in Judaism, the descriptions in the Book of Revelation in the Bible, Zoroastrian concepts of renewal of existence, and the Bodhisattva Maitreya in Buddhism.

Index

A

Abhimanyu · 135, 146, 149-150, 152-153, 156-157, 163, 165-167, 178, 188, 197, 204, 257
Abhira · 11
Acharya · 200
Achutha · 12, 93-95, 97-98
Aditi · 53
Aditya · 253
Advaita Vedanta · 93
Afghanistan · 235
Agni · 30, 32, 232, 241
ahimsa · 242
Ajanta caves · **243-252**
Akbar · 127
Akrura · 59
Amba · 116, 144, 155, **207-210**
Ambalika · 116-117
Ambedkar, B.R. · 242
Ambika · 116-117
Ananda Shesha · 4-5, 217, 239, 254-256
Anga · 122, 124, 195
Arabian Sea · 69, 79
Archaeological Survey of India · 81, 247
Arjuna · 10, 72-74, 80, 103, 105, 118, 121-122, 124-125, 134-137, 139, 141-144, 146, 150-153, 155, 157, 158-160, 164-169, 171-173, 175-178, 187, 190-191, 195-198, 200-205, 209, 216, 219-220, 224-228, 256-257
Aryan · 54, 83, 235
Ashoka · 127, 240
Ashvin · 118
Ashwatthama · 139, 165, 172-173, 182, **185-188**, 199-202, 204
astra · 146, 188, 201
   Brahma · 146, 177
   Brahmashira · 146, 187
   Naga · 177
   Narayana · 173
   Praswap · 210
asura · 88
Atlantis · 79-80
Aurangabad · 243, 248
Aurangzeb · 248
Avalokitesvara · 251
avatar · 9-11, 36, 70, 94, 239-242, 256, 261-265

B

Bactria · 235
Badami · 245
Bagh · 245
Balarama · 4, 6, 9-10, 20, 23, 25-26, 57-62, 65-66, 70-71, 124, 144, 182, 183, 212, 217, 239, **253-259**
Bali · 188
Beard, Charles · 77

Behan, Brendan · 49
Bhadra · 51
Bhagavad Gita · 10-12, 65, 103, 106, 137, 141-142, 161, 217, **223-225, 227-229**
bhajan · 93
bhakti · 12, 41, 89-90
Bharadvaja · 200
Bharat · 231-232
Bharata · 102-103, **232, 234-235**
Bharatavarsha · 232, 235
Bhima · 72, 118, 121-123, 125, 130, 134-135, 142, 144, 149-153, 155-157, 164, 170, 172-173, 176, 182-183, 186, 190, 195, 205, 219-220, 256-258
Bhishma · 105-106, **109, 113**, 115-117, 121, 129-130, 136, 141-142, 144, 149-153, 155-161, 163, 167, 171-172, 185, 190-191, 197-198, 201, 203, 207-210
Bhurishravas · 156, 168, 216
Bodhi · 88
bodhisattva · 244, 249, 251-252
Bollywood · 63
Brahman · 226
Brahmin · 73-77, 89, 117, 122, 124, 177, 194, 196, 200-201, 205, 265
Brenan, Gerald · 55
Brihaspati · 110
British Broadcasting Corporation · 101
Buddha · 12, 88, **239-242**, 245, 251, 253
Buddhism · 239-242, 245, 249, 251, 265
Buddhist · 13, 224, 227, 242, 244-245, 249, 251

C

Cecconi, Lorenzo · 252
Chaitanya · 41, **85-86, 89-91**, 259
chaitya · 245, 247
Chanakya · 28
Char Dham · 69, 81
chiranjeevi · 188
Chitrangada · 115
Chopra, B.R. · 176
Chopra, Ravi · 102
Christ · 7, 12, 249
Christian · 7, 19, 102, 227
Christie, Agatha · 215
Churchill, Winston · 126, 133
Clinton, Bill · 194
Coelho, Paul · 198
color theory · 246
Correggio · 252

D

Dalai Lama · 251
Dasharatha · 51, 53
Dashavatara · 9, 239, 253, 258
deva · 32, 53
Devaki · 3-5, 58, 61-63, 94-95, 217, 253-254
Devasena · 58
Devavrata · 106, 110-113
Devdatta · 265
Devi · 6, 96
dharma · 12, 127, 136-138, 141, 144, 153, 161, 164, 172, 200, 209-210, 219-220, 225-226, 229, 240, 263, 265

Dharma (god) · 118, 127, 220
Dhrishtadyumna · 150-151, 156, 171-172, 186, 203, 205
Dhritarashtra · 117-118, 121-123, 125, 128-130, 133-134, 142, 144, 190-191, 205, 228
Doordarshan · 101
Draupadi · 36, 95-96, 103, 123-125, 128-130, 134-135, 143, 144, 150, 176, 178, 182, 187, 195-196, 203, 219, 220-221, 256, 258
Dravida · 265
dredging · 83
Drona · 122, 125, 129-130, 134, 136, 139, 141-142, 144, 150-151, 153, 155-157, 163-165, 167-173, 175, 185, 187, 194-195, 197, **199-205**, 219
Drupada · 123-125, 143-144, 150, 155, 171, 200-201, 203, 208
Durvasa · 117, 193, 218, 233
Duryodhana · 103, 118, 122-123, 125-126, 128-130, 133-136, 141-144, 151-157, 161, 163-165, 169, 173, 175-176, 178, **181-183**, 185-187, 190, 195-198, 200, 203, 212, 256-258
Dushala · 118, 143
Dushasana · 36, 118, 129-130, 144, 156, 165-166, 176, 183
Dushyanta · **232-235**
Dvaraka · 10, 52, 54, 69, 71-72, 75, 79-82, 84, 95-96, 191, 213, 216, 255-257
Dwarka · 10, 69, 81-84
Bet · 69, 81-84
Dwarkadhish Temple · 69

E

Ekalavya · 202-203, 205
Ellora caves · 244, 247-248
Emerson, Ralph Waldo · 227
Euripides · 73, 136

F

foreshortening · 246
Franklin, Benjamin · 205

G

Gandhara · 143, 152, 182
Gandhari · 118, 144, 183, 190-191, 215-216
Gandharva · 108, 115, 233, 255
Gandhi, Harilal · 211
Gandhi, Mahatma · 19, 89, 211, 224, 228-229, 242, 259
Ganesha · 9, 20, 102, 258
Ganga · **104-111**, 160, 200
Garuda · 26, 28, 54, 80, 146
Gauda · 89
Gauranga · 87-89
Gautama, Siddhartha · 239, 242
Gaya · 88
Gayatri Mantra · 87, 233
Geneva Convention · 138
Ghatotkacha · 152-153, 157, 169-170
Ghritachi · 200
Gita Govinda · **43-44, 46-48**, 241, 253

Gita Jayanti · 13
Goethe · 46
Gokula · 4-6, 9, 13, 16, 19-20, 22, 25, 33, 69
gopi · 12, 21-22, 27, 33-36, 39-44, 55, 59, 69, 94, 255
Goswami, Jayadeva · **43-44, 46-47**, 241, 253
Goswami, Rupa · 90
Goswami, Santana · 90
Grousset, Rene · 249
Gujarat · 10, 69, 81, 213, 216, 263
Gulf of Khambhat · 79, 83-84
guna · 226
   rajas · 226
   sattva · 226
   tamas · 226
Gurgaon · 205
guru dakshina · 199, 203
Gurugram · 205
guru-shishya parampara · 199, 205

H

Hanuman · 103, 188
Hare Krishna · 12, 41, 85, 88-89, 91, 242, 253, 259
Harivamsa · 11, 72
Hastinapura · 105-106, 109, 111, 116-117, 121, 123, 125, 128, 134-135, 149, 188, 191, 195, 200-203, 207, 209, 219, 257
Hemingway, Ernest · 139
Herodotus · 166
Higham, Tom · 84
hijra · 210

Hindu · 7, 10, 12, 20, 32, 36, 51, 53-54, 66, 69, 72, 79, 80, 84, 87-88, 90, 102, 106, 124, 138, 141, 191, 194, 200, 205, 210, 213, 224, 229, 232, 235, 239, 241-242, 253, 255-256, 262-263
Hinduism · 9, 19-20, 87, 90, 102, 110, 188, 224, 227, 240-242, 245, 262
Homer · 102
Hoover, Herbert · 153
Hugo, Victor · 137
Hunter, William Wilson · 252

I

Iliad · 102
India · 3, 9-10, 12, 19, 28-29, 32, 39, 42, 44, 48, 63, 69, 79-81, 83, 86, 89-90, 98, 101-102, 104, 113, 127, 141-144, 151, 197, 199, 210-211, 213, 220, 223, 227-228, 231-232, 235, 240-249, 251-253, 258-259, 263
Indra · 29-32, 53-54, 58, 80, 106, 108, 118, 169, 196, 219-220, 232, 233
Indraprastha · 126-128, 130, 133-134, 191, 196
Iravan · 157
ISKON · 91
itihasa · 80

J

Jagannath · 90, 259
Jain · 72, 227, 235

Jainism · 232, 245
Jambavan · 52
Jambavati · 51-52, 55, 212
Jara · 70, 214, 217
Jarasandha · 4, 63, 69-72, 80, 128, 202, 217
Jataka tales · 245
Jaya · 103
Jayadratha · 143-144, 156, 165-169
Jesudas · 223-224
Jesus · 7, 9
Jobs, Steve · 194
Jones, William · 46, 241
Jyotirlinga · 216

K

Kadamba · 26, 34, 46, 255
Kailash temple · 244
Kalayavana · 70-71
Kalindi · 25, 28, 51
Kalinga · 151
Kaliya · 25-28
Kalki · 261-265
kalpa · 256
Kalra, Rashmit · 248
Kama · 44, 46
Kamsa · 3-7, 9-10, 15-16, 20, 25, **57-61**, 63, 66, 69-70, 72, 80, 95-96, 253-254
Kanishka · 127
Kanva · 233-234
karma · 137, 210, 216-217
Karna · 122-125, 129, 136, 144, 146, 151, 153, 156-157, 160-161, 163-165, 169-170, 172-173, 175-178, 181, 185, 190, **193-198**, 203, 205
Kartikeya · 20, 58
Kashi · 116, 207
Kashmir · 142, 213, 252
kathak · 42
Katyayani · 34
Kaurava · 36, 65, 72, 102-105, 115, 118, 121-123, 125-130, 133-136, 141-144, 146, 149-153, 155-159, 163-165, 167-173, 175-176, 181-183, 185, 187-189, 194-197, 200, 203-204, 209-210, 215-216, 224, 229, 232, 256-257
Kazi · 89
Keshava · 12, 58, 94
Keshi · 58, 94, 96
Kichaka · 134-135
kirtana · 89
Konark · 213
Koran · 51
Kripa · 144, 182, 185-186, 200-201
Krishna · 3-7, **9-13**, 17, 19-36, 39-48, 51-55, 57-63, 65-77, 79-81, 84-85, 87-91, 93-96, 98, 103, 105, 110, 124-125, 128, 130, 136-137, 139, 142-143, 149-152, 155, 157-159, 161, 164-165, 167-169, 172-173, 175-178, 181, 183, 187-188, 190-191, 194, 196-198, 204-205, 209, 211-218, 221, 223-226, 228-229, 239, 249, 253-255, 257-259, 263
Krishna Janmashtami · 13
Kritavarma · 143, 182, 185-186, 216-217
Kshatriya · 61, 70, 124, 194, 200, 202-203, 225

Kubja · 60, 66
Kuchela · 75-77
Kunti · 71, 117-118, 122-124, 134, 136, 176, 189-191, 193-196, 198
Kuru · 104, 118, 122, 134, 149-150, 160, 172, 191, 201, 258
Kurukshetra War · 84, **102-104**, 116, 118, 136, 138-139, 141-143, 149-150, 155, 159, 163, 171, 175, 181, 183, 189, 191, 197, 203, 210, 215-217, 219, 224, 228, 257
Kyrgyzstan · 235

L

Lakshmana · 51, 96, 103, 212-213, 255, 257
Lennon, John · 194
lila · 42
Lilliputian · 256

M

Madhava · 88, 94-95
Madri · 117-118, 143
Magadha · 4, 69-70, 72, 80, 202
Mahabharata · 10-11, 36, 65, 72, 79, 80-84, **101-106**, 110, 115, 117-118, 138, 141-142, 144, 146, 150, 182, 193, 198-199, 210, 225, 231-232, 235, 257-258, 265
Mahabhisha · 107-108
maithuna · 46, 55, 65, 110, 117, 233

Maitreya · 265
Mandela, Nelson · 19, 194
Manipuri · 42
Manjusri · 251
mantra · 88, 117-118, 146, 177, 193-194, 201
Markand · 213
Markandeya · 265
Masse, Bruce · 81
Mathura · 3, 9, 11, 13, 16, 20, 25, 57-61, 63, 65-66, 69-72, 80, 253
matki · 33
Matsya · 109, 143, 150, 171, 241
Mayapur · 86, 89
Menaka · 233
Michelangelo · 252
Mitravinda · 51
Modhera · 213
Modi, Narendra · 143
Mohammad · 12
moksha · 88, 224
Mount Govardhana · 25, 29-30, 32, 54
Mount Meru · 219
Muchukunda · 71
Mukunda · 12
Muslim · 89, 227, 241

N

Nagnajiti · 51
Nakula · 118, 121, 134, 164, 176, 182, 190, 219- 220
Nanda · 4-6, 16, 20, 25-26, 29-30, 44, 59, 95
Narada · 54-55, 57, 73-74, 187

Narakasura · 53
nastika · 241
National Institute of Ocean Technology (NIOT) · 81, 83
Natyashastra · 232
Nehru, Jawaharlal · 247
Nimai · 87
nirvana · 88, 224, 242, 248, 251
niyoga · 116
Nyaya · 87

O

Odyssey · 102
Oppenheimer, Robert · 227

P

Padmapani · **249, 251-252**
Pahari · 48
Pakistan · 141-142, 144
Panchala · 123, 125, 143, 150, 200, 203, 208
Pandava · 36, 65, 71-72, 102-104, **115, 118**, 121-126, 128-130, 133-136, 141-144, 146, 149-153, 155-159, 161, 163-168, 170-173, 175-177, 181-183, 186-190, 193-198, 203-204, 209, 215-216, 219-220, 224, 228, 232, 256-257, 258
Panditaraja, Jagannatha · 47
Pandu · 117-118, 121, 123, 127, 143, 193
Parashara · 110

Parashurama · 110, 116, 177, 188, 194, 197, 200-201, 203, 207, 265
Parijata · 53
Parikshit · 188, 191, 219
parva · 102
Persia · 235
perspective (art) · 246, 252
Ponlop Rinpoche · 13
Prabhasa · 106, 213, 216-217
Prabhupada, Bhaktivedanta · 90
Pradyumna · 212
Purana · 11, 79, 102, 231, 242
   Bhagavata · 11, 42-43, 65, 79, 232, 241
   Bhavishya · 264
   Kalki · 264
   Skanda · 79
   Vishnu · 11, 240
Puri, Ishvar · 88
Putana · **15-16**, 57, 96

R

Radha · 22, 40, **43-48**, 52, 88, 90, 94-95
Rajasthani · 48
Rajasuya · 71-72, 127-128
rakshasa · 157, 169
Rama · 9-12, 23, 51, 53, 69-71, 88, 94-96, 102-103, 232, 254-255, 263
Ramakrishna Paramahamsa · 228
Ramanaka · 28
Ramayana · 80, 83, 101-103, 232, 255, 257
Rani Ki Vav · 263
Rao, S.R. · 81

Rasa Lila · 10, 36, 39-44, 55
Rasa Lila Panchadhyaya · 42
Rasagangadhara · 47
Ravana · 72, 103, 151
Revati · 255-256
Rishabha · 232
Rohini · 4-5, 16, 217, 254
Rowling, J.K. · 173
Rukmini · 51-52, 54-55, 76-77, 95, 212, 218
rule of proportionality · 138

S

Sahadeva · 118, 121, 134, 176, 182, 190, 195, 219, 220
Sakhi · 44-45
Salva · 207
Samba · 211-213, 216-217, 257
Sanghi, Ashwin · 32
Sanjaya · 142, 228
sankirtana · 88-89
Sanskrit · 46-47, 69, 87, 93, 143, 200, 224, 251
Santayana, George · 189
sari · 36, 130
Sarnath · 251
Satyabhama · 51-55, 94
Satyaki · 143, 151-152, 155-156, 168, 216-217
Satyavati · 110-111, 113, 115-117, 210
Shakespeare, William · 24
Shakun · 233
Shakuni · 128-129, 134, 143, 152, 157, 182

Shakuntala · 102, **232-235**
Shalya · 143, 150, 155, 164, 175, 177, 178, 181-182
Shaman · 227
Shambala · 265
Shankara, Adi · 93, 241-242
Shantanu · 104-107, 109-111, 113, 115
Sheridan, Richard · 37
Shikhandi · 116, 144, 155, 159, 167, 186, **207-210**
Shinto · 227
Shishupala · 52
Shiva · 9-10, 12, 19, 59-60, 71-72, 123, 172, 187, 208, 212, 265
Shraaddha · 88
Shveta · 151
Siksastaka · 90
Sindhu · 143
Sistine Chapel · 249, 252
Sita · 94-96, 103
Sittanavasal · 245
Smith, John · 244
smriti · 102
Solomon · 51
Somnath Temple · 213
Sreekumar, M.G. · 93
sthitaprajna · 224-225
Stockholm syndrome · 213
stotra · 93
Stuna · 208-209
stupa · 241, 244-245
Subhadra · 125, 257, 259
Sudama · 73-75
Surya · 194, 196, 213, 256
Swami Gnaneswarananda · 19
Swami Nityananda · 259

swayamvara · 52, 103, 116, 123-125, 151, 155, 195, 207, 210, 212, 257
Syamantaka · 52

T

Tajikistan · 235
Thoreau, Henry David · 227
Tilottama · 66
tribhanga · 249
Trigarta · 164
Tulabhara · 54
Tulsi · 54
Turkmenistan · 235
Tyson, Mike · 115
Tzu, Sun · 147, 158, 170

U

Ugrasena · 3, 52, 61, 63, 69, 217
UN Security Council · 139
UNESCO · 247
Upanayana · 87
Uthup, Usha · 12
Uttara · 150-151
Uttarayana · 161
Uzbekistan · 235

V

Vaikuntha · 63
Vaishnava · 36, 41-42, 47, 88-90, 242, 259
  Gaudiya · 89-90, 259

Vaishnavism · 41, 90, 259
Vajrapani · 251
Vakataka · 245
Vanderbilt, Gloria · 243
vanishing point · 246
Varanavata · 123
Varuna · 30, 32, 34, 53, 71, 255
Varuni · 255
Vasant · 44
Vasishtha · 106
Vasu · 12, 106, 253
Vasudeva · 3-6, 11-12, 51, 58-59, 61-62, 71, 94-95, 124, 217, 253-254
Vayu · 118, 233
Veda · 11, 95, 110, 240-241
veena · 55
Vichitravirya · 115-116, 207
Vidura · 65, 117, 123, 129-130, 134
vihara · 245, 247, 252
Vijaya · 103
Vinci, Leonardo da · 101, 249
Virata · 134-135, 143, 150-151, 156, 164, 171
Vishnu · 4-6, 9-12, 15, 19, 24, 26, 47, 70, 79-80, 88, 90, 93-95, 98, 141-142, 226, 232, 239-242, 253-256, 258, 261
Vishnu Sahasranama · 105, 142
Vishnupada · 88
Vishnuyaksa · 265
Vishvarupa · 24, 226
Vishwakarma · 71, 80, 256
Vishwambara · 87
Vishwamitra · 233
Vraj · 13, 34, 39, 42, 44, 61, 255
Vrindavan · 13, 25-26, 28-30, 33, 58-59, 90

Vrishnis · 11
Vyasa · 102-103, 110, 117-118, 142, 187-188, 219
vyuha · 144-146, 165, 204
    chakra · 95, 145-146, 163, 165, 204
    garuda · 145
    krauncha · 146
    makara · 145
    suchimukha · 146
    vajra · 146, 251

W

Washington, George · 184
Wilde, Oscar · 42, 63, 211

Y

Yadava · 3, 20, 51-52, 59, 61, 69, 70-71, 80-81, 212-214, 216-217, 256, 258
yajna · 71-72, 150

yaksha · 208
Yama · 118, 127, 220
Yamuna · 5, 25-26, 34, 39, 40, 44-45, 111, 126, 255
Yashoda · 5-6, 16, 20-27, 33, 59
Yelton, Jack · 131
yoga · 19, 138, 168
Yudhishthira · 36, 71, 103, 118, 121-123, 126-130, 134-135, 141-143, 146, 151, 156, 161, 163-166, 172, 176, 181-182, 188-191, 196, 198, 201-205, **219-221**, 257-258, 265
Yuga · 256, 263
    Dvapara · 263
    Kali · 11, 90, 102, 261-263
    Satya · 263, 265
    Treta · 263
Yuyutsu · 118, 144

Z

Zen · 227

What's Coming Up?

Next up, we meet Shiva, one of the oldest gods of Hinduism. Shiva is different from other deities because of his complex nature and contradictions. Even the name Shiva, meaning "auspicious," may appear contradictory because of his paramount role as the cosmic destroyer. Extremely popular, he is worshipped by a large sect of devotees known as Shaivites. Incidentally, his worshippers include Rama and Krishna, who have sought his blessings at one time or the other.

In book 5 we look at Shiva in detail—including his whims and fancies. If you are a stickler for etiquette and decorum, Shiva may not be your favorite god since he is unconventional and often seen meditating naked with snakes wrapped around his arms. His unkempt appearance has put off many—including his father-in-law with whom he had a long-running feud. His personality may be complex, but his lifestyle is simple. Unlike other deities, Shiva does not reside in celestial palaces that are secured by palace guards and entertained by dancing apsaras. His abode is Mount Kailash where he sits under a banyan tree immersed in meditation. Despite being a staunch ascetic, he is a family man and achieves a comfortable work-life balance. In pictures, Shiva is often seen with his wife Parvati and their two outstanding sons—Ganesha and Kartikeya.

Like Krishna, Shiva is artistically talented and is regarded as the lord of dance. His dance, however, is not the kind that receives a standing ovation from the audience, for it means one thing—the end of the world. That said, as a patron of arts, he has been the inspiration for some the greatest monuments of India. For his followers, Shiva embodies the Hindu concept of "Satyam Shivam Sundaram" meaning "truth, goodness, and beauty." His devotees adore him because of his simplicity and because he is one of the easiest gods to please.

www.ingramcontent.com/pod-product-compliance
Lightning Source LLC
Chambersburg PA
CBHW031410290426
44110CB00011B/323